ANGELS OF THE NIGHT

Popular
Female Singers
of our Time

Also by Wilfrid Mellers

Music and Society (1946)
Studies in Contemporary Music (1948)
François Couperin and the French Classical Tradition (1950)
Music in the Making (1951)
Man and his Music (1957; with Alec Harman)
Harmonious Meeting (1964)
Music in a New Found Land (1964)
Caliban Reborn: Renewal in Twentieth-century Music (1967)
Twilight of the Gods: The Beatles in Retrospect (1973)
Bach and the Dance of God (1980)
Beethoven and the Voice of God (1983)
A Darker Shade of Pale: A Backdrop to Bob Dylan (1984)

ANGELS OF THE NIGHT

Popular Female Singers of our Time

Wilfrid Mellers

Basil Blackwell

Copyright © Wilfrid Mellers 1986

First published 1986

Basil Blackwell Ltd
108 Cowley Road, Oxford OX4 1JF, UK

Basil Blackwell Inc.
432 Park Avenue South, Suite 1503,
New York, NY 10016, USA

British Library Cataloguing in Publication Data

Mellers, Wilfrid
    Angels of the night: popular female singers of our time
    1. Women singers—20th century—Biography
    I. Title
    784.5'0092'2   ML400

    ISBN 0–631–14696–2

Library of Congress Cataloging in Publication Data

Mellers, Wilfrid Howard, 1914–
    Angels of the night.

    Discography: p.
    Includes index.
    1. Women singers—United States—Biography.
2. Music, Popular (Songs, etc.)—United States—
History and criticism. I. Title.
ML400.M44 1986   784.5'008042   85–18659
ISBN 0–631–14696–2

Typeset in 11 on 12 pt Garamond
by Alan Sutton Publishing Limited
Printed in Great Britain by Butler & Tanner, Frome

music

CONTENTS

Acknowledgements   vii

Preface   ix

I BLACK WOMEN AS EARTH GODDESSES IN CHURCH,
   BAR, BROTHEL AND CLUB

  1 Gospel Women, Eden and the Promised Land   3
     Arizona Dranes   Sister Rosetta Tharpe
     Mahalia Jackson   Aretha Franklin
  2 The Rockbottom Reality of the Blues   16
     Ma Rainey   Bessie Smith   Ida Cox
     Victoria Spivey   Sippie Wallace   Alberta Hunter
     Helen Humes   Big Mama Thornton
     Dinah Washington
  3 From Tent Show to Cabaret: The Word and the Horn   39
     Ruth Etting   Ethel Waters   Billie Holiday
     Ella Fitzgerald   Sarah Vaughan   Carmen McCrae
     Pearl Bailey   Abbey Lincoln   Betty Carter
  4 Soul, Motown, and the Fusion of Sacred and Profane 66
     Odetta   Nina Simone   Aretha Franklin
     Dionne Warwick   The Loving Sisters
     Gladys Knight and the Pips   Diana Ross and the
     Supremes   The Pointer Sisters   Esther Phillips
     Roberta Flack   Randy Crawford   Donna Summer
     Deniece Williams   Angela Bofill

II WHITE WOMEN AS URBAN AND RURAL SURVIVORS IN THE INDUSTRIAL WILDERNESS

5 The Jazz Singer as Little Girl Lost 95
Barbara Dane   Connie Boswell   Mildred Bailey
Anita O'Day   Chris Connor   Julie London
Blossom Dearie   Peggy Lee
6 The Folksong Revival and the Real Right Thing 107
Jean Ritchie   Joan Baez   Judy Collins
Hazel and Alice   The McGarrigle Sisters
7 Women and the Country Music Industry 123
Tammy Wynette   Loretta Lynn   Dolly Parton
Lacy J. Dalton   Crystal Gayle   Bonnie Raitt
Linda Ronstadt

III NOT FROM NEW ADAM'S RIB: WOMEN AS SINGING POET–COMPOSERS

8 White Seagull, Black Highwaywoman, Red Squaw: 141
Joni Mitchell
9 The Midnight Baby and the Holiywooden Dream: 169
Dory Previn
10 Society's Child in Small Town and City 187
Carole King   Janis Ian   Carly Simon
11 Into the Global Village 199
Phoebe Snow   Melissa Manchester   Laura Nyro
Tania Maria
12 The Rough and the Tough 209
Janis Joplin   Patti Smith   Grace Jones
Joan Armatrading   Marianne Faithfull
13 Magic and Technology 221
Kate Bush   Toyah Wilcox   Judie Tzuke
Annie Lennox and the Eurythmics   Sade Adu
14 Deadend Kid and Androgyne 231
Rickie Lee Jones   Laurie Anderson

Afterword: Folk, Rock and Jazz in the Unisex Global Village 253

Discography 259
Glossary of Musical Terms 267
Index 273

ACKNOWLEDGEMENTS

The author and publishers acknowledge with thanks permission granted by the publishers of various artists' work to quote extracts in the book. All other permissions have been applied for.
Extracts from poems by A. R. Ammons: permission applied for. Extracts from lyrics by Laurie Anderson: permission applied for. Extracts from lyrics by Kate Bush © Kate Bush Music Ltd. Used by permission of EMI Music Publishing Ltd, London WC2H 0LD and Castle Music Pty Ltd. Extract from lyrics by Lacy Dalton: permission applied for. Extract from poems by Margaret Danner: permission applied for. Extract from poems by Sarah Webster Fabio: permission applied for. Extract from poems by Robert Graves: used by permission of A. P. Watt Ltd on behalf of the Executors of the Estate of Robert Graves. Extract from Billie Holiday's 'Lady Sings the Blues': permission applied for. Extract from lyrics by Bunny Hull and Jim Devlin: used by permission of Carlin Music Corp. Extracts from lyrics by Ricki Lee Jones: permission applied for. Extract from lyrics by Carol King: © 1970 Screen Gems Music Inc USA. Used by permission Screen Gems–EMI Music, London WC2H 0LD and Castle Music Pty, Ltd. Extracts from lyrics by Janis Ian: permission applied for. Extracts by R. D. Laing used by permission of Penguin Books Ltd. Extract from lyrics by Lennox/Stewart: permission applied for. Extracts from lyrics by Joni Mitchell: permission applied for. Extract from poem by Octavio Paz used by permission of Penguin Books Ltd, translation copyright © Grove Press Inc. Extracts from lyrics by Melvin van Peebles: permission

applied for. Extracts from lyrics by Dory Previn: copyright United Partnership. Reproduced by Belwin Mills Music Ltd, 250 Purley Way, Croydon, Surrey. Extracts from poems by Ezra Pound reprinted by permission of Faber and Faber Ltd from *Literary Essays of Ezra Pound*. Extracts from poems by J. H. Prynne: permission applied for. Extracts from poems by Carl Sandburg used by permission of Harcourt Brace Jovanovich Inc. Extracts from lyrics by Carly Simon: permission applied for. Extracts from lyrics by Phoebe Snow: permission applied for. Extracts from poems by Wallace Stevens reprinted by permission of Faber and Faber Ltd from *The Collected Poems of Wallace Stevens*.

PREFACE

When she speaks it's like music
Universal melodies
Lullabies that will soothe you
Put your life in harmony

She knows   let her guide you
Listen if you can   you know she's wise

She's an angel of the night

Angela Bofill

I am the necessary angel of earth
Since, in my sight, you see the earth again.

Wallace Stevens

After the final no there comes a yes
And on that yes the future world depends.

No was the night.

Wallace Stevens

Angels of the Night falls into three parts. I start from the jazz explosion ignited by Black musicians in the early years of this century, in the religious context of Gospel music and in the secular context of the blues. I trace the metamorphosis of the blues into club and cabaret jazz and the metamorphosis of Gospel music into soul and rock. That Gospel and blues were instinctive creations of oppressed and alienated Blacks has a bearing on the music created by women, who have experienced their share of oppression and alienation throughout the centuries.

Part II deals with popular musics of American Whites during the twentieth century: the tardy entry of White women singers into jazz, until then dominated by Black women, and the conscious revival of rural folksong, which was to expand into the country music industry.

The third and most important part of the book is concerned with the New Eve's search for social and creative identity in her New Edenic Garden. Although we may think of the singers of Gospel, blues and jazz as *makers* in that every performance is a re-creative act, such artists do not usually invent their own words and tunes. From the sixties onwards, however, the singing poet–composer became increasingly familiar: Black, White and coffee-coloured singers, mostly young, fashioned their words and music from their day-to-day lives, using a verbal vernacular and a musical idiom that sprang from the streets and marketplace. 'Professional' skill was not necessarily relevant to their creation and performance. Through the nineteenth and twentieth centuries 'art' music had become increasingly divorced from 'everyday' life. When it staged a comeback in the demotic arts of young people, an 'alternative culture' emerged.

The relationships between art, folk and commerce are complex. In trying to disentangle strands I have been selective rather than comprehensive in my choice of singing poet–composers. No two views on who should be included and who should be omitted will coincide; my own list of candidates changed during the writing of the book. There are several who, originally included, had to be expunged for lack of space; some have been left out because with a subject so amorphous in nature, the line had to be drawn somewhere. I particularly regret the omission of theatre singers like Barbra Streisand and Liza Minelli. Some foreign – for instance African – singers who occasionally perform in English have been rejected as not part of our immediate cultural environment.

This is a book about musical performance rather than about scores. The words and music commented on here were meant to be listened to and responded to, not 'analysed': so I have based the book on recorded performances, while remembering that such performances are not finite artefacts, but individual versions of the songs, which happen to have been stabilized. Many of the artists considered I have heard in concert; but a live performance, however enlivening, is a less reliable basis for commentary than a recording, if only because performance on disc is usually more adequately audible, and is capable of immediate repetition.

PART I

BLACK WOMEN AS EARTH GODDESSES IN CHURCH, BAR, BROTHEL AND CLUB

Chapter One

GOSPEL WOMEN, EDEN AND THE PROMISED LAND

The human race has always been enveloped in versions of worlds we do not live in now. The primitive, animistic, magic world we so often impute to children, the mad, the savage and our ancestors (*and men tend to impute to women*) is more than anything a product of *our* minds, a projection of our own imagination. Our imagination may be correct. Our myths are obscure to us since we are in the midst of them. They envelop us. We are enclosed, as were our ancestors, in the dreams we cannot get outside to look at or go beyond . . . Here, we have no instruments to pierce the limits of our possibilities. The human world seems to be everywhere and always populated more by demons and spirits than by mortals of flesh and blood. Have these delusions and hallucinations survival value?

R. D. Laing: *The Voice of Experience*

In my book on Bob Dylan, *A Darker Shade of Pale*,[1] I write of his owing his cult significance to the fact that he synthesized apparent opposites: a Jewish–Hebraic–Christian–American 'patriarchy' linking up with a pre-Christian, pagan 'matriarchy' symbolically represented by the earth goddess, madonna and harpy figures that

1 London, Faber and Faber, 1984.

haunt his verses. Musically, I identify the paternal aspects of his art with White American march, hymn and country music, with Jewish cantillation, and indirectly even with the ululations of the aborigianal American, the Red Indian. The maternal aspects, on the other hand, I relate to the pre-Christian, pagan culture of the Black African enslaved in his Whitely alien land; and in this context we might recall that Leslie A. Fiedler has suggested that 'in the language of archetype the Negro stands for alien passion and the Indian for alien perception. (Or perhaps this is only another way of saying that at the level of deep imagination the Indian is male and the Negro female.)'[2]

In any case 'barbaric' Negro jazz swept the 'civilized' world because it reminded bloodless anti-physical twentieth-century man of what he had lost. It was no accident that the rediscoveries of primitivism by Stravinsky and Bartók, Picasso and Modigliani, were contemporary with the first jazz explosion in the United States. If Black music can in this sense be perceived as an alternative cultural pole to White music, it is not surprising that women, in Fiedler's term representative, like the Negro, of 'alien passion', should early have become potent jazz protagonists, vigorously functioning inside the stronghold of the paternalistic Christian Church itself. Transplanted to their new American environment, the Black Africans had readily absorbed the Bible stories and evangelical hymns of Christianity, the more so because their earthly lot was so wretched. Landowners encouraged them to look for a second chance, because hard labour in this life would be easier to accept if rewarded with pie in the sky by and by; slave owners even found it possible to justify slavery on the moral grounds that it was a means of converting the infidel. But although Negroes gladly embraced Christianity they did not so much take over the music of Christendom as re-create their own music in the light of Christian experience. Just as in Haiti they preserved witchcraft in the form of voodoo worship by reconciling African with Christian mythology and ritual, so they transformed the discipline of the work song into an orgy of religious fervour. Where Gospel music celebrated the White Christian God, Black blues and barrelhouse music were accredited to the secular world and the Devil. Yet in technique and in effect God and the Devil overlapped; in both Gospel music and the blues the shouted pentatonic[3] incantation, the hypnotically

2 *The Return of the Vanishing American*, London, 1968.
3 See Glossary of Musical Terms.

repeated riff,[4] carry both singers and listeners outside time, as the chant becomes not merely a negative numbing of pain, but a positive rhythmic ecstasy.

This is true even when Vera Hall, labouring in the fields, hollers a hymn like 'Trouble so hard',[5] unaccompanied. By omitting degrees of the diatonic scale,[6] she makes a 'gapped' pentatonic mode, achieving maximum expressivity from the sorrow-burdened words by distonations of pitch and vagaries of rhythm, in a timbre pure yet harshly penetrating. Suffering on this earth provokes levitation, carrying us 'out of this world' as, of course, religious incantation is supposed to. But the earthy quality of the Black female voice, along with the surging rhythm, also effects a *corporeal* ecstasy. God and the World, the Flesh and the Devil cease to be contradictory forces, for what is conventionally considered a 'negative' proves basic to the 'positive' impulse. The female archetype of earth goddess and eternal mother is substituted for the Virgin Mary, herself a surrogate for Christ, the Son of the Father. White patriarchy is thus undermined by Black matriarchy.

Here is the heart of Black Gospel music, whether it adapts White hymns in the form of 'spirituals', or whether it stems from communally secular music. The non-Christian African roots of Gospel music are still evident as late as the 1970s when Marion Williams sings, unaccompanied, the hymn 'They led my Lord away'.[7] Although Marion, a native of Miami who belonged to the Church of God in Christ, had worked with harmonically sophisticated Gospel 'groups', she here creates a pentatonic incantation no less primitively disturbing than Vera Hall's field holler. Infusing body with spirit, she appeals to Christ for release from the suffering that is vicariously ours; and release becomes audibly incarnate in the wild upward slides on the word 'away', and in the frantic swoops on 'Calvary's hill'. Similarly the refrain – 'He never said a mumblin' word, not a word, mmm–mmm not a word, no, no, did he say' – effaces time in inducing hypnosis, while the intermittently spoken 'nuff said's and the visceral tone on 'They pierced Him in the side' centre us in the painful present. Again God and Devil, Word and Flesh, are integrated.

4 See Glossary.
5 *Negro Worksongs and Calls.* Details of recordings are given in the Discography.
6 See Glossary.
7 *Brighten the Corner Where You Are.*

The mainstream of Black Gospel music is found, however, not in solo singing but in the communal group, which emulates the relationship between preacher and church congregation. Even today, one may hear such singing in the islands off South Carolina: an area rich in folk musics preserved unsullied owing to geographical isolation. *Been in the Storm Too Long*, recorded on John Island in 1959, enables us to experience the relationship between prayer, incantation and communal worship in field conditions, interlacing solo singers with choir and congregation in Moving Star Hall, heart of the island community. When Laura Rivers sings the spiritual 'That's all right' she is unaccompanied, chanting the pentatonic phrases in a style halfway between spoken prayer and song. Yet she imbues even this solo performance with communal implications, since she responds to her own refrains, as would other members of the community, were they present.

When Bertha Smith sings 'Lay down body' such a group is there to support her and God, each of her phrases being echoed in yelled heterophony:[8] unisons the more thrilling because inexact; parallel thirds that teeter rancidly between major and minor. Through the singing and shouting, people clap to lend rhythmic emphasis, in metrical patterns that grow cumulatively faster and more complex. Worship becomes a public activity – complemented by private adoration when Alice Wine wonderingly and hesitantly sings 'I'm gonna sit at the welcome table'. Incanted song acts as prelude to improvised prayer, beginning with a citation of the Our Father, which is everyone's property, and moving into personal confession. Alice's speaking voice veers from flat speech to pitched notes and patterned rhythms, prompted by crucial words like 'sin', 'strong', 'sorrow', rise', bird'. Indeed speech becomes near-musical composition – a phenomenon that recurs throughout the history of jazz singing, however secular its context.

Mary Pinckney singing the spiritual 'Down on me' with three members of the Moving Star Singers, a specialist if not exactly trained ensemble attached to the Church, shows the same form at a slightly more organized stage. Here personal, communal and magical dimensions coexist. Her tumbling strain-like[9] cries spring from personal anguish – 'Seem like everybody in this whole world is down on me' – yet anguish is ameliorated because in the refrains it

8   See Glossary.
9   See Glossary.

is shared with the choric group. The wildness of the singing – the three voices hardly attempt to tune their unisons or to make their thirds politely parallel – suggests that God is momentarily identified with untrammelled (female?) libido, not susceptible to human discipline. But singing 'Row, Michael, row' with the same Moving Star Singers, Mary Pinckney's daughter, Jane Hunter, manages to balance the godly with the humane. There is a practical reason for this: since the spiritual is also a rowing song co-ordination is essential. When Gospel groups work in city churches, some rapprochement with Establishment presentation becomes the norm: the basic vocal primitivism we have noted is fused not only with the hymn, but also with the parlour ballad, and incipiently with ragtime, if not with jazz.

The Roberta Martin Singers' performance of the White hymn 'Yield not to temptation'[10] is a case in point. This group, centred on Chicago, was the first Gospel ensemble to achieve commercial success; and it is relevant to note that Roberta herself, despite strong Evangelical connections, had earned her living by playing the piano to silent movies. That her musical secularity in no way inhibited her religious devotion is evident, in this 1947 number, in the quite complex interrelationship between Gospel soloist, male backing group and pianist. The soprano, Delores Barrett, is Black, but does not sound like an earth mother. Then a girl of 21, Delores displays a voice of pristine purity, with a touch of operatic bel canto. Even so, the effect is modified by her dialogue with Roberta Martin's cavernous contralto, and by the male ensemble, who encourage Delores to Gospel-style equivocation between song and speech. Her agile grace-notes decorating the melodic line and her crooning portamentos[11] hint both at a Negro preacher and at a hollerer in the cotton fields; through the vocal acrobatics the sensual here-and-now is imbued with exaltation – an effect abetted by the piano part, a jazz waltz, which is rooted in earth-pounding feet, yet persistently lopes across the bar lines.

There is a comparable equivocation in Willie Mae Smith's singing, with Bertha Smith on piano and Gwendolyn Cooper on organ, of D. B. Hardy's White hymn 'Give me wings'.[12] This fast, ragged performance is representative of the Southern Gospel style of

10 *Brighten the Corner Where You Are.*
11 See Glossary.
12 *Brighten the Corner Where You Are.*

St Louis, where Willie Mae lived for more than fifty years. Popularly
known as 'Mother' Smith, she, unlike Delores Barrett, does sound
like a Black earth goddess. Her breathy, wide-vibrato-ed, explosive
vocal production resembles that of 'heavy' blueswomen such as Ma
Rainey and Bessie Smith. Yet Mother Smith remained exclusively
an Evangelical singer who reveals the physical–metaphysical
paradox of the jazz experience. The words of the hymn oppose the
'wolves of hell' omnipresent in the world to the 'flying away' to
which love of Christ impels us. The beat is heavy, the piano and
organ sonority oppressive; yet the husky voice takes to the air as the
Lord gives her wings.

How African tumbling strain, Black American holler, White
march and White hymn are inextricably tangled in Negro Gospel
music is forcefully exhibited in the work of Arizona Dranes.[13] She
was born blind in Dallas, in 1904 or 1906, probably with a tincture
of Mexican in her Negro blood – her second name is Juanita. A
member of the Church of God in Christ, she sang and played Gospel
piano from her early teens. In the mid-twenties she attained
momentary fame by way of a recording contract, which brought,
however, minimal pecuniary reward. As she travelled through
Texas, as far as Memphis and Oklahoma, she was usually impoverished and often in real distress, but she had the compensation of
making music for her God, knowing that her social and religious
function was understood by the people for whom she performed.

What makes her fascinating is the distinction between what her
music was and what she thought it was: she was a fiery barrelhouse
pianist in what was then known as 'fast western' style, and the music
she makes is hardly distinguishable in kind from that played in bars
and bordellos by male rudimentary boogie[14] pianists like Meade Lux
Lewis, Cow-Cow Davenport and Roosevelt Sykes the Honeydripper.
Barrelhouse piano derived directly from White American march but
in being 'ragged' (with the accents of the right hand dislocated over
the left hand's pounding beat) it became perhaps the most sexy music
ever invented – the more so when the player shouted improvised
blues riffs in wild tumbling strains, over and against the instrumental
metre. The rhythmic complexities of Meade Lux Lewis are the closest
early jazz ever came to its African origins.

Yet in playing comparable music Arizona Dranes has no dubiety

13   *Arizona Dranes 1926–28.*
14   See Glossary.

about her religious zeal; her music is a peculiarly potent, because primitive, example of Gospel music's liaison between discipline and freedom – and perhaps between God and the Devil. On her discs she is credited with the composition of many numbers, though they were probably improvised to words garnered from traditional Evangelical material. She works within three conventions: as solo singer accompanying herself on piano; as solo pianist who breaks into song, supported by backing voices; and simply as keyboard soloist. All the numbers are fast, sometimes very fast; all are straight diatonic in the manner of White march and hymn, with little trace of modality. The jazz element lies in the tense relationship between rhythm and metre: as we may hear in 'In that day', an aggressively metrical American march ragged, over which she squeaks patterned riff-like phrases. Her voice, compared with that of Marion Williams or Delores Barrett, is wilfully non-expressive, reinforcing with its blare the frenzy promoted by her pianism. The orgiastic effect is magnified when she sings and plays with the backing of a vocal group: sometimes, as in 'John said he saw a number', a single blues shouter (Sara Martin) and a hot Gospeller (Richard M. Jones), sometimes, as in 'By and by we're goin' to see the King', with a semi-professional group (the Reverend McGhee and his Jubilee Singers). Their version of 'Lamb's blood has washed me clean' is wildly corybantic; and the title is justified because Arizona's hollers and the choir's microtonal howls attain, through their primitivism, a pristine vernality. The ecstasy induced by the Devil's music succours the mysterious way in which God is said to perform his wonders.

Arizona Drane's squawk might also be described as a rasp, a term Alan Lomax applies, in his quasi-science of cantometrics,[15] to the tight, nasalized vocal production endemic to male-dominated societies. When women employ such a technique they may be reflecting the emotional numbness, even agony, that living under patriarchal dominance causes them, or they may be unconsciously borrowing male tightness and toughness as a means towards survival in a hard world. Arizona Drane's rasp, like that of women in American pioneer communities, belongs to the second category. Her Mexican blood may have some bearing on this aspect of her vocal production, affecting her basically Negroid quality. She becomes a Black matriarch assuming the role of White patriarch. In

15 For an account of cantometrics see pp.238–9.

any case, she is an eccentric, being a pianist before she is a singer. The mainstream singers in female Black Gospel music tend to absorb masculine rasp into the more liquid vocalization of the African, which is orientated towards the chest and belly rather than towards the throat. Arizona Drane's singing sounds penitential if potent; a more representative Gospel singer like Sister Rosetta Tharpe[16] sounds, in comparison, as though she finds her African-biased cantillation a pleasure.

Another ardent affiliate of the Church of God in Christ, she admiringly listened, as a child, to the performances of Arizona, and emulated her when, encouraged by her mother, Katie Bell Nubin, she shouted Sanctified songs at camp meetings. The rudiments of the style are evident when she sings a traditional spiritual, 'Daniel in the lion's den', with her mother as vocal backing and with the basic instrumental ensemble of guitar, piano, string bass and drums. Rosetta begins as primitive shouter over a boogie-rhythmed piano part that is less abrasive, though hardly less exciting, than Arizona Drane's. But as the number unfolds Rosetta gradually takes the centre of the stage, her self-confidence overriding, in jazzy abandon, her mother's traditional Gospel idiom. Daniel in his den and Jonah in the whale's belly were biblically mythical figures whose imprisonment seemed to parallel the Negro's lot. The very idiom of jazz – with its blue notes[17] pressing against the harmonic prison of the White hymn and its polyrhythms striving against the metrical prison of the White march – unconsciously echoes this theme. Not surprisingly, Rosetta converts jazz to her Gospel purpose. Despite her Sanctified childhood, she had led a harried life, working during the thirties in big cities with big bands, notably Cab Calloway's. In those years most of her material was jazz standards, though she often insinuated a Gospel song into her sets, with overwhelming effect. Learning from her experience as dance-band vocalist, she yet remained faithful to her church and its music, to which she returned: unequivocally, except in so far as her Gospel style profited from her enhanced mastery of jazz line and rhythm.

Having re-entered the fold and acquired the soubriquet of 'Sister', Rosetta Tharpe attained her heyday in the fifties and early sixties. She now performed with larger, more commercially streamlined instrumental groups, and used fairly sophisticated

16 *Sister Rosetta Tharpe.*
17 See Glossary.

arrangements. Yet much of her material is still called 'traditional', and she is credited with the composition of some of it: justly so, in so far as, being a Gospel singer, she presents each performance anew, as a Message. Basic to all her songs is her impeccable enunciation; every word must be audible if its therapy is to function. A fair proportion of the verse is spoken, with the heightened declamation of a Black preacher. Preaching speech is always on the point of being sublimated into song; when she sings, her voice is edgy, but less raspy than Drane's.

Her finest numbers tend to be the most expansive, such as 'I do, don't you?' and 'God, lead us along'. Through God, the self and the people are united; and the Devil too plays his part, since the effect of exaltation increases the more jazz tension surfaces. This we may hear in 'What are they doing in Heaven?', which begins in ballad style and in organ-like sonority, but with the voice very blue in timbre and rhythm. The choric responses become almost fierce; although this is a talkin' and preachin' song, its lyricism garners strength from its jazzy open-endedness. There may even be dubiety in the putative answer to the question: *What* are they doing in Heaven?

But this is hardly Sister Rosetta's most characteristic number. Usually she thinks she knows the answers, and her confidence is her strength. Sometimes this is manifest in fast rags and music-hall numbers such as 'Blow you, the trumpet of Zion', a rousing march that carries all before it. In similar vein, 'Shine for Jesus' leads the ragged march towards the extrovert exuberance of rock. Balancing these pieces are numbers, usually in waltz time, that encroach on the terrain of White country music. 'Lilly of the valley', 'Seeking for me' and 'Never alone' recall the ballads of Hank Williams and share with him the 'sincerity' that he said was the essential attribute of a successful pop song. But the black edge to Rosetta's voice and the subtlety of her rhythmic nuances give to these numbers a depth to which Williams seldom attained. Rosetta Tharpe, as emblematic Black earth goddess, can dispense the balm that Hank Williams, being White and male, can only wishfully and wistfully yearn for. Like Hank, Rosetta knew 'the fury and the mire of human veins' at first hand; unlike him she was not, given her faith, broken by them.

The Gospel singers so far discussed worked in the Bible belts of the American plains, but the greatest woman Gospeller — the first to attain national, even international, fame — was born in New Orleans, in 1911, and profited from that richly musical, polyethnic

American, African, French, Creole, Spanish, Italian and German environment. Mahalia Jackson's grandparents had been born into slavery; some of her relatives were Black entertainers playing valses, quadrilles, polkas and 'mazookas' at White house parties, as well as blues and rags with Ma Rainey's circus. Despite the hedonistic atmosphere of New Orleans, the Jackson family was devout and when, like so many New Orleans jazz folk, they moved north to Chicago they found not only less rigorous economic conditions, but also a more strenuously Evangelical environment.

Young Mahalia soon combined religious enthusiasm with economic viability in becoming lead singer to Salem Baptist Church and a member of the Johnson Gospel Singers. She triumphed through the magnetism of her voice and personality. Television contracts brought fame and even fortune, as she became the only Gospel singer almost as well known to White as to Black audiences. Although she received materially tempting offers to perform in other than religious contexts she, unlike Rosetta Tharpe, rejected them, resolutely refusing to sing anything other than Gospel music. This did not mean that she was unaware of the dark realities of the present. For the Negro, Gospel music was inseparable from a context of oppression. Having become an international celebrity, Mahalia Jackson brought political motivation into the open. In later years her art and her faith worked for Civil Rights, in co-operation with Martin Luther King.

The magnificent voice and the fervent faith are almost inseparable; a voice of such vibrancy, over so wide a range, creates a sound that is as all-embracing, as secure as the womb, from which singer and listener may be reborn.[18] Singing one of the best known of spirituals, 'Nobody knows the trouble I seen', she begins very slowly, savouring the sorrow-burdened words, which concern the basic human condition, not merely the plight of the Black in an alien land. The breathtaking beauty of the voice and the superbly controlled transitions from speech to prayer to song heal and anneal. This gives Mahalia a chance to hit back at the hurtful world when, in the latter part of the spiritual, she swings the tune almost jauntily. 'City called Heaven' inverts this process in that heaven is a state beyond mortal coils and toils – which are none the less incarnate in the low, drone-dominated opening phrases, in which intonation is absolutely precise, even when off pitch! A vision of bliss springs from an awareness of desperate mortality.

18 *In the Upper Room with Mahalia Jackson.*

Sometimes Mahalia Jackson makes creative use of country music; her slower numbers, like those of Rosetta Tharpe, may recall Hank Williams in being a cross between hymn and parlour ballad. In 'He's my light' country idiom is intensified by the reality of the blues more potently than it is even in Hank William's finest numbers. 'I walked into the garden' is a fast and 'Come to Jesus' a slow, country waltz; in both the corny convention is reborn through the immediacy of the dialogue between soloist and chorus, the self and the people. Often the numbers are ascribed to 'Jackson' but, as with Rosetta Tharpe, there is little distinction between composed numbers and those picked up from folk or commercial sources and 'arranged' – usually by someone with the appropriately anonymous name of Smith. In every case the music becomes the performance: an act of prayer as well as or rather instead of a concert.

As with Rosetta Tharpe the emotive power of Mahalia Jackson's music is most impressive in her longer pieces. 'In the upper room' begins very slowly, with tremolando chords on organ. From that womb of sound the vocal line tenebrously emerges, gradually taking wing in coloratura of immense range, while the chorus throbs in chromatic harmony that is a sophistication of the improvised homophony[19] of plantation choirs. The performance is the experience, as the voice climbs from the sultry register of the 'low room' to the ethereal heights of the 'upper room'. Transcendence is enhanced as the tempo quickens and jazz elements – blue notes, scoops, slides, elisions and syncopations – grow more obtrusive. The final stanzas, evoking Mahalia's communion with Jee–hee–hee–sus in the upper room, sound powerfully sexy, with an audible wink that is poles removed from salaciousness. If we recall the age-old association of the ecstasy of (especially female) saints with sexuality, we will find no hint of blasphemy in this. Rather it is another example – the most potent we have so far encountered – of Gospel music's paradoxical liaison between God and Devil.

How close Gospel music may be to secular jazz is revealed in Mahalia Jackson's magisterial performance as vocalist with the Duke Ellington band, in his 'religious suite', *Black, Brown and Beige*. The Duke holds her back until the fourth movement, 'Come Sunday': in which she produces a variety of tone colour – from darkest purple to silver sheen – which remains part of the ripe Ellington ensemble. At the same time her control of line creates a serenely structured jazz

19 See Glossary.

melody; even her hummed final chorus, tugging at the heart strings, remains noble. Her ultimate improvisation on the words of the Twenty-third Psalm is deeply affecting Gospel incantation, stemming from speech while contributing to the band's euphony.

Black Gospel music, in ritualistic contexts, is far from dead; indeed the most thrilling 'live' Gospel recordings ever issued appeared as late as 1972, in a double album by Aretha Franklin with James Cleveland and the Southern California Community Choir.[20] Born in 1942, belonging to a later generation than Mahalia Jackson and Rosetta Tharpe, Aretha Franklin is best known as the most inspired of women soul singers.[21] None the less she started from a devout Evangelical background, her father being a preacher with a voice of inspirational quality, her mother a Gospel singer admired by Mahalia Jackson herself. When Aretha returned to church to record these tracks she proved how deeply the roots of soul were embedded in Gospel; she also demonstrated that there can be no rigid demarcation between the secular and religious impulses in jazz. Performing in church, with the Reverend James Cleveland as preacher, pianist and choir leader, Aretha Franklin does not merely sing: she creates an experience in which we participate along with the several hundred 'gathered together' in worship. Because she is making 'music of necessity' she sings more wondrously than she has ever done. Interaction between her genius and that of the Reverend Cleveland generates inspired and inspiring enthusiasm in choir and congregation; and the word 'genius' seems not extravagant, if one recalls its dictionary definition as 'natural ability or tendency . . . exalted intellectual power, instinctive and extraordinary imaginative, creative or inventive capacity'.[22]

The material comes from sundry sources, all retempered in the heat of the moment. Numbers described as 'traditional' may have folk origins, or may be composed hymns that have become public property through hard use. Among the most remarkable is a version of the shape-note[23] Evangelical hymn 'Amazing Grace', which opens very slowly with the choir chanting in improvised homo-phony, austerely diatonic in the style originally adopted by New Englanders. Through the concords, Aretha begins to croon snatches of vocalise, on and around each syllable of the words. Gradually her

20 *Amazing Grace.*
21 See pp.68–71 for a discussion of Aretha Franklin as soul singer.
22 *Concise Oxford Dictionary.*
23 See Glossary.

roulades[24] become more extended until she's soaring on top of the homophony, now screeching or squawking in a wilder version of Arizona Dranes's bleat, now sobbing and sighing with a warm liquidity recalling Mahalia Jackson. Chorus and congregation rise to a frenzy that, in winging lyricism, hints at 'mystical' incandescence.

No less remarkable, if more immediately physical, is 'How I got over', a number by an earlier Gospel singer, Clara Ward, who had deeply influenced Aretha's singing childhood. On this occasion Clara Ward was present in the church, along with Aretha's singing mother and preaching father; the fact is worth mentioning because it is further evidence of the tendency of Black ritual music to transform personal into communal feeling and, beyond that, into universal experience. Aretha's expressivity of timbre and malleability of rhythm are here intimately personal, though the quasi-*super*human *sostenuto* of her line wafts her among the angels. The jazz thrust of Cleveland's piano playing, reinforced by the percussionists, provides a link between earth and heaven.

If Gospel ritual is distinct from concert performance, it has something in common with pop music, so it is not surprising that Aretha Franklin incorporates into the Gospel service songs from totally different traditions. She even transmutes 'You'll never walk alone' by Rodgers and Hammerstein from a 'lonesome' jazz standard of the thirties dance halls into an impassioned appeal for Christ's succour, assimilating jazz intonation into the preaching chant of her Church. The late entry of the choir sends prickles down the spine and provokes Aretha to a cataclysmic cadenza, wide in range, startling in dynamics. Comparable metamorphoses occur when she adapts material from her own generation. Marvyn Gaye's 'Wholly holy', a Motown soul song, distinguished in its own right, becomes the more so when Aretha turns it into a hymn, with wide-spanned line over a gentle rock beat.

Throughout, the inspirational quality of worship ensures that Aretha will achieve new identity in each performance, whatever the source of her material. The traditional numbers are all 'arranged', and she is credited as arranger. One suspects that little notation was involved, the arrangements being empirical. This means that for Aretha as Gospel singer performance is composition, and she may not be off the mark in believing both to be divinely instigated. By borrowing the Devil's means, God triumphs in Aretha Franklin's Gospel music — which is also her finest contribution both to soul and to jazz.

24   See Glossary.

Chapter Two

THE ROCKBOTTOM REALITY OF
THE BLUES

Blues blues blues
  Why did you bring trouble to me?

O death please sting me,
  and take me out of my misery.

Sara Martin

I got to make it, I got to find the end.

Bessie Smith

Black woman, in her emblematic incarnations as the archetypes of
mother earth and eternal goddess, took over and matriarchized, in
her Gospel music, the patriarchy of the White Christian church. But
the basic music of the Black African, transplanted into White
America, was not religious but secular. However readily Negroes
responded to Christianity, they were segregated from their own
gods, and found the heart of their music not so much in worship as
in the painful reality of their everyday lives. Their work songs
reverted to the primitive holler, part sung, part yowled; as they
hollered to themselves in the empty fields the deep roots of their
racial heritage were stretched in an ageless pain. In the astonishing

'Wild ox moan',[1] as sung by Vera Hall – whose 'Trouble so hard' afforded our introduction to Gospel music – the tranced repetition of broken pentatonic phrases induces an immense loneliness. Distortions of pitch sound more Eastern than Western, transplanting into American English the pitch inflexions of African languages. So evocative a memory of so remote an antiquity makes the present moment's dedication to toil seem the more forlorn.

Field hollers were of course sung unaccompanied, being addressed not to an audience but to the singer himself or herself, and to the task in hand. Work songs and play songs might be unaccompanied but, being of their nature communal, could be supported percussively by any *ad hoc* banging or scraping instruments employed in the act of work. Naturally enough, Negroes picked up such European instruments, in however tattered and battered a condition, as came to hand, and were soon playing violins along with the percussion instruments on which they habitually improvised. Most crucial was their discovery of the guitar: an instrument that had affinities with the African banjo, which had accompanied the slaves to the plantations, but was musically more rewarding. The guitar could play pitch distortions similar to those found in primitive monodic musics, emulating the Black singing and speaking voice; at the same time it could offer the sensual sonority of triadic harmony. Singer and guitar could indulge in antiphonal dialogue comparable with that between leader and group in African tribal musics. The difference was that the group need no longer be present. Through his guitar the deracinated Negro was able to talk to himself, whoever might, fortuitously, be listening.

Although the blues derived directly from field hollers and indirectly from ballads, spirituals and Gospel shouts, they needed the guitar for musical consummation. At first, country bluesmen such as Blind Willie Johnson used the guitar mainly to provide drones for their African-style tumbling strains to ride over; but as they became more involved with White march and hymn, blues 'form' was gradually precipitated from the interaction of the two worlds. The twelve-bar structure of the blues – four bars of tonic moving to the seventh chord, two bars of subdominant, two of tonic, two of dominant seventh and two more of tonic – was a lowest common denominator, derived from the hymn, within which improvisation could take place. There was no clear

1 *Negro Worksongs and Calls.*

distinction between the conventions of the Church and those of the saloon and street; the blues sequence was simply the context within which the Negro was obliged to live, socially and musically. The dialogue between voice and instrument thus complemented a deeper antiphony between the Negro's experience and the alien world in which he found himself. The combination of the rigid harmonic and tonal form with the vocal line's African flexibility of rhythm and pitch represented a difficult acceptance – a part, therefore, of the reality from which, without sentimental evasion or even religious hope, the Negro started.

This is why the blues are both personal, in so far as each man sings alone of his sorrow, and impersonal, in so far as that individual experience is the common lot. Although the singer may protest against destiny, he is not usually angry, and seldom looks to heaven for relief. He sings to get the blues *off* his mind – which is why blues are often affirmative, even jolly, despite their oppressed subject matter. Robert Johnson,[2] a highly neurotic bluesman addicted to wine and women no less than to song, wailed (shortly before he was murdered in 1937, at the age of 21):

Bad time is upon me,
Everywhere the panic is on,
I feel disgusted,
All the good times done gone.

But, continuing his confessional improvisation, he goes on to a general statement:

Everybody's crying
They can't get a break.
Tell me what's the matter.
Everything seem to ache.

Tragic passion is tempered by detachment. The truth of the blues is rockbottom: at the furthest possible remove from a Stephen Foster dream of the Old Kentucky Home.

Country blues singers were usually if not exclusively male, their art growing from the ritual of agricultural work. Those who raised blues to professional status tended to be social outcasts, whether through temperamental malaise like Robert Johnson, or through physical affliction, usually blindness, like Blind Willie Johnson or

2   *Robert Johnson, 1936–37.*

Blind Lemon Jefferson. Homeless, they wandered from city to city, seeking a minimal livelihood from song. But by the twenties and thirties, when the blues had matured into the most profound manifestation of Black consciousness, the 'classic' as compared with the 'country' blues has become primarily urban and female. The term 'classic' signifies that these blues are the climax to a tradition in which many disparate streams, religious and secular, meet. There were sociological as well as psychological reasons for the dominance of women in this area. The female attachment to the Church provided solidarity in an atomized society, and the relative economic security of Black women as domestic help for affluent Whites offered a minimal basis for hope. In classic blues women sing of belonging to a maternally orientated community, even though it may be afflicted. The solace Blacks sought for the lacerations of patristic White America was to be found on the maternal bosom. Later, when female blues singers became entertainers serving a White as well as Black public, their material success could be seen as morally suspect. Black women could be accepted, even welcomed, as titillators of White men whereas Black men, as titillators of White women, were inadmissible.

A few female primitive blues singers cropped up in the days when the country blues was a male prerogative. An example of this rudimentary style is the singing of Bessie Jones, who croaks 'Beggin' the blues' unaccompanied.[3] Most of Bessie's singing life was devoted to the Church; but she recorded this track when she was still young and 'out in the world', inventing the words *ad hoc*. Significantly, she sounds like a man; her savagely 'rasping', near-baritone voice sears like a field holler. Comparable with this are two 1934 numbers by Bertha Lee,[4] then wife of the celebrated bluesman Charlie Patton. In 'Oh death' and 'Troubled 'bout my mother' they holler together in stridently hymnic vein, while Charlie strums drone chords, rather than the blues sequence, on his guitar. 'Mind reader', however, has no connection with Gospel hymnody, being a real blues on the traditional theme of sexual jealousy: a theme that, denying familial continuity, underlines lonesomeness. Bertha Lee too sounds like a man in that her vocal production is harsh, almost stern, making her protest against her lover's infidelity an act of *self*-assertion. The conventional repetition

3   *The Roots of the Blues.*
4   *Bertha Lee.*

of the first two lines of the text serves, as usual, an empirical function, giving the singer–player time to reflect, in a performance based equally on memory and on improvised invention, on what's coming next. It also reinforces the semantic point, making an affirmation, however desperate the odds, by saying things forcefully, twice.

The most impressive of these early female blues shouters was Memphis Minnie who, bellowing to her own guitar, was recognized during the twenties as peer of the male blues singers. She made a comeback during the forties, recording with the barrelhouse pianist Sunnyland Slim; from these tracks[5] we may retrospectively chart the transition from country guitar blues to the classic blues that women sang to the accompaniment of piano, a harmonically orientated one-man band, often with an obbligato melody instrument also. Memphis Minnie's 'Down home girl' presents the prototype: a voice of sterling courage, giving a fillip to the underbitch, with a barrelhouse piano part thrustfully magnifying the traditional guitar sequence. The bleat of the jazz horn universalizes Minnie's lament, which is also an affirmation. Horn, usually trumpet or saxophone, is a generic term for a blown instrument in jazz, and is perhaps so called for its phallic connotations. It extends the range and intensifies the sonority of the male urban Black's voice, parleying with the opulently maternal resonance of the Black's woman's voice. The image of an earth mother is no less applicable, though the earth has grown dingy.

Though the barrelhouse pianists contemporary with the guitar-plucking male blues singers were primarily instrumentalists, they occasionally shouted improvised blues verses against their rowdy pianism. Women seldom did this unless one counts Arizona Dranes as a barrelhouse rather than Gospel performer. But Jimmy Yancey, greatest of Chicago barrelhouse men in expressivity if not in virtuosity, sometimes called on his wife to provide an improvised vocal commentary of his piano blues.[6] Jimmy's own performances were always intimate, often unusual in favouring slow tempi, thin textures and gently undulating rhythms. When Mama Yancey stands by his piano, making up verses that give the blues experience a local habitation and a name, she intensifies the inwardness of his playing, despite or because of the fact that her vocal production is

5 *Memphis Minnie.*
6 *Lowdown Dirty Blues.*

churchy rather than sensual. This applies whether they are making their own blues empirically, as in the marvellous 'Four o'clock blues', or whether they are adapting folk material, as in 'Make me a pallet on the floor'. Even when playing a more composed piece like Leroy Carr's 'How long blues', Jimmy achieves his lonesome sensitivity by way of bare textures, hesitating rhythms and minute fluctuations of colour, to which Mama's apparently uninvolved, bleating voice makes a perfect foil. Though these tracks were cut as late as 1951, their spirit is that of the late twenties or early thirties, their emotional impact being proportional to their authenticity.

The 'classic' female blues sprang, however, from an environment different from either the rustic shacks of the guitar-twanging bluesmen or the city tenements where the barrelhouse pianists pounded. The first charismatic woman blues singer was Gertrude Rainey, another 'Ma', who acquired her maternal soubriquet at the age of 18.[7] Born in Georgia in 1886, she had the usual Southern background of hard work and hard worship. Field hollers were an aural complement to her childhood; the Church dominated her adolescence. Her path to musical professionalism was, however, through the theatre; by the turn of the century she had made her début at the Columbus Opera House in a talent-spotting show called *The Bunch of Blackberries*. In 1904 she married another Black entertainer, William Riley, with whom she travelled the South, doing a song-and-dance routine in minstrel and vaudeville shows. Blues were merely part of a repertory based on sundry types of music-hall song. After she became famous she told an interviewer that she first overheard a blues in a small town in Missouri, when she was touring with a tent show.

Her genius lay in her recognizing what the blues might mean not merely in folk, but also in relatively sophisticated, art. When, in the early twenties, she embarked on a series of 'race' recordings,[8] she revealed how the blues laid bare the soul of the deracinated Negro, and could speak potently to the souls of most inhabitants of big cities. Paradoxically, her appeal was dependent on her apparent remoteness from such urban living. Short and squat, gap-toothed, fuzzbuzz-haired, extravagantly bejewelled, she looked like some grotesque reincarnation of tribal witchcraft; and sounded not only

7   *Ma Rainey*.
8   'Race' recordings in the early days of jazz were geared specifically to the Black public, but were usually pressed and distributed by White entrepreneurs.

like 'The Mother of the Blues' but also like a cultic priestess. Despite her secular material, the liturgical flavour of her vocal production linked Africa to the Christian–American Church.

In 'Sleep talkin' blues' she is accompanied by Tampa Red on guitar and Georgia Tom Dorsay on piano. Tampa Red was a country bluesman who had gravitated into Memphis show business; Georgia Tom Dorsay sang blues but was more active in the field of Gospel music. Not surprisingly, this number reveals the relationship between secular country blues and Gospel song; and something of this priestly flavour survives in a 'low-down' number like 'Blame it on the blues', in which Ma's searing timbre absorbs the jazz 'dirt'[9] that came from the raw immediacy of her experience. Both the music and the title here point to the therapeutic efficacy of the blues.

Because the classic blues were both personal testament and communal entertainment in church, music-hall and circus, they developed naturally towards co-operation between a soloist and a band – which is a *congregation* of individuals. The most rudimentary example, in Ma Rainey's early years, is the 'jug' band, so called because the musicians and audience played on any sounding source – jugs, washboards, knives and forks – that happened to be handy. In 'Hear me talkin' to you' and 'Victim of the blues' Ma brazenly bleats with the Tub Jug Washboard Band, centred around Georgia Tom Dorsay's piano with Tampa Red and anonymous players improvising on jugs, washboards and kazoos. 'Black cat, hoot owl blues' veers towards the comedy number as practised by the old Georgian fiddlers; cats and owls are audibly given human, and specifically sexual, connotations. In 'Ma Rainey's Black Bottom' this minstrel-show idiom merges into the New Orleans–Chicago set-up of cornet, trombone, piano and drums, and does so without entirely relinquishing the dark majesty of the blues.

The classic urban blues is fulfilled when Ma Rainey sings with a ensemble featuring some of the finest players in twenties jazz. The famous 'See, see rider' has a wide-spanned tune that suggests a folk hymn, which Ma belts with magisterial power, while Louis Armstrong's cornet weaves an ecstatic counterpoint above it. In 'Chain gang blues' and 'Bessemer bound blues' Joe Smith's sweetly lyrical but no less nervous cornet substitutes for Armstrong, with Buster Bailey on noodling clarinet, Charlie Green on trombone,

9 See Glossary.

Charlie Dixon on banjo and Fletcher Henderson – later to be significant as intermediary between improvised and composed jazz – on piano; the no less legendary Coleman Hawkins youthfully provides a fundament on bass saxophone.

Though the collocation of so many jazz greats makes for great music, it's significant that Ma produces some of her most moving performances with forgotten or unknown musicians. In 'New boeval blues' the traditional words deal with the basic blues theme that relates sex to death, the boeval being at once a destructive pest and a life-creating penis. Ma's sepulchral tones reveal the grandeur of the theme, beginning with an unaccompanied moan like a field holler, then gathering potency with the slow-swinging beat.

The words of blues are often powerfully moving poetry, invented *ad hoc* by a particular man or woman in response to particular circumstances. As the tradition evolves, these words are refashioned by others, in response to their own in some ways similar, in other ways dissimilar, experience. Much the same is true of the tunes, many of which became associated with particular singers, not so much because they'd 'composed' them as because they'd acquired rights over them through repeated performance. The best singers naturally tended to be the most creatively inventive; if Bessie Smith[10] is 'The Empress of the Blues', of which Ma Rainey had been the Mother, that is because she is both the finest singer and the most adventurous 'maker'. Born some time between 1895 and 1900 at Chattanooga, 8 miles north of the Georgia–Tennessee state boundary, 'Queen' or 'Empress' Bessie belongs to a generation ten to fifteen years later, and under much greater stress than Mother Rainey's. The population of Chattanooga then numbered about 30,000, of which 13,000, were Black. Large numbers of Blacks were unemployed and all were grievously underprivileged. Bessie's talent was conditioned by the early humiliations she suffered. Complementarily, her improvisatory technique was inseparable from her illiteracy; she often remembered things wrongly, and the mistakes were a manifestation of genius.

As a child Bessie worked in tent shows and circuses, sometimes alongside Ma Rainey, though the legend that she was Ma's 'pupil' is unsubstantiated. She differs from her predecessor in that although her art preserves folk roots, she tugs on them more strenuously and more painfully. Ma Rainey made a fortune from her singing,

10 *The Bessie Smith Story.*

directed at her own race, in the South. Bessie, a later and more neurotic temperament, did not abjure her rural sources, yet became a committed American urbanite. Though her musical roots were primitive and her motive force darkly erotic (her appetite for sex being commensurate with her obsessive need of alcohol), she was, within her convention, a highly sophisticated musician. The tension between her folk origins and her citified art released her music and in the process destroyed both her and it. In this sense great jazz performers have often been scapegoats for the ills of industrial society.

Bessie Smith's 'martyrdom' has become legendary. Making and squandering several fortunes, she neither sought nor received anything but dusty answers from men, gin and drugs; and although the story that she died in 1937 because, injured in a car accident, she was refused admission to a White hospital is factually untrue, it has its allegorical relevance. No wonder she sang 'You can't trust nobody, might as well be alone'; no wonder she believed 'you reap just what you sow'. Her malaise sprang from what life did to her; her blues became an epitome of urban man's frustration, not merely because they were true, but also because they accepted this truth with pride, dignity and even a mountainous good humour to which most crippled inhabitants of big cities, White as well as Black, cannot aspire. She was not called 'Empress' merely because of her gargantuan physical proportions.

In the country blues words and tune had been made up by some, usually anonymous, poet–musician; with repeated performance by him and others words were changed, verses added, nuances of expression modified. In the band blues of New Orleans and Chicago the tunes were again often traditional, but since there were no, or at most only implicit, words, the possibilities for improvisation, by several performers rather than one, were more complex. Bessie Smith's town blues combine the intimacy of the country blues with the complexity of the band blues: for the singer is no longer accompanied by herself but by the band's rhythmic–harmonic fundament of piano and string bass, while the melody is shared between the vocalist and the band's soloist(s). In the blues of Ma Rainey, we noted, the instrumentalist sometimes takes over from the singer for a verse, offering his wordless comment on the tale the vocalist tells. He is thus simultaneously at one with the singer and apart from her: the solitariness of the blues has paradoxically become a communal experience. Such effects are more subtly employed in the blues of Bessie Smith who, even more than Ma Rainey, found great horn players eager to co-operate with her.

Her singing of 'Careless love' reveals the evolution of urban blues from rural roots, for the modally lyrical tune is derived from an old Kentucky mountain song, which in turn stemmed from an English Elizabethan source. Fred Longshaw's piano, in conjunction with Charlie Green's trombone, makes a solid, harmonium-like sonority, sounding like an amplified rural accordion or chapel organ. Louis Armstrong's cornet, on the other hand, though of folk-like spontaneity, introduces an urban intensity, for its spurting rhythms are jagged rather than easy, while its *fioriture*[11] spill dissonantly over the simple harmonic base. Bessie Smith's vocal line is intermediary. She sounds relaxed, timeless as a country singer; yet her rhythmic–harmonic ellipses make the relaxation weary – and so, perhaps, not relaxed at all. She may be careless but is certainly not carefree; the apparent easiness is only a respite from pain.

Indeed, being careless is not so far from being reckless; and in 'Reckless blues' Bessie sings, with Armstrong's cornet, in his mood of urban tension. The juxtaposition of these two blues demonstrates how the passive melancholy of the country blues acquired, entering the city, an element of nervous laceration. In its angular interlocking of the voice's intimacy with the cornet's bravura, 'Reckless blues' projects a hysteria latent within us all; traditional passivity makes possible modern reaction and even resurgence. That the keyboard instrument, again played by Fred Longshaw, is here a harmonium – rural, domestic, pious – emphasizes the nervous virility of the solo voices.

The tune of 'Careless love' comes distantly from White rural culture, as does the wheezy harmonium of 'Reckless love'. In both numbers the timbre of voice and cornet is at once folk-like and urban; while the background presence as 'arranger' of W. C. Handy indicates the role that art played in bringing the blues to fruition. Handy was an academically trained Black musician who notated accredited compositions; even his most famous number, 'St Louis blues', so refashions its traditional material as to amount to an original. The version of it by Bessie Smith and Louis Armstrong is its definitive statement – in the strict sense superb in majesty of line and control of rhythm. A different manifestation of this equilibrium between folk utterance and art occurs in 'J. C. Holmes blues', in

11   See Glossary.

which Bessie and Louis generate excitement through competition. Music-making usually contains an element of game, as is indicated in the metaphor whereby we speak of 'playing' music; in this number gameyness seems to stand as a metaphor for life's perilous pilgrimage, as we wait, open-eared, to hear whether singer or cornetist will 'make it'.

Competitiveness, however momentarily rewarding, may not be the best basis for a permanent creative relationship. Thrilling though the tracks with Louis Armstrong may be, he was not Bessie Smith's ideal collaborator, probably because his personality was as strong as hers. It was rather in Joe Smith that Bessie discovered her perfect partner, for we feel that his cornet obbligati are the spontaneous overflow of her vocal phrases. We've encountered Joe Smith – who died in a mental hospital after a short life scarcely less tormented than Bessie's – as contributor to some of Ma Rainey's most moving performances. To Bessie Smith he becomes an *alter ego*; she sings, he echoes, and although the echoes introduce inflexions that are his own, they also seem to be latent in the vocal phrases, waiting to be revealed. What his cornet adds is what Bessie left unsaid, yet because it is added by someone other than her, we can feel it as our contribution too. Joe Smith stands, in his anonymous name, for us, identifying Bessie's experience with our own, making us realize the heights and depths we might be capable of. The effect is not dissimilar to the relationship between vocal line and instrumental obbligato in a Bach aria, if so grand a comparison be permitted.

A beautiful example is 'Young woman's blues', in which the dialogue between voice and cornet transforms social protest into tragic lament, impersonal in range, yet rooted in personal experience:

> I'm a young woman
> And I ain't done runnin' around,
> Some people call me a hobo,
> Some people call me a bum,
> Nobody knows my name,
> Nobody knows what I've done.

The words' low-down medley of the outsider mood with a pride at once pathetic and formidable creates a tune that, in Bessie Smith's interpretation, is as dramatic as it is lyrical. The singer's autobiographical fervour inspires Joe Smith to perhaps his most masterly solo. The sudden modulation that enacts, musically, the licence of 'running around' demonstrates the advantage of working within a narrow and rigid convention: on the rare occasions the performer departs from it, the effect is all the more powerful.

Such tragic–ironic blues are among the supreme achievements of jazz, and although they have not often the autobiographical connotations of 'Young woman's blues', they usually spring from, and owe their universality to, topical and local circumstances. In 'Poor man's blues', the gurgling saxophones of the opening combine with the vocal line's displaced accents and pitch distortions to give authenticity to words that, in themselves, are not much more than self-pitying social criticism. That the music is at once savage and grotesque counteracts mawkishness and reveals terror – bitterly, yet without anger.

Similar tragi-comic effects occur when Bessie Smith works with instrumentalists more artistically trained, such as Fletcher Henderson, the pianist–arranger who played so significant a role in the evolution of band jazz. In 'Trombone Cholly', one of the 1927 tracks in which Bessie's companions are Joe Smith, Fletcher Henderson and Charlie Green (then trombonist in Henderson's band), we have a riotous tribute to Charlie (Cholly) Green, offering him opportunity to exploit the farce of trombone slides and burps, while attaining a lilt that turns hilarity into an elevation of the spirit; both Bessie's sturdy line and Joe Smith's sweet cornet contribute to this. If joviality is here tempered by blue reality, in 'Send me to the 'lectric chair' the opposite happens: the grimness of the instrument of death is defused by the boisterous buffonery of the presentation.

But the finest examples of the fusion between Bessie Smith's folk-style blues and semi-composed art are her collaborations with James P. Johnson, a pianist reared both on the traditions of barrelhouse music and in the more formalized and notated conventions of rag. Working in New York rather than in the jazz centres of New Orleans and Chicago, he took himself seriously as an art composer, producing a piano concerto and two symphonies, as well as several artfully notated musicals. We remember him, however, as a jazz performer and creator powerful enough to be a match for Bessie the Empress – as is evident in 'Preachin' the blues', in which his loping stride-bass supports her vibrant line, Evangelical in flavour despite an unambiguously secular text. 'Blue spirit blues' shows artfulness in transforming folk modality into a sombre

diatonic minor. The number describes descent into a hell populated
by trident-prodding demons familiar from the fire-and-brimstone
sermons of wayside preachers. That the effect is ironic, perhaps
parodistic, is part of the art: Bessie's howls and growls grotesquely
but realistically project the torments of the damned, while James
P.'s glissandi and sudden snatches of double time depict the
scurrying evasive action by which we try to escape the gallivanting
devils.

Tragically complementing this scary farce is the noble 'Black
water blues', in which the horror of the Mississippi floods inspired
the folk poet to images of startling vividness. The tune is not far
from a tumbling strain, though Bessie gives grandeur to its
declensions, while the energy of Johnson's boogie-rhythmed piano
floats us above even these troubled waters. If we compare this
performance with the most powerful of the country blues singers,
we recognize that 'art' has added another, and valuable, dimension.
When Robert Johnson sings of devils in 'Hellhound on my trail' he
does so without the salve of irony. In 'Blithe spirit' James P.
Johnson routs devils by crazy comedy, while even in the tragic
'Back water blues' he acts as exorcist by introducing boogie-
rhythmed water images that temper horror with mirth.

Some such recognition of 'other modes of experience that may be
possible' is usually a concomitant of great art, as the examples of
Shakespeare and Beethoven supremely prove. Bessie Smith in her
ghetto can hardly challenge comparison with Shakespeare in London
or Beethoven in Vienna; but one can say that, within her narrow
confines, she too is unafraid to storm the dizziest heights and plumb
the darkest depths. Moreover, she can surprise us not only within
the convention of the classic blues, but even within 'commercial'
conventions usually regarded as trivial. In her early years she sang
minstrel-show numbers, in later days the pop standards that, as
we'll see in the next chapter, succeeded vaudeville songs.

The late 'Black mountain blues' is almost a parody of the
narrative country number. Bessie adopts the folk raconteur's
deadpan stance, modified by sophisticated innuendo in her vocal
inflexions, while Ed Allen's chirpy cornet refracts these ironic
overtones. Yet the effect is not 'smart'; the rural mode is not so
much deflated as re-created in an urbanly worldly-wise spirit that
makes the song seem as old as the hills and as fresh as a new pin.
Bessie even manages to instil genuine feeling into a sentimental pop
standard called 'Muddy waters', based on the same Mississippi

floods disaster as the great 'Back water blues'. We don't know whether Bessie liked the (in the circumstances offensive) words of 'Muddy waters'; we do know, on the evidence of our ears, that she discovered pathos and terror in the human predicament behind the words and that she expressed it with conviction. She was a folk singer in the immediacy of her response, a professional show-business woman in her ability to communicate and to project that response.

This applies to her rare comic numbers also. If in 'Muddy waters' she brings to the sentimentality of a pop standard the hard truth of the blues, in 'Alexander's ragtime band' she injects into a Tin Pan Alley parody of 'nigger minstrel' mirth a near-hysteric febrility. Admittedly, Irving Berlin was much more than a hack composer; even so, Bessie's inebriation sounds more Dionysiacally corybantic than his because, with her Black experience she knows more about the pain and tension that are being released.

Sequential to this is the fact that one of the most moving and 'blue' of Bessie's performances would be not of a blues but of a pop song picked up, late in her career, from a Negro entertainer with whom she had worked. Jimmy Fox's 'Nobody knows you when you're down and out' is not a bad song in its own right; Bessie, at a time when its autobiographical implications were all too obvious, turned it not so much into a song of social protest as into a *cri de coeur*: a profound testament to her lonesomeness and still more to her bafflement at the unpredictability of fortune and the frailty of human loyalties. Her elongation of the syllable *no* in the opening phrase suggests indignation, even anger, and at the same time a pathos purged of self-pity; while the discoloration of tone on the words 'fall so low' seems to drain off the blood, almost to stop the pulse. Life is shut off, in a neutral limbo; even song breaks down, as Bessie hums desultorily to herself. But the humming is not the end. She sings again, with a wild, proud fortitude, reinforced by Ed Allen's husky cornet and ballasted by the solemn resonance of Cyrus St Clair's old-fashioned, New Orleans-style tuba bass.

The town blues, like the country blues in an earlier generation, were about *going on*, being in spirit stoic rather than religious. Not fortuitously, the blues attained their brief heyday, and became relevant to Whites as well as Blacks, during the Depression years. A down-and-out music, enduring, managed to *sing*; and it is significant that, despite the achievements of professionals like Ma Rainey and Queen Bessie, blues remained an amateur activity, a 'people's music'. To draw a line between professional and amateur status in such a field is neither easy nor helpful; in semi-folk art amateurs may be intermittently inspired and professionals may relapse into routine. Among the singers peripheral to Bessie value does not seem dependent on their degree of professionalism. Only Ida Cox[12] can challenge Ma Rainey and Bessie Smith both in contemporary celebrity and in the respect she continued to earn from jazz musicians.

Her earliest (1923) tracks slightly predate Ma Rainey's, and resemble them in being strongly flavoured with vaudeville. In 'Any woman's blues', 'Bama bound blues' and 'Lovin' is the thing I'm wild about' she sings authentic twelve-bar blues to Lovie Austin's gently swinging piano, but uses the open vocal production of the music-hall, producing an effect powerful but not, like Bessie Smith's, majestic. The genuine blues spirit surfaces when the two women are joined, for 'Graveyard dream blues' and 'Weary way blues', by Tommy Ladnier's cornet and Jimmy O'Bryant's clarinet. Especially in 'Ida Cox's lawdy lawdy blues' this combo makes raw music appropriate to Prohibition-years Chicago, the Windy City where the sessions were held. But Ida Cox differs from Bessie Smith not only in the range of her talent but also in the fact that, living longer, she was still recording in 1939–40. These tracks not only profit from electric technology but are further modified by the fact that by this date the style of the jazz cabaret vocalist is fully developed.

For this reason Ida Cox, singing genuine blues, does so in a manner into which Bessie never ventured. In 'Deep sea blues' Ida's sustained line has the jazz sensitivity of an Ella Fitzgerald, and her collaborators respond accordingly. Hot Lips Page on trumpet and J. C. Higgenbottom on trombone reflect the passion and drilled precision of Count Basie's Kansas City band; James P. Johnson at this date swings piano with a barrelhouse fervour honed to cocktail-lounge elegance, his delicacy being echoed by the linear pickin'-style guitar of the phenomenally gifted, then very young, Charlie Christian. The music hasn't the tragic grandeur Bessie Smith attains at her finest, but its fusion of the classicality of the woman's blues with the easier intimacy of cabaret jazz makes for powerfully affecting music – especially in the very slow 'Death letter blues', where Ida's voice is at its most plangent, over

12   *Ida Cox* and *Ida Cox and her All Star Band.*

Johnson's rolling boogie rhythm, haloed by whispering horns that sound both seductive and minatory.

Around these three greats, Ma Rainey, Bessie Smith and Ida Cox, are grouped peripheral minor figures,[13] some of whom emerged briefly, only to disappear, while others, longer lived, staged returns, sometimes in different guises. Mary Johnson was an early casualty, yet the few tracks she recorded in 1929 are basic to dirty, dusty Chicago where, if the verb be appropriate, she flourished. In 'Key to the mountain', when she dialogues with Ike Rogers's grumpy trombone, it is difficult to decide whether woman or instrument has the more wounding vibrato. The warmth of old New Orleans has been totally dissipated – as it has from the belting of Chippie Hill, though she sang on occasion with Louis Armstrong himself. Chippie, unlike Mary Johnson, was a survivor who returned in the mid-forties to sing in New York clubs. Her 1946 versions of 'Charleston blues' and 'Around the clock blues' reaffirm the raucousness of old-time barrelhouse and bordello, almost rivalling the blistering ferocity she had attained in her most celebrated track – the 'Pratt blues' in which she proved a worthy partner for Louis Armstrong at full pelt. Honest if not particularly inspired singing invokes a minor miracle from a superb horn player.

Sometimes this works the other way round: instrumental playing of genius may inspire an average singer to heights of expressivity. Consider the justly celebrated 'Death sting me blues' as sung by Sara Martin,[14] usually regarded as a vaudeville singer rather than a blueswoman. Here she is accompanied by a New Orleans-style pick-up group featuring King Oliver himself and the relatively arty pianist, Clarence Williams. The words, a statement of unrequited love, are poetry, combining rockbottom truth with the surprise of revelation; the inflexions of the voice have a comparable immediacy, an awareness of a particular human situation in a particular time and place. Oliver's cornet obbligato, answering Sara's voice with sobs, sighs and occasionally chuckles, makes intense, personal experience universal. We realize, from his wordless lament, that this woman's experience might be our own, and in a sense is so, since everyone is to some degree betrayed. The ringing sonority of the old-fashioned tuba's bass notes reinforces this effect, giving the music a hieratic flavour beyond suspicion of self-

13   *Great Blues Singers.*
14   *Out Came the Blues.*

indulgence. Such depersonalization, here liturgically sombre, also occurs in hilarious, near-farcical form in Oliver's chortles – with an effect not altogether remote from that of the Gravediggers in *Hamlet* or the Porter in *Macbeth*. Such tragi-comedy is not confined to the work of a supreme performer such as Bessie Smith.

Springing from a particular time and place, classic women's blues have proved remarkably durable. Five singers who embarked on their careers in the early twenties but were still active forty, fifty, even sixty, years later will provide a fitting climax to this chapter.

Victoria Spivey,[15] born in Houston, Texas, in 1910, moved to St Louis at the age of 16, scoring a 'race' hit with her recording of 'Black snake blues' and 'T. B. blues'. In the thirties she bloomed in the grime of Chicago, singing her own blues with the finest instrumentalists available, including Armstrong, Oliver, Higgenbottom, Tampa Red, Lonnie Johnson, Omer Simeon and Clarence Williams. It is not surprising that so many top-line instrumentalists were agog to play for her, for in those days her voice had the majesty of Bessie Smith's, if not her mystery. In 'Arkansas Road blues' and 'New black snake blues' she magnificently duets with Lonnie Johnson, imbuing the old guitar blues with urban sophistication. In 'Detroit blues' she sings with Lee Collins's trumpet, Arnett Nelson's clarinet, J. H. Shayne's piano and John Lindsey's bass to transform a trivial personal experience – in a cold spell in gusty Detroit – into an impersonal statement about the human lot.

Most of this early material was in blues tradition. But Victoria Spivey, like all blues singers, also had contacts with the theatre, and in her middle years worked in her own road shows and movies. She retired in 1951, after a domestic catastrophe, but in 1960 returned to the blues, founding her own recording company through which she supported, and to a degree promoted, the (electrified) male blues revival of the sixties and seventies. Old-timers like Little Brother Montgomery, Sunnyland Slim, Memphis Slim and Muddy Waters and forceful new talents like Otis Spann owed much to her company. In turn, her own late style owed something to them, though Victoria's durability has depended most on her own inventiveness. She is by far the most prolific composer, or maker, of classic blues, being rivalled in poetic and lyrical appeal by only a few men, notably Lightning Hopkins, in the revival generation of

15   *Victoria Spivey Reissues* and *Louis and the Blues Singers*.

bluesmen. Throughout her career her blues were performed and adapted by leading jazzmen, from King Oliver and Louis Armstrong to Duke Ellington, and from Ellington to revivalists like John Lee Hooker and Lightning Hopkins himself.

A scarcely less impressive tribute to durability is manifest in Sippie Wallace,[16] another product of Houston, whose brother was the child-prodigy pianist Hershal Thomas and whose father was a publisher who included his daughter's numbers in his catalogue. She played piano in Texas barrelhouse style as well as singing, and remained faithful to her roots after she had moved, in 1923, to New York. There she toured in road shows but, making a comeback in the sixties, proved that her heart was still tied to her Texan adolescence. In her famous 1966 Albert Hall concert she sang old-style blues to the old-style barrelhouse piano of old-world players like Little Brother Montgomery and Roosevelt Sykes. The years rolled back as the piano men churned out their boogie beats, twittered in jittery tremolos, capered in crazy arabesques, while Sippie, disdaining amplification, held her brazen line, beyond fate and fortune. As an inventor of blues Sippie Wallace is less talented than Victoria Spivey, who had organized her comeback; but as maintainer of a tradition that of its nature pays tribute to human fortitude she is unrivalled.

Except perhaps by Alberta Hunter, born at the turn of the century, active in the twenties and thirties, magnificently resurgent in her and the century's early eighties. She ran away from her natal Memphis when she was 11, and was soon singing in low-down dives off Chicago's South Side. She graduated from these haunts of pimps and prostitutes to classier joints such as the Dreamland Café, where she worked alongside the legendary Brick Top and Florence Mills. Like them, she sang vaudeville songs more frequently than blues, though it was her own 'Down-hearted blues' that launched Bessie Smith on her fabulous career. Alberta's relatively gentle, coolly caressing voice never developed the acerbity of a blues belter, let alone the majesty of Bessie, but she had her moments of glory, especially in collaboration with Armstrong, Sidney Bechet, and Fats Waller. Her theatrical talents were encouraged by Eubie Blake, then a writer of musicals as well as a ragtime pianist. Instigated by him, she took off for Europe to work in cabaret and music-hall. She retired from show business in 1954, to become a nurse. Fortuitously

16 *Sippie Wallace Sings the Blues.*

precipitated back into music when she was 80, she made music no less potent than that which she had produced in the thirites and early forties. Given her varied experience, it is not surprising that her art is as eclectic as that of reborn Sippie Wallace is single-minded and simple-hearted.

On her 1935 sessions[17] with an unnamed pianist and guitarist, Alberta offered jazzy cabaret numbers, such as 'You can't tell the difference after dark' and 'Send me a man', full of sexual innuendo, half sung, half spoken. Her enunciation is impeccable, as is appropriate to the intimacy of a cabaret singer, and her voice, whether speaking or singing, is at once tender and cool. In effecting transitions between speech and song she produces a wobbly moan, ambiguous in feeling, since one isn't sure whether it's portentous or risible. Similar effects are more subtly used in her 1940 sessions with Eddie Haywood, a cocktail-lounge pianist capable of swing as well as of delicate filigree – as is evident in 'The castle's rockin' ', the number that Alberta adopted as theme song. At the same time we recognize that such club jazz wouldn't have such substance were it not related to the thread of true blues that runs through her career.

Her finest music, and it is very fine, is in her 1939 tracks recorded in New York with Charlie Shavers on trumpet, Buster Bailey on clarinet, Wellman Braud on bass and a self-effacing Lil Armstrong on piano, all traditional jazz musicians of Chicago era and ethos. Most of these numbers are genuine blues in which Alberta's voice, without becoming gutsy, attains a curiously pallid vibrancy, complemented by Shavers's trumpet and (especially) by Bailey's whirligig clarinet which, veering between gabble, howl and chortle, almost rivals the playing of Bechet himself. 'Yelpin' the blues' is an especially moving example of the traditional tragi-comic ambiguity in the blues between the bestial and the seraphic; while the minor-keyed 'I see you go' approaches Bessie Smith's hieratic solemnity in imparting blue fervour to a number that is not, strictly speaking, a blues. Here the timbre of both voice and clarinet is dark, slightly minatory. Even a version of the jazz standard 'Someday, sweetheart' acquires a blue nervosity within apparent hedonism, as Buster Bailey's clarinet frolics, but like a cat on hot bricks. When he and Alberta duologue in the (real) 'Down-hearted blues' that made her name, they do so with a cool

17   *Classic Alberta Hunter.*

intensity apposite to a number as significant for jazz history as it is
for the singer herself.

A survivor comparable to Alberta Hunter is Helen Humes, born
a decade later in 1913. She acquired some fame between 1938 and
1942 as vocalist with the Basie big band, though she was
overshadowed by the figure – vast in more than one sense – of the
male blues singer Jimmy Rushing. At the age of 60 Helen Humes
made a comeback on a disc[18] dominated by the fine old-style
barrelhouse pianist Jay MacShann; and the music she sings, some of
it her own, is in the tradition of the classic blues, as is her manner of
performance. 'They raided the joint', 'For now and so long' and 'A
million dollar secret' are slow twelve-bar blues sung in a timbre
closer, in rasp and bleat, to Ma Rainey and Bessie Smith than to
Ethel Waters; MacShann's piano, Arnett Cobb's saxophone and
Clarence Brown's guitar likewise reinvoke the low-down funkiness
of Chicago in the thirties. Fast blues like 'Ooo baba leba' and 'Let
the good time roll' are unambiguous barrelhouse music; even when
Helen sings ragtime numbers such as 'My handy man' and 'Guess
who's in town' her vocal production and rhythmic drive relate more
to the barrelhouse than to the theatre shows of Ethel Waters, who
popularized the tunes half a century ago. In 'That old feeling' Helen
proves that she can handle a ballad effectively, but finds in it a raw
nerve – consider her permutations on the word 'old' – that is not
usually associated with the genre. Helen Humes offers, with the
backing of the instrumentalists, a magnificent re-creation of a lost
era, making the past present.

Re-creation may and should lead to progress; we find it when we
turn to a singer born twenty years later than Alberta Hunter,
thirteen years later than Helen Humes. Traditionally, Big Mama
Thornton,[19] like the original 'Ma' Rainey, came from Southern
Alabama and had an Evangelical preacher for father. But although
her first musical experience was in church, she seems to have severed
that connection when her mother died. Big Mama was then 14; by
the early fifties, when she cut her first disc, she was influenced by
the male barrelhouse singing pianists who were electrically
remoulding the glories of the past. She belongs to their tradition,
and although her voice has the penetration of Ma Rainey and Bessie
Smith, her wailing, screeching, gibbering vocal line is more frantic

18   *Helen Humes Comes Back.*
19   *Big Mama Thornton.*

than was the classic mode. This is counteracted by the fact that the
new–old blues is formally less rigid. Vocal part and instrumental in
'Mr Cool' are more primitive than in the classic blues, sounding like
an urbanly electric version of a Vera Hall field holler. Electric
guitars and keyboards add timeless drones rather than supportive
harmony, creating, through their hollow resonance, citified
permutations of the Negro's lonesomeness.

This trend away from the 'structured' blues was abetted by
technology. The blues of Big Mama Thornton, as of John Lee
Hooker, need the long-playing record as well as the timeless tedium
of the small hours. This applies also to fast numbers, which trespass
on rock music's territory – such as Ma's version of 'Little red rooster'
and 'Big Mama's new love'. Particularly interesting is her version of
'Hound dog' by Lieber and Stoller, introduced by her in 1952 but
later rendered famous or notorious by Elvis Presley. While Big
Mama treats the hound comically at one level, ending with
ludicrous bayings and barkings, the acuities of her edgy pitch and
the vagaries of her rhythm create a music at once passionate and
scary. This sexuality is for real, offering the heights of delight but
also the depths of despair. The snuffling outside the door threatens
as it excites, and if the hilarious postlude offers release, there is
certainly something to be released *from*. Elvis, on the other hand,
sings on the beat and on the note, with a romantic tone at odds with
the doggy lust; what he offers is a game – a lively game, but hardly
an invitation to the dangerous unknown. This may be why Elvis's
song was so successful: it offered sexual reality of a sort to the
relatively affluent teenage Whites for whom he catered, but its
danger was strictly vicarious. Big Mama's sexual magic, being
genuinely dangerous, wears better and lasts longer. Her hell hound,
if in part a comic beast, has a genuine relation to the woman who
spits out 'Ball and chain blues' to an explosive tumbling strain
reinforced by ferocious pentatonic arabesques on guitar and keyboard. In this number, later to be associated with the distraught
rock-blues singer Janis Joplin, or in the immensely slow, timelessly
meandering 'Jail blues', Big Mama Thornton demonstrates that
women's blues still speak trenchantly to a world more desperate, if
less depressed and deprived, than that of the twenties. Interestingly
enough, these tracks were recorded in Monroe State Prison. The
prison holler of the bad old days has been electrophonically reborn,
not by a male jailbird, but by a big, female songbird.

Big Mama Thornton is both a throwback to the country blues

and a leap into the steel-citied future. To round off this chapter, however, we must consider a singer whose position is equivocal. Dinah Washington, born in 1924, two years earlier than Big Mama, in the same state of Alabama, moved to Chicago in her teens, soon achieving fame as cabaret and rock singer as well as blues woman. After an active professional life she died at the age of 39, in the archetypal industrial city of Detroit. Dinah's experience in several jazz genres makes her of peculiar historical interest; but the tracks she made at the age of 21, with a sextet based on Lionel Hampton's vibraphone,[20] suggest that she may be the last of the 'naturals' as a blues singer. For this disc Leonard Feather, better known as a jazz bibliographer, produced a number of traditional-style blues, which Dinah sang as to the manner born, though with a distinctive personal timbre reflecting the 'lateness' of her style.

Unlike Big Mama Thornton, Dinah Washington is not a gutsy singer. In 'Blowtop's blues' she responds to Feather's urbanely ironic words with flat tone-colour and terse, clipped phrasing. She does wonders with the words, and it's impossible to be sure whether her little wails and gasps on 'yes' or on 'you're the *first* to know', are pathetic or risible or both. Though her statements are veiled, compared with Ma Rainey or Bessie Smith or Big Mama Thornton, they have a sinewy wryness, which Wendell Culley's trumpet clownishly echoes. In its low-keyed manner, this blues is affecting and is, in its equilbrium between despondency and hilarity, a thoroughly traditional performance. As late as 1962[21] Dinah offers a version of Leroy Carr's classic 'How long blues' that is tougher than Carr's own performance, if less moving than that of the Yanceys. Honky-tonk piano defines a thrusting boogie rhythm while the vocal line, still drained in tone, disciplines blue passion with tight, short-winded phrasing. Still finer is 'Nobody knows the way I feel this morning', a genuine twelve-bar blues on which Dinah improvises, with no lapse in intensity, over 8½ minutes. The slow swinging beat of piano and bass invokes the authentic aura of late-night Chicago bars, and Dinah Washington's voice, though not intrinsically remarkable by the standards of a Bessie Smith, can rival any blues singer in response to verbal nuance.

Dinah Washington's laconic rather than emotive way with the blues looks forward to what came to be known as 'rock and blues';

20 *When Malindy Sings.*
21 *Dinah Washington.*

while occasional instrusions of Gospel idiom – for instance the backing voices in her version of Carr's 'How long blues' – suggest the emergence of soul. Unfortunately Dinah was not able to concentrate on the blue heart of the matter since she was lured into recording so many pop standards in luscious arrangements for theatre orchestras. Yet this too is part of her 'documentary' significance. Making a personal and distinguished contribution to the blues, she sang her pop standards with a blue difference, exploiting her tart delivery and precise enunciation to ironic, and sometimes pathetic, effect, in conjunction with the lavish arrangements. She demonstrates how the blues remained crucial, even when jazz had moved far from bar, brothel and tent show to the cosier comforts of club, cabaret, and theatre.

Chapter Three

FROM TENT SHOW TO CABARET: THE WORD AND THE HORN

My hands move pianissimo
over the music of the night:
gentle birds fluttering through leaves and grasses
they have not always loved,
nesting, finding home.

Margaret Danner

These are psalms for the harp and the shining
stone: the negligence and still passion of night.

J. H. Prynne

Classic blues singers, as we have noted, inherited a heavy infusion of Gospel music from their childhood years. Embarking on professional careers as entertainers, they worked in tent shows, circuses and theatres, singing not so much blues as minstrel-show and vaudeville numbers. Minstrel shows had begun in the nineteenth century as a grotesque parody by Whites with blackened faces of Black entertainers. In the wake of the First World War inanity seemed the more excusable: singing, dancing, acrobatics, juggling and animal acts were increasingly interspersed with comic turns or burlesques satirizing 'serious' material, or treating imbecilities with mock dignity. Blacks in turn parodied the Whites' parodies, even performing with their faces reblackened!

White military twosteps were usually played on a band consisting of cornet, piccolo, trombone, tuba, violin and string bass, with an assortment of plucked strings, notably banjo, guitar and mandolin, with or without piano, according to circumstances. All the tunes were diatonic major, without trace of the modality of the blues; modulations were usually restricted to the dominant, subdominant and relative minor; clauses were symmetrical, normally eight plus eight with a 'middle eight' in a related key, and a *da capo*[1] of the first eight. Sometimes there was a more relaxed trio[2] section in the subdominant, though this did not conspicuously modify the perky euphoria. Solo banjo pieces, at breakneck tempo, were no less stimulating to whirling arms and flickering feet than were the ensemble numbers. Complementary to this march-derived music was the sentimental parlour song as perfected by Stephen Foster, either in 'three-quarter tempo', i.e. 3/4, in the shape of a slow waltz, or in 'common time', i.e. 4/4, derived from the White hymn. Psychologically, the martial and chapel-parlour types of pop music were opposite sides of the same evasive coin. We march, drunk with complacent self-confidence, but pipe a tear because reality can never measure up to our dreams: we grow old and die or, like so many of Stephen Foster's heroines, prematurely 'fade away'.

It is not surprising that American Blacks, holding on for grim life, should have evolved their own version of the White march. Ragtime, basically a piano music though often played by *ad hoc* bands, was the Afroamerican's attempt to create a 'civilized', notated music that could compete with that of his masters. Though the symmetrical rhythms of the military twostep were 'ragged' in being syncopated, the music preserved a dandified elegance: a white-toothed grin beamed from the black mask. In the music of the better rag composers there's a wistful vulnerability beneath the eupepticism – though the music remains a riposte to an alien world. It's significant that Blacks on the whole evaded the complementary White parlour song. Sentimentality was not their line, even though nostalgia for 'the beauty of their wild forebears' had to be. When they faced up to their grief, their music became African-affiliated, modally inflected, free-rhythmed blues, having no truck with pretence or pretention.

1 See Glossary.
2 See Glossary.

How Black ragtime, pseudo-Black minstrel music and White operetta merged to create musical comedy, from which the idiom of the pop standards of the twenties was derived, is demonstrated in *Shuffle Along*,[3] by Noble Sissle and Eubie Blake, the first all-Black musical, produced in New York in 1921. 'Bandana days', played by Blake and the Shuffle Along Orchestra, is a straight American military twostep, slightly ragged but indomitably eupeptic. 'Daddy, won't you please come home', despite the lachrymose lyric, is a brisk, almost bullying march, shrieked in high register, with extravagant vibrato, by Gertrude Saunders. Though the vocal style sounds to us grotesque, it has affinities with early cabaret as distinct from blues.

When the musical came to fruition after the First World War all its composers were White and most of them were Jewish. The themes the songs dealt in were, like those of vaudeville music, either hedonistic – dedicated to delight in the present moment – or nostalgic – dedicated to memory and regret. That popular music should have been thus devoted to escape may point to a malaise inherent in industrial civilization, which was White rather than Black. Even the forms comfort and conform, tunes still being contained in a rigid diatonicism and in symmetrical eight-plus-eight bar periods, though harmony and modulation may, especially in the 'middle eight', be slightly more adventurous than in the old minstrel-show music. The relationship between verse and chorus is similar to that of main section and trio in a Sousa march. The jazzy element – the 'syncopated pianism' – not only evades the reality of the blues, but politely tones down any hint of abandon that survived in Black rag.

It does not follow that the pop standard's escapism is necessarily and entirely negative. Dream-pedlars of genius, such as Jerome Kern (who was European-trained) and Irving Berlin (who was not trained at all) may demonstrate that dreams can bear witness to our hearts. And on one occasion a great composer, reared in Broadway's Tin Pan Alley, revealed through hedonism and nostalgia a profound awareness of what it means to live in big cities: George Gershwin, though White and Jewish, was unique among Tin Pan Alley composers in responding to the rockbottom truth of Black jazz and of the blues in particular – especially in *Porgy and Bess*, a musical that is also a fully-fledged opera.

3 *Shuffle Along.*

The relationship between White and Black elements in Gershwin's music helps us to understand what Blacks did to the White standard when, gravitating from music-hall traditions, they used it as basic material. Black women, no longer singing mainly to a Black public, appear on stage in Broadway theatres and clubs, presenting White music to a White audience. They seldom sing the blues, their own originally improvised creation; but in adapting the clichés of the pop standard, they remake the Hollywooden Dream in their own terms. Black 'matriarchy' demolishes the White deceits that had tried to demean it, and does so with the apparent collusion of a White public. We may trace this process in the singing by Black women of White standards, from the classic blueswoman who made sporadic assays in this direction, to an apex of achievement in the work of Billie Holiday, who, after adolescence, scarcely sang blues at all.

The Mother of the Blues, Ma Rainey, had performed much old-fashioned vaudeville material but few pop standards. Empress Bessie Smith sang a fair proportion of White pop songs, re-creating them in the light of Black experience. Ida Cox, the third member of the classic blues triumvirate, made a comeback in the forties, when she sometimes sang pop standards in their own right, displaying, in her version of 'I can't quit that man', a vocal production related to the masculine stridency with which she sang blues, but more femininely open in timbre. The elongation of syllables and the exaggerated portamentos suggest the music-hall in which, even back in the twenties, many singers – such as Martha Copeland and Rosa Henderson[4] – were most at home.

The most unambiguous instance is Ruth Etting, a torch singer in New York who found fame and fortune in the Ziegfeld Follies on Broadway. When she sings Irving Berlin's 'Shakin' the blues away'[5] she is doing precisely that: not in the therapeutic sense of a real blues singer but in a technical sense, since the number is an anti-blues – a ragged pop standard, which in its middle section parodistically quoted Negro spirituals, 'shaking it all over God's heaven' in a manner that deliberately debunked 'coon' music yet at the same time worried White publishers, scared lest it be thought irreverent, if not downright blasphemous. Ruth's voice has a music-hall bray in the lower, and a pristine openness in the upper,

4   *Big Mama.*
5   *The Vintage Irving Berlin.*

register. Throughout her range enunciation is impeccable. Whatever the view of the publishers, this number got across to its White theatre audience, who could catch every lucent if hardly golden word. A theatre singer, Ruth Etting lived out her life as if on stage. Violence in her life didn't huddle in back streets but was open to the public eye: she earned notoriety when her husband shot and wounded her pianist lover whom she bigamously married while the husband was in goal.

The commanding figure among Black cabaret artists as distinct from blues singers is Ethel Waters.[6] Born in 1900, she was singing blues for 'race' recordings in her teens; but says that she relinquished the blues because Bessie Smith, with whom she shared a double bill at 91 Decatur Street, couldn't brook competition. Whatever the truth of this, she became a celebrity when working, during the early twenties, in New York clubs and theatres, for a White public that put her in her place by dubbing her 'The Ebony Comedienne'. In fact she was more light-skinned than ebony, as were other jazz musicians, notably Jelly Roll Morton and Fletcher Henderson, who in veering towards 'art' exploited White sources.

In 1921 we find Ethel singing with Albury's Blue and Jazz Seven 'The New York Glide' and 'At the New Jump Steady Ball': rags accompanied in New Orleans style homophony, with a sonority recalling both fairground and chapel organ. The instrumental parts thus have affinities with Ma Rainey's ambience, but Ethel Waters's voice, floating aloft, is poles removed from that tough milieu. Her orientation towards 'art' is further emphasized in the following year, when she sings 'Jazzin' babies' blues' with the band of the relatively sophisticated pianist–arranger Fletcher Henderson. The number is not formally a blues, nor is it blue in feeling, despite the New Orleans–Chicago alleviation of Joe Smith's cornet and Henry Brashear's trombone.

From this tentative start Ethel Waters became, during the thirties, the first great jazz cabaret singer. It is no accident that the years of her consummate artistry coincide with her discovery of the master composers of Tin Pan Alley. Her 1933 version of Irving Berlin's 'Sultry heat' lives up to its title, for Ethel's voice, clear in enunciation and clean in intonation, embraces a range of vocal colour from adolescent pipe to maturely erotic quaver. She exploits the liquid, female aspects of African vocal production, without the

6 *Jazzin' Babies' Blues 1921–27* and *Ethel Waters 1938–39.*

masculine rasp whereby the female Black voice asserts, in the blues, the power of its maternalism in opposition to White paternalism.[7] Abetted by Fletcher Henderson's quite elaborate theatre-orchestra arrangements, Ethel Waters 'tamed' Blackness for presentation to White theatre audiences, and in the process revealed unsuspected verities within apparent cliché. Her 1938 versions of Hoagy Carmichael's 'Bread and gravy', 'Old Man Harlem' and 'Georgia on my mind' are classics in which innocence in word and tune becomes, in Ethel's exquisitely timed song that is also speech, childlike but not childish wisdom. Her phrases float over the beat, evading the blue grit of Black jazz but imbuing the line with its own truth, poised between wit and pathos. Success at this level, in cabaret song, depends on co-operation between art and performance, on the simultaneous presence of a good composer and an inventive and sensitive executant. Ethel Waters has herself referred to the improvisatory quality of her singing, even when dealing with the most standardized standards: 'I can't read music, never have. But I have almost absolute pitch. My music is all queer little things that come into my head. I feel these little trills and things deep inside me, and I sing them that way.'

Given this intimate relationship, it would clearly work best if composer and performer were the same person. This seldom happened in club jazz as distinct from improvised blues, though on one memorable occasion Ethel Waters sings a number of her own, or at least one composed in collaboration with her pianist Reginald Beane. 'Stop myself from worryin'' over you' is a mini-masterpiece, in which the ever-surprising twists and turns of melody and rhythm spring from the confused tissue of emotions – evident in the permutations of stress on 'stop', 'my-self' (emphasis shifting between the syllables), 'worryin' ' (with a wurra-wurra on the trouble spot), 'over' (again with shifting stresses), and the ultimate 'you'. We may hear, too, how the relationship between singer and instrumental soloist is modified, as compared with the blues. Louis Armstrong's cornet, in dialogue with Bessie Smith, tends to universalize the vocal line, the phallic jazz 'horn' being a life force. In this Ethel Waters number, however, her dialogue with Eddie Mallory's trumpet and Benny Carter's saxophone is conversation in a strictly social context.

Jazz conversation reaches its apex in the art of Billie Holiday,[8]

7   See pp.9, 238–9.
8   The Billie Holiday Story.

the only club singer to carry the authentic flavour of the blues into the world of the pop standard. Her life, as revealed in her disturbing autobiography *Lady Sings the Blues*[9] had a background of squalor – childhood rape, prostitution, drink, drugs – no less appalling than Bessie Smith's, despite the fact that, after adolescence, she lived not in a ghetto but in the purlieus of Tin Pan Alley. Through her life, however harried, she preserved something of Bessie Smith's dignity, and managed to infiltrate it into the often trite words of the songs she sang. She was a blue singer if not a blues singer. It is encouraging that her revelation of reality beneath apparent sham met with wide popular response; no one has doubted, then or now, her pre-eminence.

Billie tells us in her autobiography that as a child she decided that she would always tell the truth, or what she believed to be the truth, even though the world would kick her for it, and kick the harder because she was Black. Such honesty has musical implications, for although she was a pop singer Billie modelled herself on no preconceived models, and acknowledged a debt only to the two greatest improvising 'realists' of jazz:

> Unless it was the records of Bessie Smith and Louis Armstrong I heard as a kid, I don't know of anybody who actually influenced my singing, then or now. I always wanted Bessie's big sound and Pop's feeling. Young kids always ask me what my style derived from and how it evolved and all that. What can I tell them? If you find a tune and it's got something to do with you, you don't have to evolve anything. You just feel it, and when you sing it other people feel something too. With me it's got nothing to do with working or arranging or rehearsing. Give me a song I can feel and it's never work. There are a few songs I feel so much I can't stand to sing them, but that's something else again.

So even at the heart of the mechanized world of the standard, Billie Holiday was an empiricist and in this sense still a folk artist, like Bessie and Satchmo. Pop standards were the mythology of her urban world; her re-creation of them was as much an act of self-discovery as was Bessie Smith's creation of the blues.

Classic blues singers usually performed with a pianist and a single obbligato[10] player. Ethel Waters worked mostly with a small combo

9   *Lady Sings the Blues*, London, 1958.
10   See Glossary.

or theatre orchestra. Billie Holiday, flourishing during the big-band era of the thirties, sang with larger groups, functioning as a dance-band vocalist, inserting a verse-and-chorus or two within instrumental music originally meant to be danced to. This is itself evidence of her greater subservience to the Big City; and makes her response the more courageous. Not surprisingly she is most effective when singing numbers by the Tin Pan Alley greats.

Consider her 1936 version of Jerome Kern's hauntingly sentimental 'The way you look tonight'. She sings with Teddy Wilson's relatively small, post-Chicago ensemble consisting of himself on piano, Irving Randolph on trumpet, Vido Musso on clarinet, Ben Webster on tenor saxophone, and a rhythm section consisting of Allen Reuss, John Kirby and Cozy Cole. Through a vocal production veering between a nasal twang reminiscent of Bessie Smith's but tighter, and a liquid, open tone recalling Ethel Waters, Billie purges the words of self-indulgence while at the same time revealing the sense in which they speak sober, not intoxicated, truth. Her elongated vowel sounds and shifts in rhythmic emphasis evoke wonder; love touches her 'foolish heart' with a tender quiver and when she pleads that her lover may 'never, never change' the integrity of the appeal lies in its quiet urgency. Teddy Wilson's piano, coolly uninvolved, yet with an electrical swing beneath the spare surface, matches Billie's restrained commitment, and Kern's tune is strong enough to take what Billie does with it.

The same may be said of Kern's 'A fine romance', in which both words and music temper a corny love story with irony. Billie's song-speech is here near-satiric as well as ironic; or even satyric, since her veracity involves latent sexuality beneath the apparently innocuous words. The darkening of her tone on 'mashed potatoes' is potent indeed, and in a lighter way sexuality colours Bunny Berigan's cheeky cornet obbligato and Irving Fazola's fluid clarinet roulades. Billie's enunciation of the period key-word 'baby' is a study in itself. Sung by a woman to a man it carries him back to the womb, establishing her ascendancy. But it also takes on an erotic quality, and positive and negative, inviting and dismissive, impulses are inextricable. In a no less insidious sentimental number, Jack Strachey's 'These foolish things', Billie sings with Teddy Wilson and a line-up of distinguished Ellingtonians. Her presentation reveals why both lyric and tune strike home so forcefully. The flatness of her tone, her unexpected yet inevitable verbal stresses, tell us that these trivialities are indeed 'foolish', yet are also moving in that they're the tip of an iceberg or the surfacing flame of volcanic depths. What is latent in Billie's vocal line is patent in Wilson's glassy piano and in Johnny Hodges's fiery alto arabesques.

The numbers so far discussed belong to the negative pole of the pop standard's hedonistic–nostalgic dichotomy. Songs dedicated to the fleeting physical moment may be no less subtle, as we may hear in 'Eenie meenie minie mo', in which Teddy Wilson is again the elegant pianist, while Roy Elridge tootles an agitated trumpet obbligato. Billie Holiday's vocal fuses Elridge's heat and Wilson's cool, for her speech inflexion is deadpan but her cross-phrasing has suppressed passion. This is not merely a matter of cross-rhythms; the basic tempo of the vocal line is often different from the instrumental tempo, making the eupepticism of the song anything but easy. 'One, two, button my shoe', similarly concerned with happiness in the present moment, is similarly nervous: hardly surprisingly, since a girl who had received as many dusty answers from life as had Billie can't be expected to sing in unsullied jubilation. Her tone here remains neutral, offhand, yet her delayed accents lighten the sleazy atmosphere with wide-eyed wonder, so that she occasionally resembles Ethel Waters. The wonderment is enhanced by Bunny Berigan's obbligato, for he plays cornet with an open tenderness reminiscent of Bix Beiderbecke, a White man playing an innocent instrument with forlorn hilarity – a Little Boy Lost in a twenties Big City.

Brilliant though her tracks with Teddy Wilson's group are, Billie Holiday attained her apex when she became vocalist to the greatest of all big bands, the Count Basie Orchestra of the thirties. Billie's wry, strong voice complements Basie's thin, wiry piano line, counteracting the crashing industrialized might of the big band, keeping the flag of the human spirit flying, a bit desperately, but never hopelessly. Her voice now has greater acuity and more expressive malleability, whether she is performing in enlarged chamber style with members of the Basie band or with the whole massive consort. Consider how, in 'I've got a date with a dream', she sings the word 'dream' in a ghostly tone, ending in a glissando sigh, indicating that she knows in her heart just what the dream is and is not worth. The effect is complemented by Dickie Wells's reticently singing trombone, which preserves the instrument's *cantabile* dignity while imbuing it with the intimacy of jazz saxophone or clarinet. Pathos is fused with something on the verge of risibility, in a manner that exactly parallels Billie's vocal line.

It is not an accident that Billie Holiday's favoured obbligato instrument was the tenor saxophone, nor that Lester Young's playing of it should have echoed her vocal production as precisely as Joe Smith's cornet echoed Bessie Smith's. Lester Young was the supreme horn player nurtured by the Basie band. Born not so far from New Orleans in 1909, he became one of the creators of Modern Jazz, being nicknamed 'Pres' by Billie Holiday because she thought him as great as Franklin D. Roosevelt – praise indeed from a Black woman of the thirties. Like Billie, Lester was a loner, speaking through his horn of the need for love, in laconic phrasing and pallidly dispassionate tone (often achieving, through fancy fingering, fluctuating densities on a single note). His neutral style, no less than Billie's, hides beneath discretion an intense yearning. Nobody sings and plays the words 'hunger' and 'love' as Billie and Lester sing–play them, and the confused terminology is appropriate, since Young's saxophone is a speaking voice and Billie's voice, however seismographically responsive to words, sings like a horn.

A lovely example is 'Back in your own back yard', a song about the Stephen Foster dream-home. Billie's tremulous little mordents[11] expose the dream's pathos, as do the interwoven lines of Young's wistfully wandering saxophone and the fragile *fioriture* of Wilson's piano. Yet all three performers give to frailty an unexpected strength, since their lines have the fine-spun resilience of steel. 'If dreams come true' is another number about the common dream, in which Billie enters into dialogue not only with Lester Young but also with another Basie horn player, trumpeter Buck Clayton. Here the truth within the dream consists in the simplicity of the tune's statement (she wants to believe), modified by the lingering, lagging phrasing (she finds belief difficult). In 'I'll never be the same' Billie's shifting stresses – consider her singing of the words 'there's such an ache in my heart' – are echoed rather than answered, by Lester's saxophone, with an effect of impersonal regret, but also of gentle mockery.

In these enlarged chamber-style tracks the horn players are all Basie men, though the pianist remains the faithful Teddy Wilson. It is possible, however, that Billie Holiday's ultimate triumphs occur when she sings with the Basie band complete, with the Count at the keyboard, since it is then that her fortitude in the face of the brash

11 See Glossary.

city is most patent and potent. A comparatively simple instance is 'Swing, brother, swing': simple because the massed brass pulsates against the famous rhythm section of Freddie Greene, Walter Page and Jo Jones to inculcate orgiastic fervour, which Billie complements with a dark-toned, thrusting-rhythmed sexuality that lets the tiger, rather than the cat, out of the bag. The reality behind the standard's tawdry love tales is no longer camouflaged – nor is it in a superb version of 'They can't take that away from me', a Gershwin number wittily serious in verbal content and sustained in melodic–harmonic structure. Billie seems to be dismissing the love experience with a rueful smile in her recollection of 'the way you sip your tea' – sometimes stressing 'way', at other times 'you', 'sip' or 'tea', But although there is humour also in her articulation of the 'nevers' in 'we may never, never meet again on the bumpy road to love', her phrasing *enacts* the hurtful bumpiness of the road, while her portamento on 'love' is halfway between passion and regret. When she 'holds' his hand we feel the pride in the act; despite the ironies, we're left with an awareness of the renewal that love, despite its deceptions, may offer. Though the Gershwins' song intrinsically contains these complexities, no one has revealed them with the depth Billie Holiday here displays, in the context of the Basie band, from which soloists emerge to talk over and with her.

Another analogy with classical art music may be pertinent: if the blues singer and instrumental obbligato player bear to one another a relationship similar to that of vocal and instrumental soloists in a Bach aria, here there's a parellel with the baroque concerto grosso. Just as the tutti in a baroque concerto represents the public world, while the concertino of soloists is an interaction of private lives within that totality, so the massed brass of the Basie band can be seen as the brazen city, from which solo members intermittently seek new, more individualized relationships. Billie, a lone girl at the heart of the conurbation, enters into dialogue with the instrumental soloists, revealing through words *specific* personal feelings, even within a city scary because mechanized and impersonally vast. The instrument is, and is not, the singer, and their dialogue works for survival, at once affirming and transcending the self.

Occasionally Billie Holiday moved outside the range of the pop standard to which she gave so extraordinarily simple, yet simply extraordinary, a renovation. Those numbers she 'couldn't stand to sing' because words or music or both had so personal a significance for her usually lack her characteristic irony: as we can hear in her famous 1939 version of the lynching song, 'Strange fruit'. Her variety of coloration and paradoxically breathless *sostenuto* give the line an oddly venemous poignancy; in the clinching phrases 'for the sun to rot', 'for the wind to seek', she may attack notes as much as a tone flat, dead and vibratoless, whining up until she ends on centre in a way that freezes the marrow and burns like ice.

Sometimes no personal reference was necessary to spark off intensity. If the tune was strong enough, and the words elemental enough, she could become every woman's representative, as she does in most of the 'serious' Gershwin love songs, notably the 1939 version of 'The man I love' and the late, 1948 'I wants to stay here' from *Porgy and Bess*. Such near-tragic performances are an authentic big-city complement to the classic blues – as is clear if these numbers are compared with 'Long gone blues', a (probably improvised) return to the real twelve-bar blues that Billie had seldom sung since early adolescence. This track, also recorded in 1939, reinvokes the ghosts of Bessie Smith, Louis Armstrong, *and* Ethel Waters, making a line, now metallic, now voluptuous, that is an almost jubilant testimony to the human instinct for survival.

Billie Holiday was a Black woman whose singing reimbued the dreams of all women, whatever their colour, with truth. No other singer has achieved her at once painful and joyous integrity, which is still alive, if latent, in her last disc, recorded in 1958. When she sings Otis Redding's touching 'The end of a love affair' to the accompaniment of Ray Ellis's syrupy theatre orchestra (the album was called *Lady in Satin*) she sounds, wasted by heroin, like an old woman; notes creak, croak and crack, and the rhythmic flexibilities seem often beyond her control. Even so, the emotional impact is considerable. The catch in the breath in the phrase 'a little too fast', the *frisson* of fear on 'fast', the wandering elongations on 'stare' and 'blare', the sudden efflorescence, followed by collapse, in the phrase 'isn't really a smile at all' – such moments reassert the honesty that is the core of Billie's experience and leave us in no doubt that, at this stage, such honesty is indeed 'terrifying'. The end of an affair is the end of a life; Billie's drug-induced death was another martyrdom. Later Black women singers achieve marvels of expressivity as well as of virtuosity but cannot rival her unblinking veracity. This is demonstrated if she is compared with two women of superb talent, Ella Fitzgerald and Sarah Vaughan.

As starting-point let us consider Ella Fitzgerald's singing, on tracks recorded in the mid-forties, of numbers from Rodgers and Hart musicals.[12] In her 'Manhattan' both words and tune are sprightly and amusing; in 'Thou swell' a dream of young love is presented without sentimentality and with charm. Ella sings the songs straight, with none of the harsh dirty tone and few of the displaced accents of the blues, but with considerable variety of tone colour, ranging from a sexy low to a limpid high register. In 'My romance' the simple, repeated upward scale of three notes attains pathos in the mordents for the 'soft guitar', and approaches the freedom of jazz improvisation in the final chorus, while in 'I wish I were in love again' an almost indentical phrase is made to express, by Ella's false accents, a make-believe merriment. The words in these Rodgers and Hart numbers have a modest wit; the tunes are memorable if only because they are so simple and include so much repetition; the performance, with a jazz-biased theatre orchestra, is professional, enjoyable, sometimes touching. Yet it is not more than touching: we know that while 'I wish I were in love again' tells us, a little facetiously, something true about love, it is true only by evading the elements in love that are bound sooner or later, however happy one imagines oneself to be, to hurt.

This combination of naivety with sophistication also characterizes, as has been noted, the songs of Irving Berlin, who felt no need to extend his range beyond the convention of the thirty-two bar tune. In recording *The Irving Berlin Song Book*[13] Ella Fitzgerald gave classic performances of these inspired banalities, backed by Paul Weston's Orchestra, a largish theatre band that found scope for jazz improvisers of ability. The effectiveness of Ella's performances lies in a direct simplicity matching the words and music. Whereas Billie Holiday, revealing the hidden heart of pop standards, often transmuted their words and tunes to a degree that worried publishers, Ella Fitzgerald offered versions that are instantly recognizable. Bessie Smith's raucous circus-style presentation of 'Alexander's ragtime band' has already been commented on; Ella's version, not much less zippy, displays a technical virtuosity that amounts to emotional control. Accepting the brisk inanity of the ragtime march on its own terms, she revels in, rather than glosses over, its triviality.

---

12 *Ella Fitzgerald Sings Rodgers and Hart.*
13 *Ella Fitzgerald Sings Irving Berlin.*

More interesting are two songs from the Astaire–Rogers musical *Top Hat*, the title song and 'Cheek to cheek'. These Ella pipes with dippy rapture. If we are young we recognize the experience, unless we're very hard-boiled, as potentially ours; if we merely have been young we enjoy remembering what young love felt like. Either way we cannot escape the tunes because, within their narrow, stepwise-moving range, they more or less sing themselves. Yet they have their instinctive subtleties: consider how in 'Cheek to cheek', the repeated phrase is gradually extended until it reaches its highest point on Ella's half-stifled 'hardly speak'; or how, in a more tearful number, 'Let's face the music and dance', a descending scale is used to no less effect, since Ella's voice, rich and dark yet floating, really does help us to 'put aside the teardrops' while there is 'still music and moonlight and romance' – with a quivery melisma on the last word. A cheery number like 'Top hat, white tie and tails' works the other way round, for Ella's lilt, carrying us onwards, breaks into wordless scatting as she wafts us 'to–hoo–hoo heaven'. Wonder and wit are fused; and while this is inherent in Berlin's song, it takes a performer of Ella Fitzgerald's calibre fully to reveal its human implications.

The young Ella excelled in these moods of adolescent delight and bemusement. In two other Berlin numbers, 'How deep is the ocean?' and 'How about me?' she uses the composer's repeated notes, lullingly regular rhythms and symmetrical phrases to ask those open-ended questions as well as to soothe. Though such songs may not help us to grow up they do, as sung by Ella, correspond with feelings we've all had in adolescence, and we cannot deny the precision of her and of Irving Berlin's art. Unlike the facetious numbers of Rodgers and Hart, these numbers don't deny that love may hurt, but seek a vicarious pleasure from the hurt itself. So they too create an illusion that we can live on the surface of our feelings. Sincere though they may be, their truth, as compared with that expressed by Billie Holiday, is partial.

Such a comparison is unfair unless we consider what happens when Ella Fitzgerald tackles pop standards of greater substance and complexity. Late, in 1970, when her voice was past its bloom but her artistry was unimpaired, she recorded a double album with the greatest of jazz instrumentalists, Louis Armstrong, with the all-star backing of Oscar Peterson on piano, Ray Brown on bass, Herb Ellis on guitar, and Buddy Rich and Louis Bellson as percussionists.[14]

14   *Ella and Louis.*

Armstrong duets as vocalist as well as playing the trumpet, and the gravelly timbre of his speech–song complements the sensitivity of Ella's song–speech. The effect tends to be tragi-comic, as jazz often is; and a comparison of the Fitzgerald–Armstrong version of Gershwin's 'They can't take that away from me' with Billie Holiday's tells us something about the relationship between jazz, art and commerce. Billie Holiday, working within a commercial environment, never misses a trick in catching Ira Gershwin's verbal witticisms, yet she succeeds in making a serious statement about the nature of love. Ella, backed by Louis, catches the jokes too, and finds in them an underlying pathos. But her humour, compared with Billie's, is coy, the more so because Louis's comicality is on the brink of farce. Thus the professionalism of the performance becomes a defence mechanism.

The same happens in the delightful 'A foggy day', which begins with Louis speaking sweet and simple, over a ripe guitar. Ella's singing entry whirls upwards, across the beat, to effect the 'age of miracles', until the sun 'shines' through the fog in Louis's climacteric trumpet solo. Another Gershwin number, 'Our love is here to stay', also calls on Louis's trumpet as apotheosis, for the dialogue of voice and horn culminates in a solo that opens a new dimension. The performance convinces us that the love, being here to stay, deserves this triumph. Yet it *is* a performance: if less so than the version of 'Let's call the whole thing off', in which Louis's and Ella's capping exchanges of potătoes and potātoes, tomătoes and tomātoes create cumulatively risible metamorphoses of rhythm and pitch. Though we are tempted to laugh out loud at singer, player and Ira Gershwin's words, the performance is not *merely* frivolous, since it reveals that such trivialities may be mini-tragedies of incomprehension and misunderstanding. To call the calling off off is a joke that leaves us where we were – so is it, after all, funny?

Only in one of these tracks do Ella and Louis present a love experience unprotected by the irony of their virtuosity and professionalism. That is their version of Hoagy Carmichael's 'The nearness of you': a haunting tune, if not quite in Gershwin's class, whispered by Louis, crooned by Ella, in intimacy, with a consummative coda for trumpet. Though the honesty of presentation is comparable with Billie Holiday's, it is blander, apposite to a less uncomfortable world. None the less Ella's lyricism here helps to explain how she was capable of her finest achievement: the 'potted' version of Gershwin's *Porgy and Bess*,[15] made by Ella and Louis in 1957, with a cross between a jazz big band, a theatre orchestra, and a symphony orchestra appropriate to the opera the work originally was. The skilful arrangements are by Russell Garcia, who conducts.

Although Gershwin inhabited an area between art and commerce, he owes his pre-eminence among composers of standards both to his exceptional genius and to his profound understanding, White Jew though he was, of the Black reality of the blues. This is evident throughout the streamlined opulence of this version. 'Oh Doctor Jesus', which is Gospel music in Gershwin's opera, sounds yet more authentically Negro in Ella Fitzgerald's performance, its pentatonic lamentation wailed in age-old sorrow. Similarly she sings the street cries of honeyman, strawberry and crab sellers as to the manner born, and could do so because Gershwin himself never put a foot wrong in these ethnic transcriptions. Black authenticity and a composer great by any standard – not just that of 'the' standard – combine to storm heights and plumb depths, whether the numbers are ostensibly comic or tragic. 'It ain't necessarily so' we think of as a funny number, and Ira Gershwin's words are indeed witty. Yet the undulating G minor tune and the prodding rhythm are far from easy, and this is not surprising if we remember what the song is about. Crooned by Sportin' Life, who captivates us in his serpentine villainy, it undermines the simple faith that simple folk like Porgy and Bess live by; its effect is no less sinister than the happy dust with which Sportin' Life, significantly a light-skinned mulattto, dupes as well as dopes the guileless denizens of Eden. This comes across in the performance, beginning with Louis's solo which, over a panting ostinato, is more frightening than funny. Ella's swinging vocal line misses none of the jokes while revealing the terror behind them. The ultimate scat-singing duet is frenzied rather than fervent.

In the light of this we can understand why the 'tragic' numbers in this version acquire the status of art music without ceasing to be jazz. In 'I wants to stay here' Bess–Ella is torn between her need for love's security and the lure of danger; her jazz voice responds vibrantly to Gershwin's music. A straight opera singer could not do it so well, neither could she achieve the equilibrium of modality and pitch that gives intensity to Ella's singing of 'My man's gone now', from the majestic opening phrase to the improvised, pathetically

15   *Porgy and Bess.*

broken cadenza. Similarly the love duet, 'Bess, you is my woman now', is an ultimate interplay of composition and improvisation. The tune reveals hidden depths as Louis's near-speech is capped by Ella's soaring song, 'taking off' from a notated operatic duo into one of the supreme passages of improvised jazz. Similarly 'Summertime', although a lullaby for a baby, does not deny the tragic dimension of Experience inherent in Innocence itself. Louis's introductory trumpet solo is heroically fierce, telling us that the new life contains within it the moil and toil of human existence. His speech-song, compared with his trumpeting, is quietly intimate; but Ella's song line, responsive to verbal nuance, elevates the melody to something approaching the trumpet's grandeur. In the final duet chorus Ella sings the loving words while Louis scats with a suppressed ebullience dangerously tinted with lunacy. Both Louis and Ella are masters of scat-singing: which is what happens when, feeling having grown too deep or too high for words, the voice becomes an instrument. The jazz horn imitates the human voice; the voice, transcended, emulates the horn that had imitated it.

For Billie Holiday, who was born in 1915, words were always pre-eminent though she gave them, especially in dialogue with Lester Young, a horn-like dimension. Ella Fitzgerald, born in 1918 and starting out, in the same swing era, as vocalist with the band of Chick Webb, could be no less responsive to words, as her *Porgy and Bess* tracks demonstrate. But whereas Billie died in 1959, Ella survived her and, in the early eighties, is still 'alive and well'. Not surprisingly, Ella gravitated from the swing era into that of the beboppers, of whom the most distinguished representatives were alto saxophonist Charlier Parker and trumpeter Dizzie Gillespie, so called because his pyrotechnics were dizzy indeed. Their more metrically complex and elliptical melodic lines influenced Ella's aproach to the voice, her growing partiality for scat-singing being an aspect of her more abstract musicality.

This evolution reaches an apex in the singing of Sarah Vaughan,[16] the third major figure among the cabaret singers, born in 1924, six years later than Ella and nine years later than Billie Holiday. The greatness of Billie Holiday was not dependent on vocal quality nor even on technique in any conventional sense. Ella

16 *It's a Man's World, Sarah Vaughan and Count Basie, Sarah Vaughan and Clifford Brown* and *After Hours.*

Fitzgerald had a beautiful natural voice and a technique dazzling in jazz if not in academic terms. Sarah Vaughan has a voice magnificent by any standards, as capable of bel canto as of the folk inflexions of jazz. Through the years she has developed a technique adaptable to a variety of styles, in all of which she is a performer whose bravura amounts to an act of re-creation. Billie Holiday's re-creation *is* her life; Sarah Vaughan's, even more than Ella Fitzgerald's, is a show, a technical apotheosis.

Sarah Vaughan was fortunate in having her musical baptism with the big band of Earl Hines, consisting largely of front-line Ellington men. That prepared her for collaboration with the Count Basie band in its heyday, as is evident in their version of the Tizol–Drake number 'Perdido', often featured by Ellington. Basie takes it very fast, in driving powerhouse idiom; Sarah's voice, covering an immense range from visceral growl to throaty squawk, approaches the grandeur of Bessie Smith, but is more wildly whirling. Yet her savage–sophisticated arabesques are executed with total control; she knows what she is doing even in her most ecstatic flights, when words disperse into the gobbledegook of scat. In this she's a match for the Basie band, which crackles in machine-like exactitude; between them they make a music of the Asphalt Jungle.

Against such hedonism, Sarah opposes numbers in nostalgic vein, such as 'I cried for you': remarkable because Sarah's voice really does cry while incorporating lament into a sustained line that would do credit to a European-trained classical singer. The massed brass of the band, meticulous in ensemble and rhythm, here offers succour; the big-city sound, with everything in its tight-metred, euphoniously coherent place, here becomes a palliative for lonesomeness. More characteristic of her slow-and-sentimental manner is 'Alone', which flirts with danger. She begins literally alone because unaccompanied, with cadenza-like gurglings through which the tune is discernible, since the vagaries of pitch and rhythm suggest both line and implicit harmony. As soloist she belongs here to the generation of Charlie Parker and Thelonious Monk, for her harmonic sense, based on the chromaticism of the more advanced standard, is more complex than the rudimentary diatonicism of New Orleans–Chicago homophony. But the Basie band also adds its quota to the sophistication, since its womb-like sonority grows gradually more mysterious and even, in its ensemble chorus, minatory.

If there is nothing on this fine disc to challenge Ella Fitzgeralds's *Porgy and Bess*, the reason lies not so much in Sarah Vaughan's inferior art as in the fact that none of the music is of Gershwin's calibre. She does however sing some fairly slight Gershwin on a famous disc with the phenomenal young trumpeter Clifford Brown, recorded in 1954 shortly before his death in a car crash. This stands as a peak in Sarah Vaughan's achievement as a singer of Modern Jazz, developing the pop standard from words towards pure musicality, abetted by an instrumental soloist of a talent equal to hers. Consider what happens to a simple 'hedonistic' song like Richard Rodgers's 'It's crazy'. Sarah sings the first statement straight, responsive to the wit of the words but abandoning them for a hum to introduce Clifford Brown. His first chorus noodles around the boogie rhythm, then takes off in *fioriture*, which, on Sarah's return, affect her winging convolutions. Ultimately, she mingles words with vocalize in a wildly wide-flung line; the 'craziness' the verse talks of has become, in the technical sense, scatty.

'Nostalgic' numbers work in much the same way. Vernon Duke's 'April in Paris' – that quintessential song of adolescence – is at first unfolded by Sarah with a regard for the words so scrupulous that speech becomes lyrical in its own right. Elongating the rhyme words with open, sustained tone, she increasingly aspires to a horn-like state; Clifford Brown's solo seems to spring from the vocal line, capping Sarah's verbal nuances with sizzling passage-work intrinsic to the tune. This brings to the surface the sexual excitement latent in words and tone so that Sarah, on her return, can imbue regretful lyricism with something of the fervour of her 'wild and whirling' Basie tracks. In her more virtuosic way she, like Billie Holiday, gives reality to dream – as she does in Gershwin's 'Embraceable you', this time without benefit of Brown's trumpet. Her dark tone and heavy vibrato for 'the gypsy in me' leads into the *almost* disorientated scatting of her final chorus, while Jimmy Jones's piano remains discreetly elegiac.

In later years Sarah Vaughan has devoted most of her time to performing with largish theatre orchestras in luxuriant arrangements, producing what the record shops call 'Easy Listening'. It *is* easy to enjoy the cunning and craft of her performances of pop standards, escaping at the Happy Hour with Sarah and our memories, though it is no substitute for the re-creative music she made as a genuine jazz singer, especially in duo with Clifford

Brown. Even so, there are magical moments in her later work: notably the famous version of Benny Carter's 'Key Largo',[17] in which she sings not with an opulent orchestra, but with merely Barney Kessel's guitar and Joe Comfort's bass. She takes the hypernostalgic number very slowly, dwelling on words with infinite variety of timbre and inflexion – consider what she does with the word 'empty', with the internal rhymes on 'cargo' and 'Largo', with the elongated 'erase' and 'sea', with the permutations on self and not-self in the line 'till *you*'re with *me*'. The tortoise-like pace gives her time to savour harmonies subtler than those typical of the standard – which Barney Kessel's solo emotively underlines.

We have noted that these two central club singers, Ella Fitzgerald and Sarah Vaughan, weave strands inherited from Billie Holiday, the basic jazz singer, and from Ethel Waters, a vaudeville artist who sometimes sang jazz. Two lesser but distinguished contemporary luminaries tend to separate these strands; Carmen McCrae is perhaps the 'purest' jazz singer since Billie Holiday, while Pearl Bailey is the performer closest to theatrical traditions.

Born in 1922, Carmen McCrae[18] also had her early musical experience in the big-band world, working during the forties with Count Basie, Benny Carter and Mercer Ellington. Yet in natural talent she remained an intimate jazz singer rather than a show-business performer – as is evident in her 1954 sessions, discreetly accompanied by Tony Scott's clarinet, Dick Katz's piano, Skip Fawcett's bass and Ossie Johnson's drums. Singing Cole Porter's 'Easy to love' Carmen McCrae demonstrates that for her as for Billie Holiday words are the essential impetus. Her enunciation is as meticulous as her tone is pure; both seem so true that articulation itself promotes the swinging rhythm. Her lack of rhetoric discovers expressivity within trite words, the most touching number being a performance of Tony Scott's 'Misery' in which, abandoning his clarinet, the composer accompanies her on piano. Carmen's vocal line wanders in a miserably lost state that turns out not to be directionless, for this 'song of despair' is beautifully shaped as a dialogue between voice and piano, leading to a consummative cadenza left suspended on a high, not despairingly low, note.

Carmen McCrae's lyricism is always intimate; however precise her articulation, she always sings rather than speaks. This remains

17   *When Malindy Sings.*
18   *Carmen McCrae: I Hear Music* and *Carmen McCrae.*

true when, in 1970 Carmen returned to the big band, recording with a combo directed by drummer Kenny Clarke (at one time her husband), with pianist Francy Boland and a galaxy of soloists such as Benny Bailey, Art Farmer and Tony Coe. Although the band attains a brazen ferocity comparable with the Basie band and although, to compete with it. Carmen adopts a harsher timbre, words remain pre-eminent. Consider, in 'November girl', the transition from a fluttery tone on 'heartbreak' to a metallic timbre for 'you'd bettter face it'; or the broken rhythms that, in 'A handful of soul', give hesitancy to what seem like exalted arabesques as she makes 'a *bee*line for the sun'. In 'You're getting to be a habit with me', a standard featured by Frank Sinatra, Carmen builds a compulsive swing from rhythms that are almost stutters: 'You've got me in your *clu*tches, I could not do without you'. Even 'I don't want nothing from nobody', blared as defiantly as it used to be by the Basie band, stammers as it challenges, for the voice's cross-rhythms hurt.

But Carmen McCrae's most moving music remains her simplest, in chamber-music intimacy. The same is true of one of the most distinctive Black singers of the fifties and sixties, Nancy Wilson, especially when she recorded standards with George Shearing's elegant quintet.[19] In 'On Green Dolphin Street' or 'Born to be blue' her springy jazz line seems an inevitable consequence not only of the words, but also of the appealingly personal quality of her voice; Shearing's bouncy-rhythmed, exquisite textured pianism matches her line perfectly. As with most of the best jazz singers, including Billie Holiday, expressivity is allied to a delicate, perhaps defensive, irony: consider, in her version of Hoagy Carmichael's lovely 'The nearness of you', her transition from trumpet-like sustained notes to airily curling vocalise. Self-protective irony is one way for a girl, perhaps especially a Black girl, to get by in the big city.

At the opposite pole to these club singers stands Pearl Bailey[20] who, born in 1918, first earned fame as dancer as well as singer on Broadway. She scored hits in musicals, notably *St Louis Woman* (1946) and *House of Flowers* (1954), and starred in the movie versions of *Carmen Jones* and *Porgy and Bess*. Later she became a television personality; even as a jazz singer she has usually appeared with the expertly theatrical band of her husband, Louis Bellson, whose own

19 *The Swingin' 's Mutual.*
20 *Pearl Bailey and Louis Bellson.*

career embraced stints with Benny Goodman, Tommy Dorsey, Harry James and, most impressively, as drummer and arranger for Duke Ellington.

Bailey–Bellson appearances always have a strong flavour of show business, juxtaposing big-band jazz with corny ballads and occasional hymns. The theatrical approach naturally affects Pearl Bailey's presentation of jazz standards, whether in hedonistic or nostalgic vein. Her sentimental numbers usually escape jazz categorization, as when she sings 'Hit the road to dreamland' as a straight lullaby, humming and moaning through an undulating cradle-rocking accompaniment. More normally she favours the hedonistic type, singing 'That certain feeling' very loud and very hard, with a punch to match that of Bellson's loud, hard band. The coda in half-time makes the music-hall affiliation explicit, getting the punch line across. 'Solid gold Cadillac' has Pearl talking as well as singing over an infectious boogie beat. The talking takes the audience, on the other side of the footlights, into her confidence. The inflexions of the sung line are often witty – consider her sundry enunciations of the word 'gold' and the rhymed emphases on the last syllable of 'Cadillac' – but there's no hint of the pathos that Holiday, Fitzgerald or Vaughan might discover even in such a tough mama's mercenary tale. Nor is there meant to be. On its own terms the number is vocally and instrumentally brilliant.

A peripheral figure who flowered in the late fifties and early sixties is Abbey Lincoln, who fits into no defined category. One can have nothing but respect for the intelligence and sensitivity she shows in her choice of songs, usually of high quality and always suited to her gifts. Instrumentalists of exceptional talent were responsive to her personal approach – which centres on the bell-like clarity of her voice, the precision of her enunciation, and the perfection of her intonation. Not surprisingly, she is a singer who, like Billie Holiday, starts from words and their meanings, seldom indulging in the musical pyrotechnics typical of Ella Fitzgerald or Sarah Vaughan.

On her 1957 disc, *That's Him*, she collaborates with jazz musicians of the calibre of Kenny Dorham on trumpet, Sonny Rollins on tenor saxophone, Wyton Kelly on piano, Paul Chambers and the legendary Max Roach on bass and drums. Phil Moore's 'Tender as a rose' she sings unaccompanied and very slowly, yet she manages to create, from her dark tone's savouring of the love–hate relationship latent in the words, a vintage jazz experience. When she combines with the horns she exploits the traditional jazz interchange between word-uttering human voice and voice-imitating instrument, especially in the most moving track on the disc, which, not fortuitously, happens to be a version of Billie Holiday's own 'Don't explain'. Abbey Lincoln sing–speaks the words with lethal precision and suppressed passion, while Kenny Dorham's muted trumpet weaves a wandering line around the voice, over the feline tread of Paul Chambers's bass. For the final ensemble Sonny Rollins joins in, in mellifluous duet. The combination of speaking immediacy in the voice part with the impersonal dialogue of the horns gives a near-tragic dimension to the music.

Although nothing else on the disc has quite this poignancy, each track is re-creative, whether it be a well-worn standard like Harold Arlen's 'Happiness is a thing called Joe' or Grainger's 'When a woman loves a man', or a less familiar though no less distinguished number like Kurt Weill's 'That's him'. Impressive is the way in which Abbey adapts her voice not merely to the song but to the personality of the obbligato player. Her very strong version of Oscar Brown's 'Strong man' is exactly complemented by Rollins's bois-terous, blowsy tenor. In a very fast version of McHugh's 'I must have that man' her voice bops and bounces in emulation of Dorham's cat-on-hot-bricks trumpeting.

Even more remarkable is the 1959 disc, *Abbey is Blue*, to which Dorham, Kelly and Roach still contribute, though drums are sometimes in the hands of Philly Joe Jones and the saxophone player is Stanley Turrentine. In a version of Ellington's 'Come Sunday' she substitutes for the fervour of Mahalia Jackson's original Gospel performance a long-spun line that, if relatively cool, is no less moving. Still more magical is her performance of Kurt Weill's 'Lonely house', which epitomizes the heart of lonesomeness in a ponderously slow beat and in a fraily fluctuating tone, while Kenny Dorham's trumpet whispers nocturnal secrets and Philly Joe Jones's percussion ticks off the minutes and hours like a fateful clock. Abbey's obbligato players usually manifest this discretion, as though in awe of her awe of the words and music. This is what gives such pathos to her singing of Oscar Brown's modally folk-like 'Brother, where are you?' Her voice, telling the tale of the boy's lost state, is thin but steady as steel, and only Les Spann's tremulous flute and Wyton Kelly's suddenly eruptive piano reveal the pain behind the vocal line's poise.

In a more complex number of her own composition, 'Let up', Abbey Lincoln intensifies this effect, making, at very slow tempo, an appeal for courage in the face of anguish. The 'nobody knows' refrain – encouraging us to complete the line with the unuttered 'the trouble I've seen' – hints at Gospel music, though again the long line, live on the note, eschews Gospel fervency. It is, however, tense enough to exact from Tommy and Stanley Turrentine's trumpet and saxophone a reiterated African riff with a pathos proportionate to its discretion. Though not formally a blues, this number is very dark blue; and Abbey's response to word and musical phrase may give blueness even to a Hammerstein–Romberg standard like 'Softly as in a morning sunrise'. At first unaccompanied, like Gospel incantation, she is for the most part supported only by twanging string bass, like an amplified country guitar. Only exceptionally does she distort the natural accentuation of words, always with calculated effect: in 'Laugh, clown, laugh' to depict an unnaturally clownish condition, and in Herbie Mann's 'Afro-blue' to evoke, through a circular modal tune and a hypnotic ostinato on percussion, a phantasmagoric Eden.

It is indicative of Abbey Lincoln's intelligence that she often sang numbers not only by highly inventive composers such as Gershwin and Weill, but also words by 'serious' poets, such as Langston Hughes (who wrote 'Lonely house') and Maxwell Anderson, whose 'Love and the stars' was set by Weill in hymn-like gravity. Most remarkably is 'When Malindy sings',[21] a setting by Oscar Brown Junior of words by the Negro poet Lawrence Dunbar. The song deals not only in naturalistic terms with Negro life, but also with the spontaneous truth of Afro-American as distinct from Western singing. Abbey's habitual respect for words may thus flower into African ululation, echoed by five instrumentalists of several generations, from old-time Coleman Hawkins on tenor and Max Roach (then Abbey's husband) on drums to Modern Jazzman Eric Dolphy on alto, bass clarinet and flute, and the adventurous – and in 1961 very young – Booker Little on trumpet.

Though less well known than some, Abbey Lincoln is a major figure, inimitable and unforgettable. But we must end this chapter with an artist comparable with Abbey but more central in that she provides a link between the Modern Jazz of the fifties and sixties and the then future, which is our present.

21 *When Malindy Sings.*

Born in 1930, six years later than Sarah Vaughan, Betty Carter has remained faithful to the jazz spirit of the bebop era and in so doing has carried vocal jazz to an unexpected consummation. She began as a big-band vocalist with Lionel Hampton, but establishing her own supporting group, steered her bebop singing increasingly towards 'pure' musicality – far more consistently than did Fitzgerald and Vaughan, and in contradistinction to Billie Holiday and Abbey Lincoln. In her 1955 tracks[22] with the admirable Ray Bryant she may start from a response to the words but usually leaves them behind as vocal exuberance takes over. Compare her version of the Rodgers number 'Thou swell' with Ella Fitzgerald's. Ella takes it as a gleefully adolescent love song, as it may be; Betty Carter finds in the witty words an impetus to rhythmic virtuosity so stunning that it induces both hilarity and startlement. Her tricks with metre and accent are not gimmicks. The irony is conscious; the girl is laughing at as well as with herself, and this applies too to the final chorus in which she abandons words in favour of scatting pyrotechnics.

That the young Betty Carter could also present a simple song simply is shown by 'Can't we be friends', a number by Kay Swift, a rarely talented rare phenomenon – a female pianist–composer. The song is about the end of an affair, apparently accepted with wry good humour:

I should have seen the signal to stop,
Plop, plop, plop, plop,
This is how my story ends.

But although we chuckle at Betty's ambiguities of tone and rhythm (consider her permutations on the single word 'I'), we also realize (consider her handling of 'seems', 'never again', 'shame' 'cry') that renunciation hurts. So 'simple' seems an inadequate description of the song's content and effect.

Betty Carter's masterpiece in this vein is probably her 1955 version of 'Moonlight in Vermont'. Ella Fitzgerald, in her sessions with Louis Armstrong, presented it as the hoary old nostalgia standard it is. Betty Carter takes it immensely slowly, exploiting the mystery in the low register of her voice to paint what the verses call 'the romantic setting'. Against this Betty's octave leaps and abrupt changes of dynamics define the reality implicit in those

22   *The Betty Carter Album.*

'telegraph cables' that, the voice hardening, represent man's dominance over nature even in moonlit Vermont, and that carry
messages, perhaps of disastrous import, between lovers and friends,
not to mention enemies. This is an instance of how jazz performance
may be so radically re-creative as to amount to composition: a point
that has a bearing on Betty Carter's later career.

Although her work as a jazz club singer has never really lapsed
since her youth in the fifties, her meteoric rise to fame in the late
seventies was unexpected if not inexplicable. It represents an
evolution distinct from that of Holiday, Fitzgerald and Vaughan,
though it may have some affinity with Abbey Lincoln's 'conscious'
intelligence. A high proportion of the numbers Betty Carter now
sings[23] are of her own composition, making a disturbing extension
of the 'mystery' inherent in her early 'Moonlight in Vermont'. The
formal training she received at the Detroit School of Music probably
had less to do with this than her innate cleverness: evident for
instance in the careful structure of 'What is it?' a large-scale number
embracing a grim introduction built on reiterated chords ('No, no,
no, he'll never be mine'), a moony arioso in which jazz beat, though
elusive, lurks beneath the surface, and a *da capo* of the introduction
laced with the arioso. That the words too are elusive and often
inaudible matters little, since the song functions 'musically' in a
more extreme way than do any songs of Vaughan or Fitzgerald. The
dark voice of 'Moonlight in Vermont' is still more veiled: tone is
pinched in the upper, sepulchral in the lower, register. Pitch is
often microtonal, with slowly wailing glissandi and meandering
rhythms. Onanje Alan Gumbs's piano hints at jazz chromatics but
worries little about harmonic direction. Its drone-like sonorities act
as a foil for Betty's sophisticatedly primitive vocal moans.

An even slower number, 'We tried', is even more extreme in
using these quasi-primitive techniques. Betty's forlorn if rever-
berant whimpers are poles removed from Sarah Vaughan's vibrancy,
but tell us, without need of the dubiously audible words, that
the 'trying' was unfulfilled, its chances slim. The sombreness is
deepened because the voice's wavering pitch oscillates over the abyss
of Buster Williams's bowed bass. Altogether, Betty Carter's songs,
as befits their late-seventies genesis, are more distraught, and more
dangerously self-conscious, than the pop standards of the jazz age.
This applies to her infrequent fast numbers also, such as the briefly

23 *Betty Carter.*

fleeting 'Tight', or 'Happy', which is what it says it is, but in an agitated Latin-American metre that gradually transforms childlike merriment into voodooistic frenzy, the voice hooting in double-tracked duet over relentless bowed bass.

Betty Carter's highly individual remaking of Dorothy Law Nolt's 'Children learn what they live' spells out the relationship between childhood innocence, savage primitivism and the sophisticated savagery of the modern world, calling on techniques reminiscent of African street musics. So the number appropriately preludes the last and longest song on the disc, 'Sounds', again a Carter composition. The opening instrumental furiously pounds like tribal ritual music, using bowed bass to build rock-like drone patterns, again with no hint of the harmonic processes of the jazz standard. As Betty's voice moans microtonally and meanders polymetrically, the corybantic music becomes recognizably Black—instrinsically, not merely in manner of performance. Betty has no further need of the White words of White standards. The jazz singer, invoking Old Africa from the heart of Greenwich's Global village, brings the wheel full circle.

Billie Holiday had found inspiration in the enunciation of (even trite) words, creating a vocal line that inspired Lester Young's tenor saxophone to emulation, and Billie in turn emulated him. In this musicalization of words Billie turned the Hollywooden Dream against itself, embracing it within her veracity. Ella Fitzgerald and Sarah Vaughan also found stimulation in words but treated even the most trivial products of Tin Pan Alley more cavalierly, as subservient to their musicality. A third stage is reached in the singing of Betty Carter, who not only demolishes and re-creates verbal illusions but sometimes substitutes her own newly created material for the pop standard. In turning once more to the roots of Black music she completes the circle, reinvigorating the industrial – and White-controlled – world.

Chapter Four

SOUL, MOTOWN, AND THE FUSION OF SACRED AND PROFANE

It's a hell
creeping back into
the garden, shedding
your badly worn skin,
starting anew . . .

But making it
the shiny seed's
your prize and
genesis.

Sarah Webster Fabio: *A Mirror: a Soul*

We have noted that during the first half of the twentieth century there is a sharp division between Gospel music and the blues on the one hand, club and dance-hall jazz on the other. Both Gospel music and blues are 'music of necessity' in that they were created empirically, in the context of day-to-day life. Gospel music sprang from the church service or camp meeting, from the interplay of the preacher, whose speech often approximated to song, and the congregation, with as liaison between the two, the choir, which sometimes itself functioned empirically, and was sometimes 'trained', even to the extent of using notation. Though Black

Gospel became more formalized as conventions from White hymn, march and waltz infiltrated into it, its forms remained open, repeatedly returning to ritual. It was still an activity shared between celebrants and people.

Gospel is a communal music; the blues is solitary. It stemmed, we noted, from the primitive field holler, and when the Negro began to accompany himself on the White man's guitar, his approach was not at first affected. The guitar would mumble a drone, or later the tonic–subdominant–dominant formula of the hymn; the singer would improvise a ululation, usually to his own or traditional words, reflecting his immediate situation. Frequently the phrase would begin on a high note and plunge downwards, like an African tumbling strain; usually the figurations would be basically pentatonic, emerging from the natural behaviour of the human voice. In the early blues there was seldom a tune but rather a cry, wrung from guts and belly as well as from head and heart. With frequent repetition a tune might define itself, to be adapted by other singers. But the act of 'making' is paramount. Existing in the moment of creation, the blues is personal therapy and an utterance of truth: 'Tell it like it is' is the blues singer's recurrent admonition.

Whereas blues and Gospel music are thus existential, the jazz of club and cabaret grows more artistically formulated the larger the forces get, culminating in the Big Bands, which had to use notation if they were to evade chaos. Both the words and music of Gospel and blues tend to be made up *ad hoc*; the words and music of the standards that were fodder for jazz creation during the thirties and forties were, on the other hand, notated in sheet-music form, and were usually the creation of Whites of Jewish extraction. While we should not be priggish about the existence of a dream factory designed to pander to people's insecurities, we have to admit that in becoming a *factory* Tin Pan Alley – originally West 28th Street in New York, where the pop industry was nurtured in the early years of the century – was the polar opposite of Gospel and blues. Those who worked there were dedicated not to truth but to cliché, and ultimately to material aggrandizement. What is remarkable is that Blacks, and especially Black women, taking over these manufactured products, invested them with the realities of their own music. The jazz of deslaved Blacks helped dream-enslaved Whites towards their own spiritual liberation, whether or not they knew it, or would have admitted to it if they had known.

Gospel was a White American heritage infused with Black African techniques; blues was a Black heritage that used White materials for its own ends. The fusion of the two was christened 'soul' music, since it is always soulful though not often devotional. Like the blues, soul is therapeutic — but with a difference. Blues is a technique for survival: one sings to get the blues *off* one's mind. Soul brings positive freedom: one sings because it makes one feel good. At one level this reflects the Negro's slowly changing social and economic position. Faith and hope in loving one's human mate and/or God are admitted as ideals, which are distinct from dreams; it need not be assumed that man or woman, being lonesome, must also be faithless. The family is now accepted as basic, though there is no pretence that human relations can be easy.

These changes in attitude are naturally reflected in modifications in technique. The classic blues accepted the 'White prison' of a few diatonic concords within which to improvise. Soul music, deliberately returning to a more primitive stage, may dispense with these, building accompanying patterns on merely two alternating chords, or on a continuous drone, as in some Gospel music and in the most rudimentary country blues. Harmonic and formal simplification allows rhythm unfettered impetus, and gives time and space in which melody can flower.

Soul music was for Blacks a process of rehabilitation in which male singers again vigorously participated, as is evident from the career of Ray Charles, the ill-fated Otis Redding (killed in a plane crash), and of James Brown, a secular singer whose performances generated the communal frenzy of religious ritual. Women, however, also made their contribution to the new music — which wasn't really new, since it was composed of traditional ingredients in different relationship. In the women's music the process of transition is clear — not surprisingly, since women had come to dominate both Gospel and blues. Three key figures represent progressive stages in this evolution. They are Odetta, Nina Simone and Aretha Franklin.

Strictly speaking, Odetta is not a soul singer, nor a blues nor a jazz singer, though she is soulful in everything she does. Born in 1930 in Birmingham, Alabama, she had formal training in classical music, though when she embarked on a musical career, in San Francisco and later in New York, she became that paradoxical phenomenon, a professional folk singer. This has some bearing on the genesis of soul music, which involves considerable artistry in its projection of apparently untrammelled emotion. Listening to Odetta's famous Carnegie Hall concert of 1960[1] we may hear how artfully she moulds folk material, and how potent is her technical command in so doing.

Sometimes she offers what appears to be unadulterated Gospel music, as in her versions of the spirituals 'Hold on' and 'Ain't no grave can hold my body down', in which she is backed by the choir of the Church of the Master, directed by Dr Theodore Stent. The force of Odetta's voice and its range from trumpeting treble to booming bass, with a middle register now silky, now rasping, sweeps the audience off its feet, and stimulates the choir to raucous jubilation. Only the phenomenal quality of Odetta's voice and the virtuosity of her technique separate this from the Gospel meeting's 'music of necessity'. That there is a difference, however, is apparent in versions of two more spirituals, 'No more auction block for me' and 'sometimes I feel like a motherless child', in which Odetta's often stentorian voice tenderly coos, while the choir hums *a cappella*[2] chromatics. The result is beautiful, not synthetic, but it is no longer music of necessity. Similarly, when she sings a 'preachin' spiritual', 'God's a-goin' to cut you down' or a prison holler, 'Prettiest train', unaccompanied, Odetta displays the internal drive – independent of any external beat except that of her clapping hands – that typifies the real, right thing. The 'art' lies in the virtuosity. The sheer range of her voice, as her cries, gasps and gurgles invoke generations of labouring, suffering, praising Negroes, makes her a mythic figure, larger than life. This impression is enhanced by the androgynous quality of her timbre: she sounds all-inclusively human, a maternal goddess with paternalistic powers. Yet this heroic creature can sing a plantation lullaby like 'All the pretty little horses' with a simplicity that melts the heart, and that too is an aspect of her art.

How these elements from folk and Gospel flow together to produce soul is revealed in Odetta's version of 'Meet me at the building', a hymn jazzily accompanied by string bass and by church-congregational clapping; or in 'I'm goin' back to the red clay country', which also goes back to the field or prison holler, with microtonal moans and groans, wide glissandi and long sustained but wavering 'line endings' in traditional style. All these folk

1 *Odetta at Carnegie Hall.*
2 See Glossary.

techniques are, however, enhanced by almost theatrical virtuosity —
in which context it is interesting to listen to the album of early Bob
Dylan songs[3] recorded by Odetta in the late sixties. She offers a
remarkable musical experience. In the protest songs her heroic voice
blazons us to action; 'Mr Tambourine man', in her lustrous tone,
weaves a magic spell. But these versions are a long way from Dylan.
In becoming art they have forfeited their necessity.

Odetta is an artful folk singer whose varied vocal techniques
have relevance to soul. We approach the genre more directly in the
work of Nina Simone who, born in 1933 into a large Carolina
family, was musically precocious enough to rank as an infant
prodigy. Her father was an ordained Methodist minister on Sundays
and in the evenings, a freelance handyman by day. Nina was not,
however, content with her Gospel background, and taught herself
piano and organ by the time she was 7. A local music teacher
spotted her, taught her classical music for free, and established a
'schooling fund' that enabled her to attend high school at Asheville,
North Carolina, and to proceed to New York's prestigious Julliard
School of Music. Whether she needed to learn anything about vocal
technique is a moot point, but we can hardly doubt that her studies
at Julliard helped her to acquire keyboard facility and to develop her
instinctive musicianship. Technically, Nina is a brilliant keyboard
player, and her command of this one-woman band bears on the fact
that she is an eclectic artist who performs with equal conviction in a
number of genres, all subsumed into soul because they are soulful.

Sometimes Nina Simone sings Black folk music[4] in a style
similar to Odetta's: 'Worksong' is a genuine prison number, with a
driving beat on piano, which Nina always plays herself. The grating
vocal production sounds truthful, yet the pure treble she suddenly
produces at the end removes the mask. Awareness of the illusion
proves to be a deeper kind of honesty, since Nina admits to playing
a part: she both is and is not the toiling Negro in field or prison
camp. Something similar happens in 'Little Liza Jane', a country
number she takes very fast, the voice bouncing over the prancing
piano, the texture airy. Again the coda, unaccompanied, admits
that this is a serious game, half comic, half pathetic. The old
plantation number, 'Cotton-eyed Joe', is likewise transformed. The
loping beat and springy right hand of the piano are delicate, while

3 *Odetta Sings Bob Dylan.*
4 *Golden Hours of Nina Simone.*

the melismata[5] in the vocal line are lace. A plantation song enters sophisticated cabaret without losing its folk-like innocence.

In 'Black is the colour of my true love's hair' Nina sings what is often accepted as a White folk song, though it may have been composed by John Jacob Niles, the folk singer and collector. Nina leaves his notated piano part far behind, treating the pentatonic melismata as though the tune were unaccompanied, and exhibiting an astonishing variety of tone colour and flexibility of rhythm. But although her sustained tones and quavery arabesques are artful Nina avoids the self-conscious, even melodramatic, effects that Niles himself – and sometimes Odetta – resorts to. This may be Simone's secret: she sounds natural because hers is the art that hides art. We are conscious of Odetta's art as an actress's projection. Nina's art is her honest recognition that she is not a slave on a plantation or a labourer in a cotton field, though she does not deny the pain of the Black experience.

This being so, it's not surprising that she excels in blues, improvising extended piano blues with a punch and sensitivity worthy of her male counterpart, Otis Spann. When she sings the 'Gin-house blues' associated with Bessie Smith she takes it straight, over a rocking boogie bass. 'Trouble in mind' she treats as a fast barrelhouse number, shouting over the pounding boogie rhythm that emulates the railway train. This is a suicide, or at least a threatened suicide, song and the wonder is that Nina's ebullient piano and swinging vocal line do 'make the sun shine in my backyard'. The rejuvenating power of Nina's art is even more remarkable in her treatment of standards. In Irving Berlin's 'You can have him' she appears to be debunking both the unsatisfactory lover and the mild little tune. Yet at the same time the performance affirms love and care; the climax, at the return of the first eight, is almost noble! Partly it's a matter of fluctuating vocal colour, partly the rhythmic precision, which enhances the feeling even while distancing it. Again irony seems to foster, rather than deny, the warmth of loving.

Gershwin is Simone's most potent titular spirit, as he is to many singers. Her 'Summertime' begins as a piano solo with delicate yet electrically charged spring. When the voice belatedly enters it hovers sprite-like over the keyboard figuration, floating into a dream of Eden that has substance in real childhood. In a 1982 recording[6]

5 See Glossary.
6 *My Baby Just Cares for Me.*

Nina Simone makes of Bess's song of indecision, 'I loves you, Porgy', something even more heart-rending than the versions of Billie Holiday and Ella Fitzgerald. Timbre and rhythm have the intimacy of speech yet the line is always lyrically sung. The slow-rising octave scale at the approach to the middle eight is breath-taking, preparing us for the shifts of rhythm and darkenings of tone that incarnate Crown's 'handling' of her. With her we learn that he can drive her 'mad', that 'it's going to be like dying'; yet with her we come through as the clinching line 'I got my man' ends, after being each time differently coloured and more disquieted in rhythm, with a consolatory descent to the tonic. Brisk numbers on the disc, though without the emotional charge of this song, are hardly less impressive in art and craft. In 'My baby just cares for me' the clean textures of the piano part bounce over a comic dotted ostinato, creating a euphony that almost suggests a Bach invention – a residue, perhaps, of Simone's Julliard training. Above, the voice's rhythmic speech is nearly song, happy yet aware of ambiguous peril in that word 'cares'. Bach-like textures appear again in 'Love me and leave me' – also notable for the perfectly poised triplets (on the words 'independent of you') against the duple beat.

In such performances Nina Simone establishes herself as a great jazz singer. Perhaps it is the discretion of her art and the spontaneity of her feeling that make her a soul singer also, though her soulfulness has to a degree counteracted her jazz expertise. Her jazz has coped with the personal malaise of a life sometimes desperately harried; her soul music has carried her towards public statements that stress – justifiably, some will think – political import at the expense of musical value. In mid-career Nina Simone became a committed and courageous worker for Civil Rights, and has performed and written protest songs merging the manners of White American march and hymn with Black Gospel music, sometimes with an infusion of Motown rhythmic vivacity. The music reflects her life-style: indignant over her people's lot, she left the United States for Europe, working as jazz and cabaret singer, and eventually settled in Africa, her ancestral home. Visiting Europe periodically, she still magnificently sings jazz, as some of the records commented on testify. But she now regards her social–religious–political songs as her mainstream, as is understandable and admirable, though it will be regrettable if the public aspects finally oust the private aspects of her art.

Although it is possible to establish a division between Nina Simone's 'private' jazz singing and her 'public' soul singing, she was at the height of her powers when, in the seventies, she could be near-simultaneously a great blues and jazz singer and a rocking exponent of soul, with a charisma that imbued her with the quantities of a female shaman not only for her own race, but for anyone living in our giant technocracies. A comparable fusion of the genres occurs in the work of the finest singer of the next generation, Aretha Franklin, whom we have already encountered as an inspired gospel performer.[7] She was born in Detroit, grimmest and grimiest of big cities, in 1942 – late enough to have been 'exposed', during adolescence, to the music of the great male soul singers, including Ray Charles and Otis Redding. Since her father was a Baptist minister, it is not surprising that her first musical experience should have been as Gospel singer, travelling with him on evangelizing tours. Pastor Franklin was an esteemed minister with a large and devoted flock, but if this brought a degree of material comfort, so that Aretha's childhood was never grievously impoverished, she was not unaware of ghetto life in nearby streets, where drug pushers, pimps and conmen flourished as they do in all big cities. Personal loss – her mother left the family when Aretha was 6, and died a few years later – deepened Aretha's sense of the blues, and that her music synthesizes Gospel and blues is evident from her earliest tracks. Like a jazz singer she sings from the present moment's personal feeling. As she said, using words close to those quoted from Billie Holiday, 'If a song's about something I've experienced or that could happen to me, it's good. But if it's alien to me I couldn't lend anything to it.' Like a Gospel singer, however, she does not sing alone but with a 'backing group' of a few choric voices, usually female, the relationship between soloist and backers paralleling that between preacher and congregation. The themes of Aretha's songs, unlike those of Gospel music, are usually secular, the choric backing giving public support to her private experience. She is the representative of the tribe, with whom she seeks solidarity. The tribal rather than congregational line-up accords with the later date of soul, since rock music, as distinct from blues, was now established, proffering consanguinity to the (orginally exclusively White) young, alienated from their industrial milieu.

This bears on the main technical distinction between jazz and

7 See pp. 13–14.

rock: whereas the heart of jazz lies in tension between the regular beat and the malleability of the melodic lines, in rock the beat's dominance is irresistible. The needs of the individual are now subsumed in the will of the tribe – which may induce in the singers and dancers jubilation or anger or both. Although blue subtleties of phrasing and jazz sophistications of harmony have no more place in rock music than they have in the music of authentically primitive peoples, soul, as distinct from 'hard' rock, at least recognizes that compromise is desirable. In more than one sense, the young must hang together; their communality, however fervent, must not destroy individual awareness – the reality that soul is 'all about'.

Nina Simone improvised blues but did not write the material of her songs. Aretha Franklin improvised Gospel music but usually (not always) found her soul material from other sources. This makes sense if we accept that the rhythm-and-blues singer, even if soulful, is dedicated to the tribe first and foremost. How this difficult equilibrium functions may be appreciated by listening to a sequence of Aretha Franklin songs, grouped according to their affiliation with Gospel, blues and jazz standard – and to soul proper, if it exists.[8] In each category Aretha chooses her songs intelligently, recognizing what 'turned her on', rejecting anything 'alien' to her.

Significantly, two of her vintage performances in Gospel terms are of songs by highly individual creators. 'Let it be' by John Lennon and Paul McCartney had religious, if not Christian, overtones in its original form, for it preached a message. The tune and sturdy triadic harmony, veering between C major and the Aeolian mode,[9] hymnically justify the exhortation – which Aretha re-creates in the spirit of her father's church meetings, beginning with a chapel-organ sonority which, reinforced by electric guitars and keyboards, sweeps us into the open air for the camp gathering. The beat is enhanced by more excited percussive patterns; the choric backing swings more animatedly, and Aretha as soloist takes off in jazzy flight. Her roulades are pentatonically folk-like, without the verbal expressivity of jazz singing; her tone, like that of the traditional Gospelizer, is hard, even fierce, for it must penetrate over wide spaces, potentially to multitudes. The parallel with her genuine Gospel performances is obvious, though in this rocking soul number the beat is mechanically, even martially, tighter and

8   *Aretha's Greatest Hits.*
9   See Glossary.

the homophony of the backing voices more stream-lined. The Gospel performance is music of necessity; Aretha's 'Let it be' is a brilliant artefact.

One can say as much of her version of Paul Simon's beautiful 'Bridge over troubled water'. Though this is a personal song, Aretha's version begins impersonally with choric voices and electric guitar and keyboard. When she enters as soloist her arabesques are Gospel-styled, her tone pure, as she steers the backing voices into gentle ecstasy. Again public and private experience are in equilibrium: as they are in 'You're all I need to get by', the number that set the seal on her celebrity in 1967. This is more rhythmically animated, with a jazz-tinged ostinato from the Gospel quartet. Aretha's solo line, long, sinuous, convoluted, creates a quasi-religious affirmation out of sexual commitment.

The songs so far referred to belong to the rhythm-and-blues generation and category, to which Aretha has given a Gospel renovation. The elements in her art that spring from jazz and the blues are evident in another of her 'greatest hits': 'Dr Feelgood', the composition of which is credited to her and her husband, Ted White. At a (for her) unwontedly slow tempo, the song, though not strictly a blues, is pervaded by blue, low-down funkiness, her Gospel-style roulades, dependent on the words, acquiring jazz expressivity. The lyric, about Feeling Good, amounts to a statement of the soul singer's creed. Another hit, 'I never loved a man the way I love you', is a slow swinging barrelhouse number in 12/8, in the manner of the male blues revival of the sixties. The obsessive choric ostinato drives Aretha to lyrical flights, which are sometimes yelled rather than sung; again she creates religious exaltation from sexual passion. Private experience stimulates public celebration – which happens also when she sings standards by composers of her generation, rather than from the twenties or thirties. Singing Burt Bacharach's 'I say a little prayer' she allows it its own identity, as it deserves, while welcoming its growth, over a gently syncopated beat, into Gospelized lyricism.

If such a thing as the definitive soul song exists, it must surely be Otis Redding's 'Respect', which, as sung by its creator, came to stand for a generation. As the title indicates, it is about the Negro's growing self-awareness and self-confidence: the former means that the song springs from personal feeling; the latter that it is also a statement on behalf of the race. This comes over in Aretha's performance no less than in Otis's. Her voice is passionate as well as

strident, yet the drums' hammering turns personal utterance into
universal testament, in which the choric voices participate. As in
most rock numbers metrical patterns triumph through their
consistency; very few, and then only rudimentary, harmonies are
necessary to the affirmation. Although there is no 'development'
and no imprisoning form as in the pop standard, a positive
statement accrues from repetition, always the same yet always
mysteriously transformed. Like authentic primitive musics, rocking
soul exists within the moment; it is what it does. In 'Call me', a
number for which Aretha seems to be wholly responsible, she
achieves orgiastic excitement from a country waltz, her arabesques
stimulating the backing voices to tribal frenzy. It appears to be
merely a sexual love call, but that 'merely' begs the question. There
is little difference between this and the Godly love calls in her
Gospel music, though the rapidly mounting modulations in the
coda are a more conscious contrivance than would be appropriate, or
feasible, in a congregational meeting.

How the Black rhythm-and-blues soul singer may be affiliated to
jazz and the world of the White pop standard is revealed in the career
of Dionne Warwick. [10] Born in 1941, she sang Gospel at the New
Hope Baptist Church, New Jersey, from the age of 6 throughout
her school years. She received some formal training in piano and
'theory' at the Harti College of Music, Hartford, Connecticut, but
her rise to fame dates from her collaboration with Burt Bacharach.
Whereas Aretha Franklin sang Bacharach numbers only occasionally,
Dionne Warwick became identified with his music – which is to the
sixties what the standards of Gershwin, Berlin and Porter had been
to the twenties and thirties. Many of the numbers Bacharach
composed especially for Dionne became hits. One has only to recall
'Anyone who had a heart', 'Trains and boats and planes', 'Message
to Michael', 'I say a little prayer'. The transition from the pop
standard to Broadway theatre was inevitable. Bacharach's musical
Promises, Promises, included some of his and Dionne Warwick's most
memorable songs. Even so, there is a difference between a
Bacharach ballad and those of the jazz age proper. His tunes are
broader, the beat more open, the harmonies not less sophisticated
but more spacious. A Bacharach song needs time in which to expand,
and the reason is that it is contemporary not with jazz but with soul
and rock – and with the long-playing record.

10   *The Dionne Warwick Collection.*

As singer, Dionne Warwick responds appropriately. She respects jazz heritage in her control of line and rhythm but seeks broad effects rather than the intimacies of the jazz-club singer. Out of Kerr's 'I'll never love this way again' she makes a grandly swinging affirmation of faith in loving that, whatever its sexual content, suggests chapel as much as club. Similarly her bold line and blistering tone give majesty to Barry Manilow's 'All the time', helping us to understand the obsessional appeal of his songs; some of them have more musical substance than the Manilow circus reveals. The Gospel connection is strongest in Dionne's version of the Carol Bayer Sager number 'It's the falling in love', in which her line, firmly shaped, without frills, solicits ecstatic response from the backing voices. The rituals of gospel and soul come to terms with the contemporary pop standard and with Broadway. In this Dionne Warwick's music contains the seeds of several divergent but common-rooted developments over the past twenty years. Her historical relevance is the more pointed because she is not herself a composer but a catalyst.

The rhythm-and-blues soul singer usually functions, we've observed, with backing voices that represent the solidarity of the tribe. In the early days of the century Blacks sang in unisonal chorus to emphasize the subservience of the personal to the communal; when however, they heard Whites singing European harmony they recognized in it a more complex idea of community – the reconciliation of diversities and contradictions into a 'civilized' whole. Black people enslaved responded avidly to this concept, seeking togetherness at the heart of misery. At first, the harmony of the plantations was cruder, less harmonious, than its White models, as can be heard when Black spirituals are contrasted with pious White hymnody. The part-singing was heterophonic rather than polyphonic, wild with chromatics and false relations; yet although this raw empiricism survives in Gospel music, it is gradually tamed and conventionalized as the Black man gains in confidence. Sequences of parallel thirds lend a comforting euphony – until the four-part homophony of the Evangelical hymn is transferred to secular use in the 'close harmony' of barber-shop music, so called because that is where it flourished. It follows that although the central line through soul music is traced by solo singers of exceptional magnetism, the evolution of the soul-singing 'group' is no less significant. In these groups the lead singer, usually a woman, may be a distinguished soloist in her own right who now functions as initiator of group action. The choric backing moves forward. In Gospel terms the choir takes over from the preacher, while in secular terms devotion to the social group matters more than personal fulfilment.

Originating in the Church, this music had commercial implications when Black-owned record companies, centred on Detroit, where Aretha Franklin was born, promoted the music – at first for Blacks but then, on an impressive scale, for Whites also. Motown and Tamla were record labels that came to designate specific musical styles, but their motivation was economic as well as artistic, since the point of the Black commercial enterprise was that the music should yield financial returns to the Black performers who had been exploited, if not overtly cheated, by White entrepreneurs. With pointed irony the music, appealing to Blacks, achieved its ultimate commercial triumphs with a vast White public. This will be revealed as we follow the process through the work of the Loving Sisters, Gladys Knight and the Pips, and Diana Ross and the Supremes. Though the Loving Sisters[11] came to prominence later than Gladys Knight they must be discussed first since, consistently God-orientated, they appealed most directly to a Black audience.

Led and produced by Gladys Givens McFadden, these loving sisters were four in number, sometimes boosted by the male voice of Leonard McFadden. They were accompanied by anonymous but expert rock and blues instrumentalists on electric guitars and keyboards, occasionally reinforced by accoustic bass in revivalist style. Gladys McFadden writes or invents almost all the material, which absorbs evangelical fervour into Gospel and blues. In slow numbers, such as 'Why', blues orientation is explicit in the beat, in the rudimentarily funky harmony, in the microtonally inflected pentatonics of the vocal and solo guitar lines, and in Gladys McFadden's vocal production. The Sisters' responsorial role, however, carries the blues towards Gospel, winging between earth and heaven. In fast numbers, such as 'Cry loud', Gospel affiliation is overt. Elecrophonic presentation gives an urban ferocity to a rustic camp meeting, but the frenzy – especially Gladys's superb solo line – counteracts mechanization, the more so when the percussion – as in 'It's Jesus y'all' – acquires Afro-Caribbean sprightliness. The continuity of the metrical patterns, without beginning, middle or end, becomes tribal, and we recall that African musics, though not

11   *The Loving Sisters.*

specifically Christian, are metaphysically religious as well as physically corporeal. The Loving Sisters' numbers, like most rocking soul music, never conclude but use technology to effect a fade-out, emulating the eternal present of authentic ritual musics.

The Loving Sisters flourished in the seventies. Gladys Knight and the Pips[12] began as long ago as 1958, but are the more modern group in that they steered Gospel towards secularization. Gladys Knight, born in 1947, was a child prodigy who sang at Mount Mariah Baptist Church in Atlanta at the age of 4. Her father and mother had both been members of the famous Wings over Jordan choir, and since the family was large and close-knit, it was no surprise when brothers, sisters and cousins banded together to form gospel groups. Gladys's precociousness led to professional dates and recordings; by the time she was 12 she and her Pips (so called after the nickname of a cousin who managed them) were on the way to fame. Her material was now mainly secular, concerned with sexual love and the traditional obsession of the blues with lonesomeness and alienation. The musical idiom, however, was based on Gospel's responsorial technique. Gladys was the soloist; the backing Pips were male, but were loving brothers who served the same function as the Loving Sisters in representing the community. Unlike Gladys McFadden, Gladys Knight is not a composer but found her material in Motown standards. Her instrumental backing is the same as that of the Loving Sisters, with the addition of soaring strings for the ballads that are no part of the Sisters' repertory.

In the Pips' music there is little evidence of the sacred aspects of Gospel style, and almost no trace of the blues. Their songs fall into two basic categories, which often overlap. Many numbers may be described as rock–soul ballads by professional composers like Curtis Mayfield, Jim Weatherly and David Gates. These songs have clearly defined tunes, sometimes modally inflected, over quietly syncopated ostinati, with harmony that is fairly sophisticated when compared with drone-dominated Gospel music. Gladys Knight usually sings the first verse solo, in a style more restrained than Gladys McFadden's though with clear articulation and poised swing rivalling Aretha Franklin as soul if not as Gospel singer. The Pips' choric support strengthens as the verses unfold, and what has begun as personal love experience ends with communal implications. 'Ends' is again hardly an appropriate word, for the numbers usually

12   *The Best of Gladys Knight and the Pips.*

drift into a fade-out or die on an unresolved chord. David Gates's affecting 'Part-time love' and Jim Weatherly's 'Best thing that ever happened to me', as performed by the group, offer a 'way of life' for the disorientated young, overriding alienation and sexual disquiet. In this sense the music serves some of the functions of Gospel, though the dissipation of the numinous element makes the music 'easier' and less rewarding than that of the Loving Sisters.

The Pips' second 'category' is closer to Gospel in being rhythmically orgiastic and non-harmonic. Jerry Goffin's 'I've got to use my imagination' exploits a rudimentary African beat, while Curtis Mayfield's 'On and on' does what its title suggests, and creates frenzy through hypnosis. Johnny Nash's 'I can see clearly now' unites every aspect of their work. The main melody, in ballad style, is lyrical, with modal shifts, and is initially presented by Gladys in warm lucidity. The prelude and postlude, however, transform Gospel homophony into *a cappella* barber-shop music, and the interaction of solo and chorus builds a momentum that is the closest the Pips approach to a Loving Sisters-like exaltation.

In their later work Gladys Knight and the Pips eschew sensitivity in favour of toughness. After their comeback in 1979 they make a music enlivening yet also, in its technical polish, heartless and even, oddly enough, soulless. On the album *Taste of Bitter Love* the reiterated riffs, especially in the Ashford–Simpson numbers, prove ultimately stultifying. This may be evidence that their Way of Life is more contemporary than that of the Loving Sisters; their secular ritual is more pragmatic, not so much to be listened to as to be acted out in bodily gyrations. It is only fair to add that their version of the Leiber–Stoller 'I who have nothing' is a soul song of sombre trenchancy, in its tense, tied-up beat and in Gladys Knight's abrasive yet winging vocal line, haloed by burblings on quasi-African flute. The personal–communal dualism of soul survives, though in this secular context its aspect is grim, even glum.

This is not, however, the inevitable outcome of soul's secularization: as is evident in the often joyous music of Diana Ross and the Supremes, the most commercially successful group, White or Black, in the story of Motown and soul. This success owes much to Diana Ross's physical beauty; her versatility also contributes, for her talents embrace all the elements – blues, cabaret, theatre music and gospel – that had gelled to create soul. The double album *An Evening with Diana Ross*, recorded live in Los Angeles in 1976, 'exhibits' this versatility explicitly. Diana pays homage to her heroic predecessors, Bessie Smith and Billie Holiday, Josephine Baker and Ethel Waters, singing numbers associated with them, in her own version of their manners. Though her voice is not particularly beautiful, it fascinates through its precarious balance between childlike wonder and wry sophistication, and her mimetic gifts are considerable; not for nothing has Diana Ross, like Ethel Waters in the previous generation, proved herself an award-winning movie actress.

Singing a sexual blues, 'I need a little sugar', she has the aural presence of Bessie Smith; in 'Lady sings the blues' her little-girl-tough-mama timbre cunningly evokes Billie Holiday, whom Diana impersonated in the film telling her sad story. In 'Aux îles Hawaii' her demotic French twangs like Josephine Baker in Parisian cabaret, while her version of Arlen's 'Stormy weather' recalls Ethel Waters in inhabiting an area between blues bar, jazz club and Broadway. She reminds us too of another singing actress associated with this splendid song: Lena Horne, a superb jazz cabaret singer during the fifties and sixties – especially when handling numbers of pith and point like Noel Coward's 'Mad about the boy'. Now in her sixties, Lena is still a woman of potent theatrical presence, even more beatuiful than Diana Ross, with a still-mellow voice to match her physical allure.

Diana Ross, however, is hardly deficient in magnetism. The anonymity of her mimetic skills makes her the more effectively representatative of the tribe: as becomes patent when she sings Motown standards with backing groups – supremely with the (originally all-female) Supremes. With them, especially when performing numbers by the Dozier–Holland song-writing team, Diana carries the secularization noted in the work of the Pips to an ultimate. The numbers are usually fast and rumbustious, metrically regular, diatonic major in tonality. In *A Darker Shade of Pale* I coined the phrase 'the White Euphoria' to describe the vacuous jollity generated by White singers and players, keeping their peckers up in the blue-grass country. By the same token Motown becomes a music of Black Euphoria, that much more wilful than the White variety because there had been more pain and poverty to overcome. The assets of the music lie in its corporeal ebullience. Its merriment, if mindless, is real while it lasts – even though, or perhaps because, it contains, as noted earlier, an undercurrent of irony in that it inverted precedents in being a Black music commercially exploiting Whites!

The ultimate expression of this motif appears in Jamie Gordon's Motown anthem unabashedly titled 'Money, that's what I want'. Using Gospel techniques to reverse Gospel's ethical burden, the music proves that the words mean what they say, as braying vocal lines and bouncing beat pay homage to Mammon. For most Blacks the song is a fairly hilarious joke; for Diana Ross and the Supremes, who give its definitive performance, it was also a dream that came true. A further climax to Black Euphoria occurs when Diana sings with voluble choric backing an Ashford and Simpson number featured by Gladys Knight and the Pips in their late, 'hard' phase. The cataclysmic orgy, regular in metre, diatonic major in tonality, deafening in decibel level, lives up to its title: there 'Ain't no mountain high enough' to contain it.

A trace of Gospel ritual survives here, though secularization brings with it a more artful self-consciousness. Such self-consciousness leads to a third stage in soul and Motown, represented most notably by the Pointer Sisters. Born at dates between 1946 and 1954 in the Black community of Oakland, California, the four sisters — Ruth, Anita, Bonnie and June — had a churchy background, for both their parents were ministers. As children they all sang in church, though when, with their parents' approval, they decided to become professional, they turned to secular material. Their first LP, which appeared in 1973 under the simple title of *The Pointer Sisters*, presents music radically distinct from that of the groups so far discussed, for their rocking soul is orientated towards jazz, and is art before it is ritual. The number placed first on this disc suggests the shape of things to come, for Alex Toussaint's 'Yes, we can can' evokes the aura of old New Orleans, with inspiriting drumming from Gaylord Birch, bluesy pentatonic wails from Willie Fenton's guitar, and from the girls a complex interrelation between solo lines and tuttis. This is not the conventional Motown antithesis between lead singer and backers, but a balanced ensemble with each voice momentarily becoming a soloist while contributing to the whole. The sisters form a *concertino*, comparable with that of the baroque concerto grosso;[13] remaining individuals, they define the social intercourse that makes for community, even for 'civilization'. The continuous ostinato patterns, the lack of harmonic development, the bluesy inflexions of solo voice and electric guitar, hark back to the roots of jazz; the polish of the

13   See Glossary.

ensemble, on the other hand, is the product of highly developed art – and proves that virtuosity has nothing to do with literacy, for at this time none of the Pointer Sisters could read music.

Two long numbers carry this sophisticated primitivism a stage further. 'That's how I feel', having no words beyond its title, consists of concerted homophony and pentatonic vocalises over a male-voice ostinato, emulating a funky string bass. The girls scat with ear-boggling variety of timbre from growl to blast to peep, and their virtuosity never loses improvisatory spontaneity. In 'Wang dang doodle' the Sisters remake a barrelhouse blues of the Chicago old-timer Willie Dixon, aided by pianist Tom Salisbury, who has every excuse to let his hair down as his fingers frolic. 'Pain and tears' is even faster and more furious in barrelhouse rowdyism. Despite the primitive materials – 'Wang dang doodle' repeats the same ostinato for more than seven minutes – these tracks not only sustain musical interest but enhance it as, without developing, they *go on*. This is a triumph both for the technical skill of the instrumentalists and for the Sisters' variety of vocal timbres. 'River Boulevard', another Southern-sounding number, this time by B. Mauritz, begins in slow blues style with fine traditional solos from piano and electric guitar, garners rocking percussion and homophonic voices wild in effect yet disciplined in execution, and mounts to Dionysiac abandon before the slow fade-out that is the only possible cessation to its 'eternal present'. This is not fortuitous ritual like some of the Diana Ross numbers commented on above; its effect of total spontaneity is dependent on its totally realized art. In this there is a parallel between the Pointer Sisters as a group and Nina Simone as a soloist. [14]

If this is true of Pointer Sisters numbers that refer back to the roots of jazz, it receives more explicit form in numbers appropriate to what emerged as their typical image: that of jazz, even dance-hall, singers of the thirties and forties, rather than of the wild old days. They dressed the part, with exuberant hats and teetering-heeled shoes; and their get-up matched the elegant precision of their vocal harmony. Not surprisingly, their most representative songs are their own, such as 'Jada' and 'Sugar'. Both numbers are enchanting, loping in the agility of Tom Salisbury's piano, while the girls' voices swing over the beat, sometimes individualized in varied timbres, sometimes co-ordinated in honeyed euphony. Jazz

14 See pp. 65–8.

spirit, here redolent of polite cocktail lounge rather than of grubby barrelhouse, is still active, so the music, though cheerful, is never mindless. That this is a more significant achievement than Motown's Black Euphoria is demonstrated in one of the Sisters' biggest successes, 'Cloudburst': although this number dazzles, there is no danger of its precision being equated with mechanization. The rhythmic lift of Tom Salisbury's fluttery piano is an irresistible *jazz* performance, which is complemented by the girls' dizzy scatting. Polish enhances rather than disguises jazz 'reality'.

The significance of the mimetic gift was commented on earlier in relation to Diana Ross's arty secularization; a similar quality is implicit in the Pointer Sisters' virtuosity. This initial LP includes one number, with the apposite title of 'Old songs', that deliberately debunks phoney images of Blackness, for it consists of parodies of genuine or pseudo old-time 'coon' and plantation songs of the Stephen Foster vintage. 'Swanee River' is dismissed in pert barber-shop corn; 'No place like home' is ragged in both a technical and metaphorical sense.

Such procedures figure more prominently in the 1974 disc *That's Aplenty*. The opening number telescopes 'Bangin' on the pipes', an old-time barber-shop number sung in close harmony, with a fast, fortyish rag, 'Steam heat', pounding in boogie rhythm. Parody works both ways: as in the juxtaposition of 'That's aplenty', an early twentyish boogie, with 'Surfeit U.S.A.', which guys New Orleans jazz, and behind that the military music of White America, including that of the redoubtable Sousa. There is a serious satirical point behind the double-dealing in both double numbers as sung by these brilliant Black girls, but the palpable wearing of masks places the songs in the category of theatre music and of the entertainment business.

At a more musically interesting level there's a satirical if not parodistic element in two numbers for which the Sisters introduce the Modern-Jazz pianist Herbie Hancock in place of the impeccable Tom Salisbury. 'Salt peanuts' is by two of the 'greats' of Modern Jazz, Dizzy Gillespie and Kenny Clarke, while 'Little pony' is by Nick Hefti, a talented composer of the same generation. Both numbers are taken at breakneck tempo. That a piano can flicker so fleetly does not surprise us; that the girls' voices, bubbling and bopping, scatting and scurrying, can keep up with it, never putting a quaver wrong, would be difficult to credit were it not meticulously audible. Such virtuosity acquires a satirical edge merely by being incredible.

With these tracks in our ears we're apt to detect a satirical tinge in the Sisters' singing of an old Son House blues, 'Grinning in your face', which has a primitively heavy beat that may slightly mock its original, yet builds up a powerful emotional charge. The Sisters produce an individualized homophony in which the tumbling-strain-like entries overlap in wild heterophony, ending in wails more frightening than funny. Jesse Ed Davies's electric guitar and Paul Jackson's thudding bass are not to be laughed away, while the bluesy White singer Bonnie Raitt contributes ominously on slide guitar. The deepest dimension to the irony may lie in the fact that these sophisticated girls collaborate with the bluesmen on equal terms. This particular mask or hat, among the many sported by the Pointer Sisters, fits.

Different hats are worn with equal conviction in the last three tracks on the disc. The Sisters' own 'Fairytale' could be described as a parody of White country music, and the title makes its point. Yet if it's a parody, it's acutely intelligent, with an admirable tune that Anita as lead sings with inflexions that almost kid us into thinking not that she is acting a part, but that she is in fact White. Because the music is good it is more than mimetic – as is Bonnie's solo version of 'Black coffee', a number made famous by the White night-club singer Peggy Lee. Bonnie sings it no less sensitively than Peggy, but more mysteriously, eventually carrying it out of the cocktail lounge into a wild forest of feeling, much as in 'Fairytale' Anita gradually lures corny country music into scattily dangerous territory. The long (8½ minute) number that rounds off the disc sets the seal on this. In origin 'Love in them there hills' is a Whitely euphoric country song. The Sisters, with Herbie Hancock on electric keyboards, Paul Jackson on bass and Bill Summers on African talking drums, shekere and congas, turn it into ritual that inspires the ultimate in corybantic extravagance, and does so by way of precise rhythmic control. Again the parody – of White country music *and* of African ritual – is double-edged. As White America is whirled back to darkest Africa, we admit that America has become a 'fairy tale' without being sure that an African Jungle is really the 'better place' we want to be in. It may be another fairy tale; the dubiety applies to Blacks as well as Whites.

During the seventies some such fusion of mechanized Motown with soulful rock became the central line through Black pop musics, whether created by quasi-tribal groups or by solo singers with vocal backers. It is significant that perhaps the most distinguished example of the genre should in fact be called *Performance*, a 1974 disc by Esther Phillips, who was born in Galveston, Texas, in 1935, with the conventional Evangelical background, but moved to California in 1949. All the numbers on this album are by professional Motown composers, expertly put over by the singer, backed by cunningly arranged instrumental forces and by two trios of voices. It wouldn't be an exaggeration to say that the album is 'about' the uneasy relationship between Black folk-jazz and commercialized Motown. Thus the final, most substantial track concerns betrayal in a love affair. Esther sings it in the authentic style if not form of a classic blues, her roulades being dark in timbre, sinewy in rhythm. Such intrusions of fierce humour as occur are, like those of the real blues, a therapy for endurance, ballasted by the chortlings of jazz horns.

In 'I feel the same', however, love-loss makes a different impact, for although Esther howls like an old-time blues belter and Gospel shouter, comedy is exaggerated to the brink of farce. We, her audience, White as well as Black, delight in a shock of recognition in her performance; but a performance is what it is, rather than an experience. This becomes explicit in the number actually entitled 'Performance'. She asks that when her performance, which 'they' cannot truly understand, is over she may be taken to a place 'where the waters are always fresh and cool', and the music mirrors the words' medley of pathos and clownery. 'Disposable society' deals with the same theme in a social rather than a personal context. Our plastically disposable community has 'thrown away the best in me, they've thrown away sincerity'. The refrain's catalogue of the products of planned obsolescence – 'automobilies with disposable wheels, wigs instead of hair' – is presented in savage farce yet with complex effect, since it is by way of Motown vivacity that Esther keeps her head above water.

Performance represents the apex of Esther Phillips's career. It was probably inevitable that her later work should grow tighter as her affiliation with the Black Euphoria of Motown strengthened. On her 1979 album, titled simply *Esther Phillips*, the satirical flavour is piquant, even in a slowish number like 'I'll close my eyes', by Rowe and Burgess, in which the vocal line, bathed in luscious vibraphone and celesta, is sung with a vibrato as wide as that of an organ's *voix humaine*. But the typical Esther Phillips number has become melodically sprightly and rhythmically robust. Esther's voice, over the clattery metrical patterns of Motown, is pinched, her enunciation terse, on the whole merry but not, since the songs have satirical overtones, mindless. 'Mr Melody' is a prototype for Esther's later music; her inspiriting version of the Hilliard–Garson 'Our day will come' proves that her mirth has both nerve and sinew. Quite sophisticated modulations disturb the orgiastically continuous textures – whereas the 1974 disc was content with drones and rudimentary blues basses, except in the parodistic 'On such a night'. The burden seems to be that 'their' day will indeed come, but that no one is pretending that the coming will be easy. Esther reveals human impulses that routine Motown deliberately disguises.

A number such as 'Our day will come', in so far as it has politicial implications, suggests another, non-ecclesiastical platform for the ritual that pop music aims at. In West Indian reggae, created for a local audience in a self-enclosed environment, 'euphoric' Black pop music, sung by men, has become overtly political. In an American context, especially a White context, political motivation has usually conflicted with commercial viability – which is one reason why post-Motown trends in soul music have, especially among women, favoured soulful expressivity rather than rocky aggression.

Roberta Flack, for instance, born in Washington, DC, in 1939, came of a lower middle-class Black family but displayed talents precocious enough to lead to her becoming a music major at Howard University. Later she worked as a teacher, and found no problem in discovering affinities between a Bach chorale and Black Gospel harmony; nor did she forget her academic training when her natural vocal abilities steered her towards a professional singing career in the late sixties. She sang numbers of some sophistication, usually making her own quite elaborate arrangements.[15] Though she doesn't compose her own numbers, she chooses her songs with tact, covering an eclectic range.

Singing a plantation-style number like McDaniels's 'River', she exploits a piercing intonation recalling Nina Simone, with the choric backing also sounding Negro. When she performs the Macdonald–Salter's 'When you smile' she adapts her voice to 1930-ish ragtime as adeptly as the Pointer Sisters; whereas in 'No tears in the end' she is as deeply soulful in melody and springily rocky in rhythm as Aretha Franklin. Yet she can also sing a number of the White singing composer Janis Ian[16] with a pure-toned

15 *The Best of Roberta Flack* and *Killing Me Softly*.
16 See pp. 177–82.

wistfulness sounding nearly as White as Janis herself. She gives an exquisite performance of Janis Ian's 'Jesse', poising the line over chromatic harmonies, and is no less 'White' in her 9 minute re-creation of 'Suzanne', most famous number of the Canadian singing poet–composer, Leonard Cohen. Here she creates mystery out of what might have been mindless meandering.

Roberta Flack's eclecticism suggests that the artfulness of her performances involves a wearing of masks such as was commented on above with reference to the Pointer Sisters, if in less extreme form. Yet Roberta preserves more personal character than the average rock–soul performer of the younger generation, of which Randy Crawford is representative.[17] All of Randy Crawford's material is recent and much of it is specially composed for her by Cecil and Linda Womack, Cecil being the lead guitarist in her expert band.

Like Motown music, Randy Crawford's numbers are admirable for dancing to. Her precise verbal rhythms, sharp enunciation, and unvaried timbre, no less than the metrically exact instrumentals and well-drilled backing voices, encourage physical movement – not merely in numbers like 'Happy feet' and 'Lift me up' that specifically refer to dancing. But if Randy's music is fine for the feet it is less rewarding to head and heart; it tends to become a *substitute* for ritual, often effective, seldom affecting. When the songs have distinctive quality it is not easy to tell how far she is responsible for it, how far it is a consequence of the arrangements and the sometimes quite interesting composition. The biggest hit, 'Nightline', is also the most thoughtfully composed number, with a bluesy, pentatonic solo line punctured by chorically and instrumentally shifting triads faintly reminiscent of Carl Orff and the 'process music,'[18] of his more minimal successors. 'Bottom line' has a clever basic idea, with a tune noodling around a nodal point, enacting the girl's determination to get her man. Here Randy's remorseless line fits the verses. Indeed it may be her lack of variety, as opposed to Roberta Flack, that makes her a spokeswoman for the younger generation, as well as a product of her production team.

Processing and packaging is slight here, however, compared with the case of Donna Summer, whose musical contribution is engulfed in the selling of her image as a sexual bombshell. Her

17   *Nightline.*
18   See Glossary.

musical talents are not strong, though she plays some part in the creation of most of her numbers, and is credited with both words and music of some of them. Her 1979 album, *Bad Girls*, is representative; the music works best when fairly fierce and rock-influenced. The title song, about young whores in the traffic-racked city, has powerful rhythmic momentum, and Donna belts the pentatonic-tending line with an appropriately brazen timbre. More characteristic of her manner as composer, however, are moderate-tempo numbers that build up cumulatively, with much repetition: such as 'There will always be a you', which opens in stratospheric coloratura, is harmonically unambitious, but has a touching shift to make the stars fall from her eyes. In these gentler songs Donna's performance is apposite to the music: not striking nor vocally beautiful, but unpretentiously affecting. A more overtly erotic number, 'My baby understands', is entirely by Donna and prompts a more impressive performance, harsh in tone, winging in line, with corybantic backing voices.

These fairly simple songs tend, however, to be grossly overproduced – the list of credits seems interminable. And the same may be said of the later, much more sophisticated disc, *Four Seasons of Love*, in which Donna is backed by the brilliant electric group the Munich Machine, plus a sizeable, impeccably drilled chorus. The four movements, which follow the four seasons, have something in common with process music in being both minimal and repetitive. The synthetic electrical sonorities are succulent for spring, warm for summer, ripe for autumn, stark for winter, and the sounds are beautiful if one isn't exasperated by the repetition. Donna's voice lightly flutes for spring, spurts in air-borne coloratura for summer, darkens for autumn and descends to a lower register for winter: a naive concept that works because, having reached winter, the music – said to be all Donna's – at last arrives at a sustained tune, floating out of the intricate metrical patterns and pentatonic doodlings on flute and synthesizers. The reprise of spring at the end almost justifies the repetitiveness, for it makes us feel that we have ourselves become part of seasonal process and non-progress. This glossily manufactured product is a long way from the Gospel antiphony it started from, but may be a valid seasonal ritual for a mechanized world.

Another Black rocking soul singer of Donna Summer's generation, Deniece Williams, doesn't write her own numbers but is vocally better endowed than Donna, with a coloratura range that genuinely extends her lower and middle registers. The songs she favours also have more musical substance, attaining a metrical complexity that often sounds West Indian or African, especially in White's 'Baby, my love is all for you', the hit from her 1979 album, *Song Bird*. The combination of Deniece's soaring, sometimes screaming, vocal line with percussion induces exaltation, though this music too tends to be overarranged.

That overproduction is not unavoidable is clear from the discs of Angela Bofill, a young singer who has survived being launched as another sexual bombshell by way of sterling, unpretentious musical abilities. Her 1979 disc, *Angel of the Night*, includes a high proportion of her own numbers, in electrophonic arrangements where gimmicks are subservient to art. Words, voice and music cultivate a far from vacuous charm. This is manifest in the opening number 'I try', which allies minimal words about loving and caring to a simple but haunting tune, intermittently intensified by an unexpected harmonic shift on key words and phrases, such as 'Can't you see you're hurting me'. The clarity of Angela's enunciation is crucial to the effect; every word rings true as a bell and we believe she means it, her voice being youthful, yet without babyish affectation. Both music and singing are strong enough to support, perhaps to promote, the fine jazz obbligato of Eddie Daniels's saxophone.

Although a girl of the city night, Angela Bofill feels no need to restrict herself to the urban fusion of Motown, soul, jazz and Gospel. She also makes a simple ballad addressed to a child, possibly hers, sung merely to acoustic and electric piano. 'Rainbow child' sounds like a cross between an Evangelical hymn and an old plantation song. The little tune is memorable in the same way as the best balladic numbers of Janis Ian, and Angela is more characterful than Roberta Flack in transmuting Janis's White idiom: consider how she points keywords – 'inside', 'always', 'watching' – with a suddenly darkened piquancy. In this disc the concluding number, 'The voyage', carries Angela momentarily beyond the city, for her verses are a tune matched by folk-like incantation in the vocal line. Towards the end Angela wings from her habitual tawny tone into coloratura, over tinkling drones on electric piano and synthesizer that sound Polynesian as well as Caribbean.

When Angela Bofill sings other people's songs she adeptly makes them hers. 'Angel of the night', by Bunny Huff and Jim Devlin, has a fine tune chanted by Angela with such clarity that we can believe that when this angel of the night speaks she makes music that 'puts your life in harmony'. Jack Perricone's 'What wouldn't I do' generates, through its modal tune and reggae-like metrical vivacity, a euphoria that is deft but not daft. Most touching of all is 'Love to last', which is about growing up to learn that a lasting love may be possible, and is all — not merely in a sexual context — that ultimately matters. Again Angela sounds at first like a Black Janis Ian in ballad style, but grows more exuberant as the wider implications of love become manifest in the reggae beat, reinforced by the Gospel-like backing voices. The naivety of the conception is part of its truth; this applies too to the versification, which may turn clichés into metaphors, and makes a spontaneous virtue out of false rhymes and metrical laxity. In general, of course, pop lyrics work within or on the periphery of established art conventions; only rarely, however, does one feel that their failure to conform is precisely the point. The Beatles, especially early Beatles, offer the supreme example; Angela Bofill's verses, in conjuction with her music, are at least comparable in effect — which is why these Angels of the Night sound ultimately *beneficent*, bestowing a slight grace on the devil-haunted nocturnal city.

PART II

WHITE WOMEN AS URBAN AND RURAL SURVIVORS IN THE INDUSTRIAL WILDERNESS

Chapter Five

THE JAZZ SINGER AS LITTLE GIRL LOST

What ails Christianity is that the old Mother-Goddess religious theme and the new Almighty-God theme are fundamentally irreconcilable.

Robert Graves: *The White Goddess*

I'm not a poet. I'm only a very small child, crying . . . Even my sorrows are everyone's poor common sorrows . . . And I die, a little bit, each day. Just as all things do.

Sergio Corazzini: quoted in *The Blues Line*, ed. Eric Socheim.

The singers so far discussed have all been Black, and we do not have to look far for the reason: Gospel song and the blues – the roots of Black musics – are emblematic of the rediscovered 'matriarchy' that threatened the White 'patriarchal' world,[1] the more so as it reeled under the impact of world wars. In the blues explosion during the century's first two decades no White woman could have intuitive knowledge of blues idiom. The first to do so was Barbara Dane,[2] a product of the White folksong revival of the fifties, who could belt a country banjo song like 'Little Maggie' with a tone as virulent as

---

1   See pp. 3–4.
2   *Folk Festival at Newport.*

that of the most primitive mountain singer. It must have been her folk rather than jazz-club training that made her vocal quality a shade grubby; certainly when she sings an authentic Black blues, such as 'Dink's blues', what comes out might be mistaken for the real thing. Beginning immensely slowly, as though singing a field holler, she wails with wide portamenti, inching up from nearly a semitone flat to land dead on pitch. Her blue false relations lacerate, her timbre vibrates. Momentarily, she has made the coloured sorrow hers.

But White women didn't normally sing jazz until Black women had taken over, in club and cabaret, the White woman's world and its all too 'standardized' music. Then, inevitably, White women began to compete. Although they did so frailly, it was by way of their forlornness that they made a distinctive contribution. Not fortuitously, the first White woman to achieve 'phenomenal' success in the dance-band world of the thirties was Connie Boswell,[3] whose fame sprang not from solo singing but from performance with her singing sisters. Presenting the standards of composers like Irving Berlin and Jerome Kern in close harmony, they created a cosiness appropriate to the love-nests the songs mostly inhabited; barber-shop rather than Gospel-meeting homophony offered security. Together, the Sisters could face the intransigent city; separately, they might have quailed. The slickness of the arrangements – Connie Boswell's own – serves as a pseudo-sophisticated mask for tender hearts.

For a long time even tough White 'mamas' like Sophie Tucker were affiliated to theatre and cabaret rather than to blues. Aparently accepting paternalistic economic dominance, White women were not obliged to confront the 'rockbottom reality' of the blues, however swaggeringly a Sophie Tucker emulated, or parodied, male charisma. In any case swagger was superficial; slowly, White women discovered that their urban industrial world was more inimical than they'd thought. By the forties, having come to see themselves as little girls lost in a scary industrial wilderness, they were at last able to profit from the courage of the Black woman. This is manifest in the work of Mildred Bailey, a White woman born in 1907, who worked during the thirties and forties with such Black stalwarts as Mary Lou Williams, Teddy Wilson, and sundry members of the Basie band.[4] Though she also sang with the big and small bands of

3   *Connie Boswell and the Boswell Sisters.*
4   *Mildred Bailey.*

(White) Benny Goodman, who did so much to encourage desegregation in the jazz world, she remained aware of her Black affiliations. Indeed she was closer to Bessie Smith, Black Empress of the blues, and to Billie Holiday, Black Queen of club jazz, than was her namesake, Pearl Bailey, though Pearl was Black and Mildred White.

Her relationship to these Black heroines is evident in the tracks she made in 1939 and 1940 with a group she called the Oxford Greys. The presence of Mary Lou Williams, one of the most bluely potent of Kansas City pianists, abetted Mildred Bailey in her acts of revocation. When she sings 'There'll be some changes made' she adapts a number made famous by Bessie Smith ('Nobody knows you when you're down and out'), and approaches her aural 'presence'. Though she hasn't Bessie's imperial quality, she has her fearlessness in the acceptance of down-and-outness. Her vocal quality, in being Whiter, is also more pallid. When she sings 'Gulf Coast blues', a real blues over a compulsive boogie rhythm, with a superb Kansas City-style solo from Mary Lou Williams, her voice recalls Billie Holiday rather than Bessie Smith; and this vulnerability, half innocent, half disillusioned, is still more patent in a version of 'St Louis blues' with John Kirby's orchestra, including Billy Kyle as pianist, and the illustrious Charlie Shavers, Buster Bailey and Russell Procope on horns. The number is taken quite fast, the vocal line breathless, the instrumental parts garnering the 'Spanish tinge' often applied to this piece. (Jelly Roll Morton said it was a basic ingredient in all jazz, though he spoke from the context of New Orleans.) The tangoid flavour threatens to become comic, and Red Norvo's footling xylophone solo debunks the jazz tension the blues had started from. None the less this performance, carrying Mildred Bailey into a cabaret-style jazz club, places her in the environment congenial to her. Her Bessie Smith-style numbers, recorded with Mary Lou Williams, may be her finest music, but her most representative tracks are those made, also around 1940, with Teddy Wilson, a pianist without Mary Lou Williams's earthiness, but with a cabaret-style elegance that always swings. We have met him as Billie Holiday's most empathetic accompanist. He's irresistible in a 1940 version of 'I'm nobody's baby', giving *élan* to what might have been doleful words. Mildred Bailey's permutations on 'no–body' become a gleeful game, which sets Teddy Wilson capering, and promotes a nervously agile solo from Roy Elridge's trumpet. In dealing with love loss, the pop standard seems to have acquired some of the therapeutic efficacy of the blues – as also happened when, in 1937, Mildred recorded 'Heaven help this heart of mine' with members of the Basie band, including its famous rhythm section of Freddie Green, Walter Page and Jo Jones. Again, Mildred Bailey's line recalls Billie Holiday, being at once piteous and joyful.

This tensile quality becomes blander and more noticeably White when she sings with the big band of Benny Goodman, which empoyed Fletcher Henderson as arranger as well as pianist. In a fascinating version of 'Smoke dreams' with Red Norvo's orchestra this White band style veers into cabaret and theatre. Eddie Sauter's elaborate arrangement employs distonation to induce an alcholic haze; Red Norvo's xylophone enhances the irreal atmosphere, while Mildred Bailey's vocal makes illusion paradoxically precise. What comes out is cabaret music at once ironic and dreamy – not in Duke Ellington's class, but comparable with the jazz 'tone poems' he created around the same time.

Although Mildred Bailey's singing tends to lose its jazz quality as it loses its pseudo-Black timbre, this need not be the case: as is indicated by Anita O'Day,[5] who, born in 1919, came to the fore with Gene Krupa's band in the early forties. Indisputably a jazz singer, she is also indisputably White, yet to define what her White vocal quality consists in is difficult. Her voice, like a Negro woman's, is deep in register but differs from the typical Black timbre in that, lacking 'belly resonance', it sounds gruff rather than vibrant. This physiological factor contributes to her emotionalism. When she unwontedly improvises a real blues called simply 'Anita's blues', with the admirably blue trio of Kirk Lightsey, John Dena and John Poole, she exploits the traditional pentatonic formulae, yet creates a music expressive not – obviously – of the Black's alienation from the White world, but of her own, perhaps romantically regretted, alienation from the 'alternative culture' of Blacks. Her phrases are forlorn – to use the adjective we started from – in being splintered until, growing wild, they turn into scatty scatting. The effect is deflationary – as is the stunt number 'Boogie blues', which is not in boogie rhythm and not a blues, but a frantic caper in 3/4, with pyrotechnic pianism from George Ingdahl, complementing Anita's vocal gymnastics.

A comparably satirical note enters Anita's treatment of standards. In 'Is you or is you not my baby? she mimics, even mocks,

5   *Once Upon a Summertime.*

Black vocal intonation; 'Night and Day' she begins unaccompanied, evoking Cole Porter's fevered jungle only to explode fever in crazy comedy when the tempo gets fast, and the voice burbles to the accompaniment of pseudo-African drumming and double-bass. One isn't sure whether the cavernous tone of the repetitions of 'making love to you' is erotic or ludicrous. It could be both, as love-making often is. The ambivalence underlines the vulnerability at the heart of Anita O'Day's White performance.

Not surprisingly, Anita is most effective when singing numbers that lend themselves to irony while having a core of truth. 'Love for sale', the song of a youthful prostitute, she sings lyrically yet with distonations of pitch and disturbances of rhythm, creating a paradoxically tough wistfulness appropriate to the subject. An old-time standard, 'Sweet Georgia Brown', complements 'Love for sale', since sweet Georgia is rubicundly innocent, though the displaced accents and pitches give the music an unease both screwed up and screwy. The vocal wails at the end – tight rather than uninhibited – are at the opposite pole to those of a soul singer like Aretha Franklin. A Black(ish) song sung by a White in White America is of its nature uneasy. Disquiet pervades Anita's 'Whitest' songs also; she cannot present a sentimental ballad like 'A nightingale sang in Berkeley Square' without guying it, not just in her performance, but in her spoken introduction too.

Chris Connor,[6] born in Kansas City in 1927, eight years later than Anita O'Day, had an adolescent initiation into jazz when a student at the University of Missouri. Moving to New York in 1949, she sang with the band of Claude Thornhill, a harbinger of 'cool jazz', and briefly with Stan Kenton's big band. In temperament, however, she was an intimate club singer and as such she achieved recognition in the fifties and early sixties. Though her fame never equalled that of Anita O'Day it ought to have done, for she displayed Anita's originality without need of defensive satire. Though Chris Connor's tone is pallid, her line is more sustained than O'Day's, and she feels no need trickily to dislocate rhythm and pitch. Respecting the words, she makes them sound respect-worthy. The impression is of a White girl who has learned from Blacks – especially perhaps from the comparably intelligent Abbey Lincoln – how to get her own back by accepting, but renovating, the clichés she's been encouraged to live by.

6 *When Malindy Sings* and *I Hear Music.*

A key number is her 1959 version of Erroll Garner's 'Misty', a song amenable to her tenuous vocal production. 'Look at me, I'm as helpless as a kitten up a tree,' the song begins, and Chris's voice flutters in helplessness, quivers with the kitten, clings to the cloud, yet never breaks the gossamer-like line. When she 'walks my way' the rhythm strangely strays; the 'violins' oscillate as they 'begin to play'; the 'misty's of the refrain are each time subtly varied. Despite vagaries of rhythm and pitch the slow song has a shape, attaining genuine climax in the third stanza by way of emphasis on the words 'just' and 'I'; however 'hopelessly' lost, she comes through, un-scathed. This quintessential White woman's song – as it becomes in this performance – is another testament to jazz resilience for, however frail, the little girl lost in the big city not only survives, but smiles.

As she does in 'Love', a brisker 1950s number, with brass as well as piano trio. This is a rather frightened song telling us that love may be almost madness, 'a life of sadness and pain, wild or tame'. Yet Chris's cool line, occasionally piping, then smokily veiled, accepts love's madness, as she had accepted its mistiness, without resorting to irony. Typically she can sing a sentimental number, 'Try a little tenderness', on its own terms, proving, through the purity of her enunciation, the spontaneity of her rhythm, and the distancing faculty of her swing, that it is not *merely* sentimental. Her variations of the word 'tenderness' itself insist that love is women's 'whole happiness'; and the admission is forlorn! Ellis Larkins's delicate pianism contributes to this expressivity. A 1955 version of 'Blame it on my youth' again broaches the little-girl-lost theme, this time with filigree piano from Ralph Sharon, her regular pianist, and with Herbie Mann's fluttery flute to complement her vocal quavering. Yet the lost girlishness never degenerates into sloppiness, since the line is fine-spun, even sinewy. The substance behind her sensitivity is still more sharply defined in the 1955 version of 'The thrill is gone', herein Kai Winging's and J. J. Johnson's trombone duo supports the still fluttering flute and piano with grave polyphony, while Chris confesses to disillusion in a line responsive to hurt, yet of airy grace.

Around the same date the image of White woman as little girl lost is given a more intimate twist in the singing of Julie London.[7] On her 1958 disc with Jimmy Rowles's Orchestra she sings standards

---

7 *Julie.*

all at moderate tempo, in a tone of dewy wonderment. Though the timbre is beautiful and the phrasing genuinely jazzy, she is too limited in mode to compete with Anita O'Day or Chris Connor, let alone with the white singer who has carried the lost-little-girl image to its ultimate. Blossom Dearie has been active as jazz singer and pianist for more than twenty-five years and conforms to Peter Pan mythology by growing no older. But she gets wiser in her artfulness, and differs from the singers so far discussed in this chapter in that she is self-reliant, needing only her own voice and piano, though in clubs she often sings with the conventional backing of string bass and drums. For many years she has performed, as do most club singers, other people's numbers, but has selected and put them over so personally that they have become her property. More recently she has started to compose her own songs, cunningly related in mood and manner to those appropriated from others. Her artful art may mark an end to the club jazz of White singers, much as Betty Carter, who has also become a composer, signals the end of the club jazz of Blacks.

Blossom Dearie's songs[8] conform to the basic categories of hedonism and nostalgia. The hedonistic numbers are witty in the manner of Cole Porter, though she favours composers of a later generation, such as Frank Loesser, Dave Frishberg and Cy Coleman. Similarly her nostalgic–sentimental numbers have their prototype in Irving Berlin, but are by more sophisticated composers such as François Legrand. The poise of her art depends on the fact that nostalgia and wit overlap, being more or less equated with innocence and experience, and with her voice and piano. Her winsome voice is that of a child, capable of open-eyed tenderness and of sudden, comically affronted surprise. Intimately sensitive to words, she at the same time heals distress in jazz swing, which is also the beat of the heart. She is no less a natural as pianist than as singer, her rhythmic sense being as potent as it is refined, while the textures of her improvised pianism are at once rich and elegant.

Her harmony is of the post-Earl Hines and Ellington era – she gives idiomatic prformances of Ellington's 'Satin doll' and of Billy Strayhorn's 'Lush life' – with more than a hint of the luxuriant grace of Bill Evans. The 'experience' of her chromatic harmony complements the 'innocence' of her vocal lines in much the same way as Delius's chromatic harmony seems to yearn for a linearly pentatonic

8 *Blossom Dearie at Ronnie Scott's* and *Sweet Blossom Dearie.*

Eden. This is why there is a general affinity between Delian harmony and that of post-Ellington jazz, though in relation to Blossom Dearie the parallel startles, if only because Delius is not a composer characterized by wit!

In assessing Blossom Dearie we may begin by comparing her version of Legrand's 'Once upon a summer time' with that of Anita O'Day. This slow waltz is a basic nostalgia song about young love lost. Anita takes it rather briskly, talking as much as singing, brushing aside sentiment along with sentimentality. Blossom takes it slower and doesn't attempt, in her *sung* enunciation of the words, to hide the heartache. Yet her piano playing, swinging the waltz jazzily, speaks irresistibly for life; through the fusion of regretful chromatic harmony with springing rhythm and vernally blooming vocal line nostalgia is reanimated. The sudden, unexpected tinge of minor in the final cadence is an aural image for learning by experience; though the little girl hasn't become in the least hard-boiled, she will not again be so easily fooled. So perhaps, although Blossom sounds like a little girl in a big city, it's hardly accurate to call her 'lost'. That her songs effect small rebirths is evident too in her exquisite version of Lerner's 'On a clear day you can see forever', wherein the air-borne vocal line opens vistas above the nasty realities of an urban world. Philippe Gerards's 'When the world was young' and Frank Loesser's 'Baby it's cold outside' likewise reveal how Blossom Dearie's childlike truth depends on her awareness of the cold outside.

This again has a bearing on the fact that her nostalgic–sentimental and her hedonistic–witty numbers are opposite sides of the same coin. Clever Dave Frishberg often provides the witty songs, the delicious 'Peel me a grape' and 'I'm hip' being his, though it is now impossible to think of the numbers in isolation from Blossom's performance. 'Peel me a grape' is sung by what used to be called a gold-digger – a member of an 'experienced' occupation which, in Blossom's lilting vocalization and pianism, sounds as open as the day. 'I'm hip', a portrait of the with-it wide-boy of the sixties, makes us laugh aloud through the comicality of its rhyme schemes, the piping perkiness of Blossom's treble, and the bounce of her swinging piano. Yet she misses none of the pathos of the boy's slavery to fashion, revealing that in his cockiness he is a little *boy* lost, even if she herself knows what she's doing. Cy Coleman's 'When in Rome' she treats in the same way as 'Peel me a grape'. The words are cynical, yet Blossom's singing and playing imbue cynicism with jazzy delight, thereby discrediting false values. What really matters is being alive, in Rome, in spring, singing and dancing. Frishberg's 'Wheelers and dealers' makes the same point, being explicitly about the distinction between price and value.

Related to this is the fact that one of the earliest of Blossom's compositions is her tribute to 'Sweet Georgie Fame'. The words, by Saundra Harris, are wittily surprising; Blossom's piano playing, though slowish in tempo, carries a suppressed electrical charge, while her arching tune, no less than the quality of her voice, distils innocence. She convinces us that although pop songs and stars fill her with 'suspicion', Sweet Georgie Fame is a nice boy and a 'real good musician.' The near rhyme is half comic; the tune melts the heart, and that she quotes 'London Bridge is falling down' evokes childhood while reminding us of the city perils. Blossom Dearie's slight songs operate on many levels – which is why they have worn well. A comparable case is 'I'm shadowing you', which makes a sly comment on the America of the Watergate years, giving a faintly sinister political undercurrent to a love song. But the minatory repeated notes of the sung melody and the piano's snaky undulations don't obliterate humour. Awareness of the darkness of experience cannot dampen the light of innocent day.

In her own compositions of the late seventies and early eighties Blossom opts for the nostalgic–sentimental somewhat at the expense of the witty category. In the double album she produced for the 1977 Appleblossom Festival at Shenandoah[9] the key song – 'Winchester in appleblossom time' – is a very slow waltz evoking an Eden that is probably her own childhood. Her blithely scatting melismata suggest both chirruping birds and babbling kiddies, while the diaphanously spaced chromatic harmony glows. (Is it an accident that the key is A major, in European music traditionally associated with radiance, wonder and childhood, from Bach to Mozart to Schubert to Britten?) Not much jazz feeling survives here; there is still less in 'Touch the hand of love', which, in a very slow dotted rhythm, remotely recalls the rural hymnody of chapel and village green.

Jazz spring surfaces again in 'Sunday afternoon', a palpable recall of *temps perdu*, again with floating pentatonic arabesques, bird-like scatting and impeccable enunciation, but with potent swing in the piano interludes. The slow tempo in these songs allows for maximum

9 *Winchester in Appleblossom Time.*

attention to words and for pianistic adventure: consider the tug at the heart-strings given by the harmonization of the word 'snow' in 'The summer is gone'. The extended piano tremolandos at the end are a new technique for Blossom, needed in order to sustain sonorities that carry us, womb-like, back to the forgotten garden. Even when, on these discs, Blossom sings other people's songs, she treats them introspectively. Cy Coleman's 'It amazes me', which can be taken wittily, here savours the wonder in the words: the harmonization of the high note at the end indeed amazes, though it is brushed aside by the piano's downward scale. Ramses Shaffy's 'Sammy', with its piping refrain, makes the youth a creature reborn, in 'a New England everlasting and unfallen, with dew on the grass'.

The *Winchester* double album promotes doubts lest Blossom's regression to childhood should lead to a decline in her jazz impetus: the very slow tempi, despite the incidental delights in vocal line and pianism, are enervating if one listens to the songs in sequence. But a later disc[10] seems to be redressing the balance, partly because she has recourse to earlier numbers with which she is identified, presenting them with renewed and renewing flair. White woman's jazz singing and piano playing have reached in Blossom Dearie (who is indeed dear and blossom-like) an ultimate in refinement; the genre ends not with a bang but a whisper.

Yet the fact that Blossom Dearie sings and plays jazz authentically itself testifies to white woman's unconscious aspiration towards blackly primitive sexuality: an image given mythic form in Marilyn Monroe, who sometimes sang in a pipe even more babyish than Blossom's, while being overtly a creamy White (not Black) Earth Goddess who, in Arthur Miller's film *The Misfits*, danced a tree ritual, naked by moonlight. Though a misfit, she was also a dream-image at the heart of modern mechanization: who effects a transition from the jazz singer proper to artists, such as Judy Garland, Liza Minelli, Barbra Streisand and perhaps Anita Harris, who operate through theatrical sense and personal magnetism rather than through purely musical qualities.

Limits of space prohibit discussion of such artists. None the less, since the boundaries between art and entertainment are now so hazily defined, it will be appropriate to end this chaper with the ambiguous case of Peggy Lee.[11] Singing a preponderance of slow

10 *Needlepoint Magic.*
11 *Black Coffee.*

ballads, Peggy often finds herself in the 'Easy Listening' category in record shops. She *is* easy to listen to, especially late at night. Even so, one learns to recognize that she may demand close attention, being in fact a jazz singer, and a fine one, comparable with Blossom Dearie except that she doesn't play her own piano or compose her own songs. Her material consists of standards of the Jazz Age, often by its best composers such as Gershwin, Porter and Rodgers. The themes of these songs are as usual polarized between laughter and tears; the heart of her art, as of Blossom Dearie's, in that the poles are interdependent.

That Rodgers's 'There's a small hotel' is an escapist song Peggy doesn't deny when she presents it as a 'Continental' waltz, setting the sentimental scene. When she hots it up into duple-rhythmed jazz the bubbling music tells us that the answer to the query 'Who wants people?' is that these lovers do, in wanting one another. All she needs to get this over – and that all is much – is the precision of her enunciation, intonation and rhythm and the subtlety of her coloration, which, like Blossom Dearie's is both expectant and fearful of experience. Gerard's 'When the world was young', sung by Peggy Lee, takes us close to the core of Blossom Dearie's blossomy April in Paris or New England – consider what Peggy and her trumpeter do with that 'hive of bees'. Gorney's 'You're my thrill' she takes so slowly that the pulse seems not merely to falter, but to be on the point of breakdown. Yet she preserves balance between the 'thrill' and the 'chill' and doesn't evade the fact that, in this awed moment, desire may mount higher!

'Jazz 'reality' surfaces in witty numbers like Cole Porter's 'I got you under my skin', in which the jokes enhance rather than disguise de–zi–er that is no less mounting. The point becomes explicit when, with perfect timing, Peggy sings 'use your mentality, wake up to reality'. This is exactly what she does, here and in another Porter number, 'My heart belongs to Daddy', which she takes fast, a bit scared, with a tremulous trumpet obbligato that none the less rises to a triumphant climax. Her version of Gershwin's 'It ain't necessarily so', sung in *Porgy and Bess* by the dope-peddling Sportin' Life, is a great jazz performance, taken with a snaky lope that gives her time to savour the very funny jokes while revealing their subversive import. Jonah's whale wails; the final, long sustained 'so' – after her multiple variations on 'ain't' and 'neces*ar*ily' – acquires unexpected pathos, hinting that although it may *not* be so, one can't help wishing it were. The familiar equivocation between illusion and reality is still present – as it is even in 'Easy living', a very slow ballad apparently destined for Easy Listening yet recurrently surprising in its rhythmic recognition of fraility within the ease. It almost debunks itself in the abrupt waltz rhythm of the coda. Least easy of all are two nocturnal numbers – 'Black coffee' and 'A woman alone with the blues' – which seem palpably to invite indulgence. But Peggy's command of verbal nuance denies amorphous generalization. She is on the mark in saying that she is 'hanging out my dreams *to dry*', and is helped to this end by the passionately impersonal commentary of the anonymous saxophone or trumpet.

The jazz singing of Peggy Lee, like that of Blossom Dearie, seems to exist for its own sake, though projected to us as audience, in that it is experience in the making. The difference between such basic jazz and dance-band singing (as practised by Bing Crosby and Rosemary Clooney)[12] is that the latter is a show inconceivable *except* in relation to its audience. A singer such as Peggy Lee, even in moving from club jazz to commercial theatres, matters because she preserves emotional, and perhaps intellectual, integrity from the heart of the big city's Dream Factory. This was an achievement as rare as it was difficult – so it is hardly surprising that alongside this urban tradition there should have evolved a deliberate reversion to 'obsolete' rural values. In this folksong revival White women played a significant role, rediscovering lost traditions and reanimating them in paradoxically industrialized terms.

12 *Bing Crosby and Rosemary Clooney*, RCA DPS 2066.

Chapter Six

THE FOLKSONG REVIVAL AND THE REAL RIGHT THING

Early spring —
why was the fire and dew of it all
spoken in your eyes and voice?

Carl Sandburg

Poetry withers and dries out when it leaves music too far behind it.

Ezra Pound

America had been born on the crest of the wave of Europe's post-Renaissance expansion. European man — not woman — confident in his sensuous and intellectual powers, sought new worlds to conquer and create. Since post-Renaissance Europe was a collocation of paternalistic communities, it is not surprising that America was itself patriarchal. Pioneer men sought a male-dominated celebration of the controlling will; the role of pioneer women was to endure. James Fenimore Cooper's men, whether White scouts or savage Redskins, treat women as fragile accessories to be huddled under tables while men get on with the serious business of shooting one another. Significantly, the great loves in American literature are not heterosexual but those between Natty Bumpo and Chingachgook, Ishmael and Queequeg, Huck Finn and

Jim. The mythical American New Adam, Walt Whitman, is androgynous; Henry James's Great Good Place, envisaged in the story so named, is a male club from which women are barred; even the heroine of Ernest Hemingway's *For Whom the Bell Tolls* has been shorn of her hair, wears men's clothes and, under the sobriquet of 'Little Rabbit', acts as mascot for male soldiers.

But the American distrust of women probes deeper than a belief in their inutility in the struggle between man and an actively belligerent nature. If to the Puritans America seemed a new Eden where man was offered a chance to establish the Kingdom of Heaven on earth, woman was the Serpent who here, even more ruthlessly than in old Europe, destroyed that hope with the seed of corruption. For Nathaniel Hawthorne, Hester, who lives on the *outskirts* of town, contiguous to the 'jungle', is the Scarlet Woman, unconscious vessel of original sin. Edgar Allan Poe's Lamia is a vampire who sucks out men's souls. In Herman Melville heterosexual love is often tainted with incest. Even today the Puritan mythology of the Fall pervades Vladimir Nabokov's *Lolita*, and is latent in Raymond Chandler's tough detective heroes, whose physical and moral courage fluctuates according to their resistence or submission to the blandishments of sexy sirens. The theme has entered 'pulp' literature, from Mickey Spillane downwards; against that backdrop it is not surprising that American women, having even more to live down than European women, belatedly became conscious of their identities, and collaterally of their rights.

In old agrarian traditions patristic domination had been less aggressive than in urban traditions. Christianity did not, at its more 'vulgar' levels, eschew magic and superstition; in American folksong masterful men and emotive women often functioned on equal terms. Some account of this was given in *A Darker Shade of Pale's* discussion of the transplantation of Anglo–Irish–Scots musics into American soil. Women such as Almeda Riddle, Sara Cleveland, Aunt Molly Jackson and Sarah Ogan Gunning cover a wide range of folk styles from rural ballads and love songs to songs of industrial action and of political protest. In a sub-conscious, il-literate society they sang the same songs as men, but experienced the themes of alienation and deprivation, of the oppression of earthbound folk by a civilization increasingly mechanized, with a more nervous sensitivity. With the women singers rural protest against industrial encroachment both geographical and spiritual was a reassertion of instinctual values. The ground was tilled from which an appeal for women's rights in a male-dominated world might sprout.

The beginning of this process may be traced in the career of Jean Ritchie, a genuine folk musician who came of a large singing family in the Kentucky mountains. As an authentic folk singer Jean veered to the 'euphoric' rather than 'deprived' style, defusing old songs of their elemental passions, cheering up the dolorous ones by singing them briskly, their modality rendered diatonic. Often she succoured them with instrumental support – with the guitar, banjo or autoharp that habitually encourage eupepticism in White country music. The cosiness of Jean Ritchie's versions of traditional songs was no doubt a product of the cohesiveness of family music-making: one could hardly feel lonesome among so many dancing and singing relatives,[1] about whom she has written in her autobiographical *Singing Family of the Cumberlands*.

Gravitating from her folk origins into professional music, Jean Ritchie inevitably contacted the industry that has commercially exploited country life. Such exploitation is not necessarily to be deplored. Country values are inescapably modified by urban culture, both because the town encroaches on the village and because the media penetrate to the remotest areas. Clearly country music then loses some of the qualities that distinguished it when it was 'music of necessity' within a small, self-enclosed community whose values it at once made and reflected.

Having once become professional, country music is sound to listen to as well as to participate in. The effect of this is paradoxical: if it means that from one point of view the music approaches the status of 'art', it also means that folk material, released from functional purpose, may rediscover primeval, magical strains that legendary Celtic songs had forfeited in confronting the realities of pioneer life. When Jean Ritchie sang as a country girl in her local environment she cheered the songs up to bolster herself and her hard-working folks. Now that external dangers no longer threaten, she can re-explore the mysterious undertow to ancient rhymes and runes. If she and we cannot experience them with the religious–mystical conviction they originally carried, we can allow them to reinvoke the psychic depths that post-industrial man had forgotten, to his cost.

That strange and wondrous song from the Appalachians,

1 *British Traditional Ballads Sung by Jean Ritchie.*

'Nottamin Town', survives today as a children's rune, though its words have the 'terrifying honesty' and psychological acumen of William Blake. Jean Ritchie pipes the hypnotic modal tune in her limpid treble, but the weaving tapstry of the dulcimer and the trance-inducing beat of the string bass encourage us to experience the song vicariously – which is as much as, or perhaps more than, we've a right to expect in our cerebralized world. The 'beauty' is here a bonus – as it is in 'The riddle song', a survival from folk tradition in the form of a children's game, sung in question-and-answer form by Jean Ritchie with Oscar Brown. Again the modal tune is not altered, though the fairly sophisticated harmonization and the interlacings of obbligato flute imbue it with wistfulness, and to that degree separate us from it. It's irrelevant to prefer the real thing, since that is no longer available. We must accept this revocation of Eden as a vision of a lost world.

Revocation of a different character is manifest in the title song of this album, 'None but one'.[2] This time the words are not traditional, but by Jean. They describe, however, a folk ceremony she encountered in the old world, at Haxey in Lincolnshire; for the music she calls on a genuine English dance tune, 'Nonesuch', archaically modal in contour, circular in structure. The accompaniment is at first given to a droning non-harmonic dulcimer, but gathers harmonic momentum as the band's beat grows incrementally assertive. The experience re-created in the pagan, pre-Christian Haxey ceremony is literally that of transcendence: people dancing in magic line or circle surrender personal identity as the Many become the One. Jean sings *about* an experience that undercuts the conscious mind into irrational levels, and invites us to live through the experience anew. The song demonstrates how a folk festival – the same may sometimes be said of a pop festival – aspires towards ritual transcendence, and occasionally achieves it.

In this example Jean's vocal production is harsher than in the songs she sang from the heart of her family group. Here tradition is artistically and ritually re-enacted, not remembered from an however distant past. Memory, rather than re-creation, seems active when Jean deals in Christian material, presumably because Christian tradition is still to some degree alive. She and her friends sing the shape-note hymn 'Wondrous love' in traditional style, with

2 *None But One.*

open tone, in balanced, fourth- and fifth-founded homophony. This recorded version is probably not conspicuously different from a performance in Jean's family circle, by the fireside, as the cool of the day. 'Now is the cool of the day' is the title of another hymn, with words and music newly composed by Jean Ritchie. That it stems from a long tradition is patent. The opening monodic incantation is modal, sung with pure tone and diction, with decorative rather than expressive ornamentation. The choral refrain is harmonically more sophisticated, and expressive, than the verse, though it is no less haunting. The equilibrium between folk and art music is delicate. Art distances us from the folk experience, while folk simplicity validifies the art.

This Jean Ritchie composition, rooted in traditional values and techniques, was probably made empirically rather than written down. Most of Jean's composed songs, however, have closer affinities with commercialized country music, without sundering their roots in old Kentuckian rurality. In 'Flowers of joy' the lovely modal tune encourages us to take the words as a conventional love song. But the shift from modal minor to diatonic major in the refrain, the barber-shop parallel thirds, the swinging beat and electrified bass transform the number into a folk–pop song with a social message. The tribal aspects of folk culture become a ritual of wish-fulfilment: what happened, in the dark backward and abysm of time, at the Haxey ceremony, and what Jean reanimates in 'None but one', is in 'Flowers of joy' a statement of intent. As Jean puts it, 'My songs are about the struggle to find God, the Oneness we have somehow lost, the way to get Home.'

This is evident more crudely in straight country songs, such as 'See that rainbow shine', which are as unambiguously diatonic and metrically unadventurous as those of the Carter family. Jean's explicit anti-city song is an ironic paradox, for the words of 'Black waters' tell of the despoilation of her Kentucky mountain country to a square-metred, diatonic-major country waltz fashioned by the very urban forces she's deploring. This paradox will be further explored in the next chapter dealing with women working within the country-music industry.

Jean Ritchie is a country woman by birth, and the city has transformed her. Joan Baez,[3] on the other hand, is a city girl with a university education, and has used for her own ends rural musics from the Appalachian mountains, the West Virginian and Kentucky slagheaps, the Oklahoma flatlands, the Arizona badlands, the

3 *Joan Baez in Concert* and *Joan.*

Alabama cotton fields, and the balmy orange groves of California. Her generation of city young, buoyed up on affluence, could affect to spurn the American Way of Life, discovering in folk music ideals of emotional integrity that the mechanizations and machinations of civilization seemed to deny. Whereas Jean Ritchie is a folk singer first and an artist second, Joan Baez is always an artist whose art distances folk experience in the process of presenting it – using the verb in the senses both of putting it over and of making what's past, present. That Joan Baez never capitulated to the country-music industry is indicative of moral strength; it is also a limitation in that it implies that, as intelligent commentator on other and older musics, she is an outsider singing to outsiders. In her early years, during the sixties, she did not create her own songs but became, in the eclectic artistry of her performance, a representative of today's Global Village. Pertinently, she is of mixed – Irish, Mexican and American – descent.

When she sings an authentic ballad like 'Geordie' her clear, penetrative tone resembles the 'folk' production of Jean Ritchie, though her ryhthmic precision and control of tone colour combine with the symmetries of her guitar part to create an unfolk-like elegance. The music sounds wistful, as folksong seldom is; that Joan Baez exploits the wistfulness, whereas Jean Ritchie only hints at it, is a measure of her greater modernity. She can do the same for a Black ramblin' song or a White blues, like 'Baby, I'm gonna leave you'; even the initial tumbling strain becomes, in tone quality and rhythmic control, beautiful rather than wild. Whether she sings a modern moonshining number like 'Copper kettle', a Black Gospel song like 'Kumbaya', a White evangelical hymn like 'Gospel ship', or a pot-pourri of African, American and Latin American sources such as 'Danger waters', her artistry is consummate.

That she imbues demotic material with civilized art is the heart of her appeal to the large, White, fairly educated, city-dwelling public who, listening to her songs, recognized in them values purer and truer than those of our mechanized world. Thus pathos is her art's essence: her performance reveals at once the integrity and the vulnerability of rural values. When she sings 'Black is the colour of my true love's hair' the line is radiant in tone, pure in intonation, but it is poised over a guitar part whose rhythm contains a distant threat. The song's beauty, and its emotive quality, cannot be separated from its conscious art.[4]

4 See also p. 66.

In so far as they proffer values distinct from those of Western technocracy most of Joan Baez's numbers are protest songs, though musically their protest tends – as in the once familar 'What have they done to the rain?' – to be gentle. In political terms, however, Joan has been active on behalf of most radical causes, and started composing her own songs from the fervour of her political convictions. She was disappointed in her hope that her Vietnam cycle would become a rallying point for action – which may be why she, like her friend and contemporary Bob Dylan, moved from protest towards love.

Most of her seventies songs come into the category appropriately called 'confessional'; the 1976 album, *Gulf Winds*, has some literary distinction in its loose, ruminating stanzas, illuminating with poetic flashes her childhood, her relationship with her parents, her usually failed love affairs, her approach to one-parent motherhood. Musically, she absorbs country music, rock and art music into folk sources, but doesn't entirely convince owing to a deficiency in melodic invention. The tunes are too subservient to the words' autobiographical revelations, so 'natural' that they often consist mainly of speech-inflected repeated notes and stepwise-moving, usually drooping, scales. 'Seabirds' manages to make a virtue out of its lack of melodic memorability, for it deals in alcohol-inspired dreams of freedom; triads hazily fluctuate beneath a fragmented tune, which flowers into a refrain as the seabird topples on the wind. The most successful number, however, is the title song, 'Gulf winds', which tells of Joan's relationship with her parents, in 'speaking' phrases modally undulating between triads of tonic, supertonic and flat seventh, but attains heart-easing lyricism in the refrain, pentatonically appealing for peace of mind. Here she seems to be consciously emulating Joni Mitchell, the finest of the women singing poet–composers who will be the subject of Part III.

Judy Collins's career follows a path in some ways parallel to Joan Baez's, in some ways divergent from it. Born in Denver, she too is a city woman; was trained as a concert pianist, and graduated from the University of Colorado, and from art into folk music, because she had a voice of remarkable natural beauty, allied to an instinctive sympathy for British folk traditions. In her early days her singing is closer to folk origins than is Baez's.[5] 'Wild mountain thyme' she sings unaccompanied in the verses, with expressive inflexion yet in

---

5 *A Maid of Constant Sorrow.*

impersonally bell-like timbre. The banjo accompaniment to the refrain is hazily romantic rather than cheerily euphoric, so the Scots melody, slightly Americanized, preserves its vernality. For 'The pricklie bush' Judy calls on a voice more raucous yet no less authentically in folk tradition, as is the words' debunking of passion. Her version of 'Bold Fenian men', searing in tone, relentless in rhythm, is monophonic except for a hint of heterophony from a remote harmonica: a romantic overtone that doesn't deflate intensity, though it distances the experience, as if the music floated from a far-off time and place, as indeed it does.

Joan Baez wittingly treated her folk material with nostalgia. Judy Collins takes it straighter, singing tragic ballads with an impersonal force that occasionally recalls the great Jeannie Robertson. None the less her versions of old songs modify the tradition, which is remade by the romanticism of her accompaniments. This happens not only in love songs but also in fiercer ballads, since she treats them dramatically, even melodramatically. Her very slow performance of 'High Germany' presents the vocal line in Americanized old Scots, but the guitar part, beginning with isolated chords that build up incrementally, turns the song into drama re-enacted. Still more startling is her version of 'Tim Evans', a murder ballad in the old tradition, though composed fairly recently by Ewan McColl. Judy Collins's version of folk idiom may be closer to the real thing than Joan Baez's. Even so, in transforming ballads into a species of theatre, she makes of them an 'artistic' performance – as indeed do Ewan McColl and John Jacob Niles, both folk scholars of repute.

That Judy so vividly relives folk idioms may explain why she could effect an unselfconscious transition from folk revival into pop music.[6] Only occasionally does she venture into post-Nashville country music; seldom does she indulge in a Baez-like anti-city song such as 'The coming of the roads', the tune of which is remote from folk tradition in being dependent on its harmonization. But Judy now frequently sings numbers by pop stars, making them more folk-like in the process; her version of Dylan's 'Mr Tambourine man' reveals the affinity of the great song with Celtic idiom. At the same time Judy, inspired by her contemporaries' example, begins to make her own songs which, like Baez's are usually confessional and often concerned with childhood. 'My

6 *Judy Collins' Fifth Album* and *Amazing Grace*.

father' is especially touching and 'Albatross', though not characterful enough to compete with Joni Mitchell's several songs on
the same theme, effectively uses the image of the solitary seabird as
an image of human, especially female, isolation and aspiration, the
vocal line meandering between stepwise-undulating woodwind.

It is significant that Judy Collins's most impressive work is a
throwback to real folk music with a difference. In 1972 we find her
singing 'Farewell to Tarwathie' unaccompanied, with the same
biting resonance, the same grand span to the phrases, the same
command of a slow yet life-giving pulse that prompted comparison
with the old-time Scots singer Jeannie Robertson. We'd accept this
performance in a collection of the real right thing; yet the record
sleeve describes the song as being 'arranged and adapted' by Judy
Collins. The arrangement and adaptation prove to be a technical
gimmick: she adds to her voice taped noises of sea, wind, seabirds
and sea beasts – so that, listening, we're carried back on a trip
through time and space, to live in a world that is past, yet
miraculously present through modern technology. Similarly, in her
version of the shape-note hymn 'Amazing Grace' she at first sings
monodically, in authentic idiom, then gradually adds choric
support, in unisons and octaves, in organum,[7] in heterophony, in
homophony, so that the lone utterance leads to a community's
rebirth, in which we vicariously share.

That educated folk singers – the paradox is apt – continued to
sing traditional music in something like traditional styles during
the years in which country music was becoming an industry meant
that 'real' folk music survived and could itself become, in no
discreditable sense, commercially exploitable. The singing of Hazel
and Alice offers impressive proof. Hazel Dickens was born and
reared in the coalmining area of West Virginia, her background thus
being similar to that of Aunt Molly Jackson or Sarah Ogan
Gunning, whose bleakly authentic singing was discussed in A
Darker Shade of Pale. Hazel moved to Baltimore in search of
employment; contacted the urbanized rurality of country music,
but never forgot the stark musical as well as social veracities she
sprang from. Musically, she didn't need consciously to emulate the
exaltation of her mountain origins or the material and spiritual
penury of her mining-country experience since her voice is their
aural incarnation. She entered professional music by the back door.

7 See Glossary.

As a friend put it, 'Hazel's going to be around to tell the tale' — which is what she does, whether she is singing to miners and their families at welfare-rights benefit parties, at communal junketings or, by way of radio and record, to tens of thousands.

Alice Gerrard spent her childhood in a more comfortable farming area near Oakland, California. Less indigent than Hazel, she attended Antioch College in Ohio; moved to Baltimore (where she met Hazel) and then to Washington, DC, and now lives and farms with her husband and family in Pennsylvania. Her background was less raw than Hazel's: she was the daughter of a congregational minister and of a tough north-west farming woman. In the community she was reared on classical music for piano, voice and violin, mingled unselfconsciously with fiddle-scraping, banjo-strumming, guitar-picking country musics. Her own songs stem from her awareness of people as people; as Hazel put it, Alice listens to the best of the old-timers and the best of the new, but what comes out is her own 'people's music: so close down to earth I sometimes feel she grew out of the ground.'

Hazel and Alice[8] must have teamed up because they recognized that their qualities and abilities were complementary. They are genuinely modern folk singers who, unlike Baez and Collins, still belong to the rural world even as they refashion it, making no distinction between traditional material and their own creations. Hazel tells us that she wrote — the old-fashioned term 'made' would be more appropriate — the words and music of 'Pretty bird' at a time when she was 'going through a lot of changes'. The words are about escape to freedom from whatever chains may bind one. Yet she sings the tune monodically, in archaic-sounding timbre, wild in melismatic convolutions around its primitvely pentatonic roots. Far from being Whitely Euphoric, this freedom sounds melancholic, perhaps because, though a synonym for heaven, it is recognized as ideal rather than real. The piercing line tells us that even if deprivation is no longer a physical fact, there will never be 'any place where the cold winds don't blow'; freedom envisaged must be its own reward. In this sense the song's ideality *is* reality — which is why the words have the flavour of genuine folk poetry while being an immediate consequence of Hazel's 'changing times', and is why the melody sounds immemorially ancient yet fresh as a daisy. Incredibly, this song was not merely recorded, but new-minted, in 1972!

8 *Hazel and Alice.*

Alice's music springs no less indigenously from her environment – as we may hear in 'A few more years', a tune from the Primitive Baptist hymnal used by her preacher father. The words are glum about our earthly lot but relish a heaven where 'dangers cease, And surges swell no more'. If this is escapism in a sense different from Hazel's subjective but paradoxically impersonal hymn to freedom in 'Pretty bird', the performance lends it dignity. Alice sings the tune very slowly, in traditional style, while Hazel 'lines out' with a tenor part, usually in parallel thirds or fourths. Vocal production is harsh, yet the melismatic embroidery exults. Hazel and Alice are, however, not normally as rudimentary as they are in these two numbers. Usually their music compromises between old and new, as in 'Two soldiers', the tune of which comes from the Kentucky mountains, though the words are attributed to the Connecticut novelist Virginia Frances Townsend, while the autoharp and guitar accompaniment mutate the tune into a diatonic waltz.

Often Hazel and Alice cross the border into the sentimental or jolly world of country music, as they do in their version of J. B. Coates's 'The sweetest gift', a corny mother-ballad, or of Wilma Cooper's 'Tomorrow I'll be gone'. These numbers Hazel and Alice picked up from blue-grass recordings of the sixties; what is remarkable is that they temper country euphoria with the earthiness of their ancestry. They absorb, rather than imitate, commercialized country music – even when singing, with painfully stretched rhythm and distended pitch, 'Hello stranger', a number by the venerable A. P. Carter himself. There's a similar grittiness in Hazel's own 'My better years', a country waltz accompanied by wailing dobro, autoharp and guitar. The out-of-tuneness itself lends dolorous veracity to the experience of separation, which Hazel says is autobiographical. Like a blues singer, Hazel is thus using her music therapeutically – as is Alice when, in her 'You gave me a song', she undermines a diatonic country waltz with modal shifts and a scrawny folk fiddle.

In the light of this it is not surprising that Hazel and Alice should have an instinctive empathy with Black folk musics. In 'Mining camp blues' the two women sing a Black blues attributed to and sung by Trixie Smith. Alice emulates Trixie's original line in the vocal lead, but substitutes bluesy folk fiddle for cornet or clarinet. The sound is further countrified by Hazel's rasping tenor part, and by Jimmie Rodgers-style yodels in the refrain. Hazel's guitar at first sounds bluely Negro but grows homphonically country-White, as the

blues is translated from the Deep South to the poor-White mining community from which Hazel emerged. Alice's 'Custom-made woman's
blues' is an even more ecletic performance, halfway between blues and
raggy minstrel-show music, with Alice's bleat recalling Ma Rainey
who, we noted, started as a circus entertainer. The fiddle obbligato
reminds us of the lacerating line of Eddie South, yet neither voice nor
violin is consciously copying its Black prototype. This blues is an
intuitive *cri de coeur*; the words are committed to Women's Rights.

The complementary roles played by Hazel and Alice are indicated by the fact that whereas Hazel sings her 'Pretty bird'
unaccompanied, Alice's solo contribution is instrumental: a banjo
piece she made up to entertain her little son and, after trials and
errors, decided to call 'Kansas galop', thereby relating country
banjo to big-city boogie. Yet the functions of Hazel and Alice are
interchangeable: archaic vocal monody and modern blue-grass
instrumentalism together create a music simultaneously old and
new. A more recent singing duo, the sisters Kate and Anna
McGarrigle, are not thus differentiated, though Anna is perhaps
more in tune with rural musics, Kate with relatively urban jazz.
Between them they evoke the small-town community that bred
them with an authenticity no less convincing than that of Hazel and
Alice though, given their later date, they are a shade more artful.

There is however a radical distinction between the McGarrigle
Sisters and any of the singers so far discussed, in that they are
bilingual and of French-Canadian stock. The family came from the
Laurentian village of St Sauveur-des-Monts in Quebec, but moved
to Montreal in 1958. While still at school the sisters performed folk
music in coffee houses, mingling Canadian *chansons* with Gospel
hymns, blues, and numbers by Black Leadbelly and the Reverend
Gary Davis, and by White Woody Guthrie and Bob Dylan. In the
mid-sixties they began to compose their own songs which, despite
their heterogeneous sources, display a personal aura. When they
crossed the border into the United States, it was evident that the
cohesive and distinctive character of their music owes much to the
fact that there is a branch of French-Canadian culture in the
American South. Though the McGarrigle Sisters have never lived in
Louisiana, their art is affiliated to the Cajun music of that State,[9]
both in its White forms and in its Black permutations, which tend
to be more dangerously merry than the White varieties.

9 See also *A Darker Shade of Pale*, pp. 68–9.

In the Promised Land? Scene in a black church at Grafton, near Yorktown, Virginia, during the New Year watch meeting. Engraving after a sketch (1880) by Joseph Becker. (*BBC Hulton Library/Bettmann Archive*)

'O clap your hands, all ye people': Mahalia Jackson in action. (*David Redfern*)

'Wholly holy': Aretha Franklin in action. (*Melody Maker*)

'A young woman who ain't done running around': Bessie Smith in 1925.
(Frank Driggs Collection, New York)

Afro-gypsy in the circus tent: Gertrude 'Ma' Rainey with her Georgia Jazz Band 1923, including Georgia Tom Dorsay (piano), Al Wynn (trombone) and Ed Pollack (trumpet). *(Frank Driggs Collection, New York)*

'The Ebony Comedienne': Ethel Waters in 1929.
(Frank Driggs Collection, New York)

Black woman in café society: Billie Holiday at the Café Society, New York, 1939. *(Frank Driggs Collection, New York)*

The Big Band sound: Ella Fitzgerald and the Chick Webb Orchestra at the Apollo Theatre, Harlem, 1937. *(Frank Driggs Collection, New York)*

Voice and horns: Sarah Vaughan with Coleman Hawkins and Illinois Jacquet at Mildenhall, Suffolk, 1954, during a tour of US service camps *(Max Jones)*

'Grinning in your face': the Pointer Sisters, 1974.
(Frank Driggs Collection, New York)

An 'angel of the night': Angela Bofill. *(Arista/Eurodisc)*

Little girl lost: Blossom Dearie.

A(r)cadians from Quebec: Anna and Kate McGarrigle. *(Frank Driggs Collection, New York/Warner Bros WEA)*

A seagull in the city: Joni Mitchell. *(Geffen/CBS Records)*

Midnight baby: Dory Previn. *(United Artists/EMI Records)*

Blonde bombshell of the marketplace: Dolly Parton.
(BBC Hulton Library, UPI/Bettmann Newsphotos)

'Very happy and very high': Tania Maria.
(*Frank Driggs Collection, New York/Concord/Polygram*)

Society's child: Janis Ian. *(Frank Driggs Collection, New York/Verve/Polygram)*

Smashed woman: Janis Joplin in the film *Janis*. (*Frank Driggs Collection, New York/Universal*)

'Me and myself': Joan Armatrading, 1981. *(Melody Maker/photo Graham Hughes)*

A dreaming with Kate Bush: 1979. *(EMI Records)*

'Block-busted blonde at the real end': Rickie Lee Jones. *(Melody Maker)*

'Moving on', eurythmically: Annie Lennox. *(Lynn Goldsmith/LGI/RCA Records)*

Big science androgyne: Laurie Anderson.
(Melody Maker/Janette Beckmann, New York)

A changeling: Toyah Wilcox. *(David Redfern Photography)*

'Why can't we live together?': Sade. *(Tochi Yajima)*

Though Black Cajun music, known as 'zodico',[10] remains outside the mainstream of country music, it is by no means irrelevant to the music of the McGarrigle Sisters,[11] who, centred on urban New York or Los Angeles, fuse their French-Canadian heritage with elements absorbed from the Southern States. Thus 'Travelling on for Jesus' is a traditional Black Gospel number from the Bahamas, but Kate's vocal line has the piercing purity of a White American mountain singer, while the swinging bass line and the guitar and piano harmonies compromise between the suavity of Cajun music and the grit of jazz. In Wade Hemsworth's 'Foolish you' the sisters sing a straight country number, though White Cajun euphony pervades the hymnic sonority of the introduction, and the chittering banjo smooths the ruffled brow of folly, if not of care.

In 'Jigsaw pattern of life' Anna makes a conventional country valse, disturbed by an agile bass line that promotes shifting harmonies. The spicy sonority of guitar, mandolin, banjo and accordion is Acadian, and not radically distinct from that of a number in Louisianan French, 'Complainte pour Ste. Catherine', in which Anna is joint composer with Philippe Tartarcheff. Fiddle, accordion and harmonica resonate over guitar and percussion in racy Cajun style, though the almost vibratoless vocal line sounds as much Appalachian as Louisianan. In 'Blues in D', however, Kate's voice veers between this vernality and the sultriness of a Black blueswoman, while the instrumental parts embrace improvisation from Joel Tapp on New Orleans clarinet and from old-time Red Callender on bass. This is a most fetching amalgam of traditional jazz, zodico and country music. The touch of Evangelical hymnody in the final plagal cadence[12] sounds, though unexpected, inevitable.

Despite their relation to demotic traditions all these songs, except 'Travelling on for Jesus' and 'Foolish you', are newly composed. Yet McGarrigle originals are closer to folk traditions than to country music and pop, for the McGarrigles, like Hazel and unlike Baez and Collins, belong to the world they artfully evoke. Kate's 'Talk to me of Mendocino' starts as a nostalgic country tune but unfolds (in a poetic arrangement by Michael Small) into a hymnic melody wonderingly wandering yet well shaped, so that nostalgia sharpens into a perennial human need. Similarly, Anna's

10   *Cajun Swamp Music Live.*
11   *Kate and Anna McGarrigle.*
12   See Glossary.

'My town' presents her small-town Canadian childhood through the sounds of parlour piano, haloed with harmonica, mandolin and guitar, while evolving a tune sustained enough to reach a climax that counteracts regression.

Being younger and closer to urban society than Hazel and Alice, the McGarrigles can absorb jazz at a more sophisticated level. Even finer than Kate's 'Blues in D' is her 'Tell my sister', in which the wide-spanned, bluesily harmonized melody stimulates haunting alto and clarinet obbligati from Plas Johnson. In 'Go leave', which Kate sings to the accompaniment merely of her acoustic guitar, she starts with an arpeggio-supported country tune sung in a childish treble, but gradually darkens her voice and bluely intensifres her guitar's harmony. Later we'll note similar effects in the work of an urban pop rather than folk singer, Janis Ian. But although the 1976 McGarrigle disc is later in date than Janis's formative albums, it is improbable that there was any direct influence. Kate McGarrigle's songs spring unsullied from the world wherein she was nurtured.

This is confirmed by a later album, *Dancer with Bruised Knees*, which is more overtly Cajun than the first disc. It includes two exquisite arrangements of Acadian folk songs, first in free, two-part canon unaccompanied, then supported by delicate polyphony of Cajun instruments – button accordion, harmonica, recorder, man-dolin, violin and organ. The modality of the tunes is unsullied; the Cajun sonorities sound diaphanous, like early Renaissance music, or like Carl Orff's adaptation of these sonorities in his instrumental music for children. A number of merry songs lope in Louisianan boogie rhythm. Kate's 'Homage à Grungie' is vocally enchanting, with dazzling harmonica playing by Chaim Tannenbaum. Her 'First born' celebrates new birth with a tune trotting blithely down the scale, but buoyed up by Warren Smith's congas and Stephen Gadd's bouncy drums. Anna's 'Be my baby' is no less vivacious, synthesizing many Southern genres, since the Acadian bass is tinged with Tex-Mex rhythms and a Caribbean flavour of reggae.

The White hymn reappears in Kate's 'Walking song', in a plainly diatonic 12/8, with poetic accordion from Gordie Fleming, and in Anna's 'Kitty come home', which begins as a country hymn with arpeggiated accompaniment but grows almost grandly impassioned when Kate, having obeyed her sister's injunction, supportively plays chapel organ. Anna's 'Dancer with bruised knees' and Kate's 'Come a long way' instil traces of blue unease into country swing, though the darker Black and blue elements evident in earlier

McGarrigle numbers are absent from this album. We may find this a limitation, or we may construe it as a small victory for the sisters' confidence in their world and their art. On the evidence of their 1978 disc the latter seems the more plausible interpretation, for *Pronto Monto* is an album renewing in its very eclecticism.

The first number, Anna's 'O my heart', sets the mood, for its light beat has the gaiety of reggae, over which the tune delightedly bounces. From befogged Los Angeles she makes us believe that she and her man will 'stay together, together but not tethered, or not too much, though times seem tough too tiresome, we still must not succumb'. The hint of prevaricating caution in the words makes the radiance of the music the more enlivening. There's the same vulnerable innocence in Anna's 'Bundle of sorrow, bundle of joy', which pays homage not to her lover but to her baby. The tune lilts over flowing quavers on piano, while a rustic clarinet traces a wistful obbligato. The song renders the joys *and* sorrows of simple folk articulate: 'The young grass grows up through the old, the lilac lives again.'

If these songs are Whitely Euphoric, they are neither mindless nor heartless, and the reason for this is manifest in numbers that are taunted by wit or annealed by suffering. Kate's 'Na cl' is a joke song relating sexual to chemical union. Its wit is bracing, never cynical, and the modern 'scientific' jape is the more effective because the tune is old-timey, with a raggy boogie rhythm over an old-fashioned tuba bass. Irony characterizes Kate's 'Side of fries' also. Tune and rhythm are again raggy and the Cajun sonorities are even more than usually eclectic, with bucolic Louisianan (rather than New Orleans) clarinet piping with Tex-Mex fiddle and saxophone, and with electric guitars plaintively tinged with squeeze-boxes. Though this little narrative song is comic it is also acerbic, and provides a link to numbers in which innocence is not impervious to anger, as well as pathos.

'Pronto monto', with a text by Philippe Tartarcheff, is a song of farewell in which dulcet lyricism is toughened by the Tex-Mex–Louisianan sonorities and tangoid rhythms. Desperation creeps into Kate's appeal to her lover to 'come back, baby', for after a slow-swinging verse about the pain in her heart the refrain has a lurching rhythm over a tonic–dominant–tonic ostinato; the contrast between Grady Tate's pounding drums and Chaim Tannenbaum's winsome harmonica contributes to the effect. Anna's 'Dead weight', unusually an anti-man song, is also uneasy in its dismissiveness, with abrupt modulations and a shoulder-shrugging coda; our ears recognize how the man's 'charm's wearing thin', as his 'voice rings like tin'. But the gem of the collection – a number in which pathos reveals tragic depths – is Kate's 'Stella by Artois', a song of love loss whose nostalgia is bleak rather than indulgent. There's a blue tinge to the ballad's lyricism, which is Louisianan despite the verse's internationalism. The rustic clarinet sings as it whimpers, George Young's exquisite playing complementing Kate's voice and piano. This sad little song and the tender jollity of 'O my heart' are opposite sides of the same pure silver coin. The McGarrigles preserve their folk-like integrity while fusing many disparate influences. In so doing they are distinguished from any *young* folk musicians in the contemporary scene.

Chapter Seven

WOMEN AND THE COUNTRY MUSIC INDUSTRY

Obey your menfolk, so that you may not be touched by the sorrows.

Mwana Kupona

So far we have discussed women folk–pop singers who stemmed from the old rural order either because, like Jean Ritchie, Hazel and Alice and the McGarrigle Sisters, they were born and bred in rural areas or because, like Joan Baez and Judy Collins, they were educated city women who sought in rural music an alternative way of life. The rockbottom reality of the singers in the former category was sturdy enough to weather their transplantation into an urban world, in which their agrarian values were reborn with minimal loss of integrity. But not many were strong enough to bring this off; it is probably not fortuitous that the McGarrigle Sisters, a late example of such 'people's music', were originally outsiders with a French-Canadian ancestry remote from the Southern American small-town life they evoke.

More commonly – because more easily – rural singers were absorbed into the country-music industry, founded on radio stations disseminating country culture throughout urban centres of the vast continent. Not surprisingly, the most commercially exploitable forms of country music are those instrumentally accompanied types epitomized as the White Euphoria, rather than the starker, mostly unaccompanied forms epitomized as the Monody of Deprivation.[1] We do not have to look far for the psychological reasons for the success of this commercial enterprise. Though we are apt to think of America as a concourse of industrial cities, it remains, in the context of its geographical scope, a collocation of small-town communities. These are motivated, but also confined, by small-town spiritual and cultural values – to which the music of the White Euphoria complacently administers. Even suburban inhabitants of big cities may find relief in such aural cosiness. The more brutish city life becomes the more welcome seems the amnesia of a country music that, electrophonically amplified, laves us in its audible cocoon.

In *A Darker Shade of Pale* this theme was approached via a discussion of the Carter Family, who were genuine old-time country folk who transferred the realities of their music into the commercialized country music of the Grand Ole Opry, making no distinction between old folk songs, Evangelical hymns, sentimental parlour ballads and newly composed numbers.[2] We have referred to them in connection with performers such as Hazel and Alice and the McCarrigle Sisters, who likewise lived ambivalently between worlds. As the media encroached, however, folk authenticity weakened, and rural performers became prepackaged 'images' of vicariously mythic import.

Tammy Wynette[3] has concentrated almost exclusively on one image, that of Woman as Doormat: the inevitably blonde woman who not only serves and suffers while man obliviously fulfils his destiny, but also finds her only satisfaction in so doing. Clearly the image is man-made. The moderate-paced, two- or three-time metrical beat, the major diatonic harmony, the electrically souped-up sonority are conforming, comfortable and comforting, designed to wake an echo in the millions of women conditioned to share her acceptance, whatever the cost. Interestingly enough, Tammy has not practised what she preaches; she has been four times married and divorced, and sings of that calamity in music that doesn't even marginally vary her recipe. 'The divorce sale' tells the terrible tale in music indistinguishable from her biggest hit 'Stand by your man',

1 For a discussion of the concepts of White Euphoria and Monody of Deprivation, see *A Darker Shade of Pale*, pp. 44–51 and 59–71.
2 *The Carter Family* RCA DPM 2046; and Columbia HL 7280.
3 *Tammy Wynette.*

which sold 2 million copies to women mostly between the ages of 25 and 45. Standing by your however-contemptible man is presented as a virtue in itself. Presumably the nauseous image cannot survive much longer, though Tammy's discs still sell briskly and her music still sounds, beneath its quaveriness, complacent.

Tammy the doormat did not of course create her own songs, though women working within the country-music industry began to do so as they became aware of their female identity, if not of their rights as women. Loretta Lynn,[4] the Coalminer's Daughter, makes her own songs, seeing them as statements about reality as she knows it, and for her reality has been hard and tough.

She was a mother at 14 and a grandmother at 28. Although, singing her famous 'I'm a honky-tonk girl', she doesn't seem exactly to relish the profession, she is proud of not being cowed into Tammyish submission. She stands on her own feet, however erring, and although the convention she sings in is as cheerily diatonic, as square-rhythmed and as moderate-paced as that of Tammy Wynette, her manner of performance is different indeed. Her vocal production grates rather than quavers; her rhythm, if regular, is wiry – so the songs' cockiness becomes acceptable as an affirmation in the face of nasty odds. Yet Loretta Lynn, being part of a commercialized industry, betrays another kind of deceit. Having become a millionairess, owning large stretches of Texas, she has in no way modified her coalminer's daughter image. She too works to a recipe, if one less obnoxious to us than Tammy Wynette's. None the less, she remains a powerful figure in the story of country music: halfway between the real folk singer turned country musician, such as Hazel and Alice, and the woman singer of the country-music industry who graduates into art.

Of that category the prototype is Dolly Parton[5] who, born in 1946 in the mountains of East Tennessee, grew up in conditions of extreme indigence. She sings much of her own material, and many of her songs spring from her childhod environment. The number that made her famous, 'Coat of many colours', concerns a ragbag coat her mother patched together for her, which exceeds in glamour not only the biblical Joseph's but also, more significantly, her own later finery. The song is nostalgic for childhood's Eden and for 'the happiness of not having', but is genuinely powerful in that it makes

4 *Coal Miner's Daughter* MCA 10; Loretta Lynn's Greatest Hits MCA 1.
5 *The Dolly Parton Story.*

the past present. Dolly's vocal style – the line penetratively emotive, yet also screwed up – preserves the intensity of old-time mountain music, being true to its simplicity. The tune is narrow in range, anchored on the repeated third; harmony favours subsidence to the subdominant at the expense of active movement to the dominant. Instrumentally, Dolly translates folk sonorities into the jaunty togetherness of blue grass. Her equation between personal and communal experience amounts to a female, 1970s version of Hank Williams's vintage songs of the forties. Both balance – slipperily rather than, like Blossom Dearie, ironically – between reality and wish fulfilment.

This is evident not merely in autobiographical songs like 'Coat of many colours' but also in Dolly's routine production.[6] 'I don't want you around me any more' dismisses fraudulent love in a manner that manages to be tough, like Loretta Lynn, without being strident, and tremulous, like Tammy Wynette, without being self-indulgent. Inseparable from this is the fact that Dolly's image is not dishonest: neither in the sense that Tammy's is in promulgating an untruth about human experience, nor in the sense that Loretta's is in that the message she preaches is contradicted by her life-style. Dolly, after her penurious origins, rejoices in success and the extravagance it makes possible, projecting her pleasure, half comically, into her peroxide-mopped, vast-bosomed, wasp-waisted, gaudily clad stage person. At once a little girl of the mountains and a (not at all dumb) blonde bombshell of the marketplace, she doesn't allow the latter to corrupt the former. Loretta Lynn is a demotic singer whose truth couldn't square with the engulfing world of commerce; Tammy Wynette is a demotic singer seemingly happy to be miserably engulfed; Dolly Parton is a poor girl who made good, as well as rich, since her folksong evolves, *through* industrial exploitation, into art. It is significant that for the album that marks her emergence as a singing poet–composer of conse- quence, Dolly not only writes her own words and music, but is also her own arranger and co-producer. Folk culture, commerce and art discover that they may succour rather than destroy one another.

Among the songs on the appropriately titled 1977 album, *New Harvest: First Gathering*, 'Applejack' is ostensibly a revocation of childhood. Because its nostalgia is accepted for what it is, this song reanimates even as it saddens us. Dolly's voice itself does this, being

6 *New Harvest: First Gathering.*

at once tender and voluptuous. Around her vocal line country guitar and harmonica weave a Dream of Long Ago that becomes a re-created and recreating present: literally so, for Dolly has persuaded a raft of famous old-timers – including Kitty Wells, Roy Acuff, Chet Atkins, Ernest Tubb and Grandpa Jones – to join her in the chorus. Two love songs stand at opposite but complementary poles: 'You are' is the kind of tribute any man would welcome from a woman – intimately expressive in melody, yet safeguarded from sentimentality by the surging refrain; against this, 'Holdin' to you' is an anti-man song disfigured neither by malice nor by self-pity. Black inflexions toughen Dolly's vocal expressivity; driving rock rhythms affirm through the song's negation.

Dolly Parton's talent is centred where it ought to be: in the memorability of her tunes. In 'How does it feel' a country ballad becomes a rock hymn that validifies love through the firm repeated notes in the tune, the steady beat, the sustained chords. Similarly, 'Getting in my way' injects into country music the exuberance of rockabilly; excitement builds up incrementally, to climax in Dolly's scatting melismata. 'There' is also re-creation, this time of White, and possibly Black, Gospel music. The tune is strong; the scoring imaginatively extends the sonorities of Evangelical homophony and of country church organ. The heaven this music seeks is no wishy-washy pie in the sky but the simple pieties of Dolly's childhood ripened to maturity; the child-like voice merges into the resonance of the choral and instrumental sonorities and, out of its innocence, generates delight.

'Light of a clear blue morning' is likewise an affirmation, which, from the intimacy of Dolly's spoken–sung verses, surges into a paean to freedom. In the first stanza Dolly's blue inflexions on the phrase 'long hard flight' and her melismata on the words 'all right' make a personal commitment that justifies an instrumental and choric development one might almost describe as 'grand'. In the last stanza Dolly's dizzy pentatonic roulades, echoed in parallel thirds, enact the flight of the eagle into the free heavens. That 'it's gonna be alright' is audible in the music, as folk and country merge into jazz and rock. We may call the synthesizing agent Art – worthy of a capital A, if that doesn't seem too pretentious for the simple sincerity that shines through Dolly's opulent image.

Only one woman country singer can rival Dolly Parton as singing poet–composer. Lacy J. Dalton earned renown with her first disc, issued in 1980 under the basic title of her name. She writes many of her songs, which she performs with a band of fiddles, guitars, piano, drums and intermittent harmonica; a backing vocal group, the Jordanaires, appears in some numbers. Lacy Dalton, tougher than Dolly Parton, allows no little-girl pipe to enervate her White big-mama voice; but her songs, like Dolly's, come into the confessional class and, if not directly autobiographical, amount to a self-portrait.

Two songs are addressed to her 'mama' and 'daddy'. The first, 'Crazy blue eyes', confesses that she's a wild woman who will always love losers, preferring the feckless desperado to the man of substance. Lacy's belting voice and her roulades on words like 'almost insane', 'body' and 'heart' tug against the social conformity that the fastish country waltz represents; in the coda Lacy's distraught passion almost approaches that of the magnificent rock–blues singer, Janis Joplin. The song addressed to her father, 'High like an angel', hints – punning on the word 'high' – that in having the devil in her soul she is following in her mother's gypsyish footsteps. She seems to be rendered 'crazy' rather than happy by the driving beat. Not only Lacy's voice but also the savage drums threaten countrified solidarity.

In 'Beer-drinking song', however, she makes a number for buddies from Texas that is what it says it is: a rousing, rousting bellow to drown sorrows in, accepting the norm of a fast country waltz and bringing it off because the tune is as strong as the rhythm. This is a pub song that would work well in the bar, and would continue to do so after many repetitions. The instrumental sonorities are excoriative. Lacy's White big-mama voice sounds nearly Black – again in the manner of Janis Joplin.

The other side of the disc touches on personal as well as communal aspects of life. 'Losing kind of love' is about a one-night stand with a man she's willing to use as substitute for a lost lover. The beat is fairly quiet and the figuration undulates, though Lacy's voice is tense – especially (ironically enough) on the word 'easy' and in the 'losin' kind of loving' ' refrains. 'Turn my head around', a song of exhaustion and worriment, begins unaccompanied, as raw as a field holler, but turns into bluesy barrelhouse music in which Lacy's voice tears us and herself to shreds; her climax on 'trusted' and 'busted' is the closest she comes to the fever of Janis Joplin. The coda lets loose the tigers she'd spoken of in the initiatory songs to her father and mother. It may be significant that she places this number last on the disc, and that it follows an appparently euphoric country number called 'Are there any cowboys left in the good old U.S.A.?' The answer would seem to be that there aren't and a 'mere' woman, such as Lacy, has done well to survive.

A personal application of this will for survival occurs in 'Turn my head around', which asserts that despite the odds she *knows* that 'relief is on the way':

Lord, I'm prayin', I'm prayin' I'll be found
By someone who can turn my head around.

We almost believe that the Lord will respond to so vigorous a Gospel injunction, though the evangelists' God is not the 'Someone' she's waiting for.

Lacy J. Dalton's 1981 disc, *Takin' It Easy*, includes more songs by other people yet amounts to a more personal statement. Tommy Williams, Don Sheffield, Sam Levine and Dennis Good on fiddle, trumpet, clarinet and slide trombone brilliantly figure in the band, for which the arrangements are now quite sophisticated. Lacy's own 'Takin' it easy' has a jogging country rhythm complicated by the Tex-Mex acridity of the scoring and by the harmonic–tonal structure that is far from rudimentary. In 'Everybody makes mistakes' Lacy used the mindless reiterations of country music to psychological ends, the repetitions being exasperating rather than jolly. Her own 'Golden memories' and 'Let me in the fast lane' dizzily adapt the hedonism of blue-grass music, with Tony Williams's hoedown fiddle sizzling in lunatic distonation, and with intricate cross rhythms against the vocal line. In all these Dalton numbers instrumental co-operation is far more potent than it is on the first album.

Yet rather oddly the most impressive, even the most personal, tracks are not Dalton originals. 'Wild turkey', by Moffat and Seber, is given a particularly exhilarating interpretation as shanty-town honkytonk, celebrating its outlaw lover–hero with heterophonic bubblings and blurtings on fiddle, trumpet, clarinet and slide trombone. In Hobbs's 'Feed in the fire' the moderate beat releases a long, balanced tune, sung with an affecting directness again qualified by instrumental moans. The final number, 'Who killed Dewey Jones' daughter?', attributed to Chambers and Jenkins, comes over as a quintessential Lacy J. anecdote, involving rape, mayhem and murder against a background of social oppression. At first spoken, the voice part grows into a powerfully sung and swung lament that explodes into fury in the chorically backed refrain, through which White big-mama Lacy interjects stormy pentatonics. The upward modulation through a third before the penultimate stanza, though a cliché of pop standards, here has devasting effect – a tribute both to the music and to its performance.

Although Dolly Parton and Lacy J. Dalton are the only women country musicians classifiable as singing poet–composers, there are many who, stemming from country tradition, make a personal contribution while singing other people's songs and occasionally creating, or contributing to, a number of their own. The closest to country traditions is Emmylou Harris,[7] nurtured in Alabama and Virginia – and on the songs of Woody Guthrie. She usually performs with the traditional set-up of acoustic guitars, mandolin, banjo, dobro, harmonica, fiddle, string bass and drums, in varying permutations, often with vocal backing. Sometimes she calls on old-time material – as when, in 1977, she performs A. P. Carter's 'Hello stranger' in a manner vocally and instrumentally slicker than the original but with a simplicity no less wide-eyed. Hank Williams's quasi-Louisianan 'Jambalaya' sounds in her version more jauntily Edenic than in his original. When she sings slow country ballads either in four time (Buck Owen's touching 'Together again') or more frequently in slow waltz or 'three-quarter' tempo (Louvin's Cajun-style 'When I stop dreaming') she takes sentimentality at its face value, and this is a strength. Similarly in fast blue-grass numbers (her own 'Amarillo', Gram Parsons's 'Luxury liner') she takes unabashed delight in her hedonism and in the virtuosity of her instrumentalists.

Occasionally Emmylou ventures into alien fields, embracing them within her own territory. Chuck Berry's rockabilly 'You never can tell' fits comfortably into the American small-town scene, and if the Lennon–McCartney 'Here, there and everywhere' intimates a more mysterious dimension, that is because genius will tell. Even so, the native Americanism of Emmylou's singing sounds appropriate to and worthy of that marvellous song. Her *gently* raspy country voice convinces through its lack of affectation, though she lacks Dolly Parton's variety of timbre and therefore of mood, and makes no approach to Lacy Dalton's vigour. She moves us by being a precarious survivor, not a shaping force. It may not be an accident that many of her best songs are collaborations with her manager, and that both before and after her rise to fame Emmylou Harris sang

7 *Elite Hotel* and *Luxury Liner*.

as backing voice to others, making a justly celebrated contribution to Bob Dylan's album, *Desire*.

Country singers, like urban jazz singers, tend to grow musically more satisfying the more they veer towards jazz 'reality'. For the most part Crystal Gayle[8] sings modern country songs to a quite elaborate backing of strings, guitars and electric keyboards. The numbers – such as 'Westward wind' or 'Someday soon', a song about a rodeo-riding lover – are not intrinsically remarkable, and Crystal sings them straight, without expressive vocalization intended to reveal meanings of dubious substance. None the less her performances give more than superficial pleasure, first because of the natural beauty of her voice, and secondly because of her jazzy swing and phrasing. When she lights on a number that has musical and emotional truth, such as Hamilton's superbly bluesy 'Cry me a river', she gives a great jazz performance, supported only by piano, bass and drums, which are all she or the song needs. Again, she doesn't 'do much' to the tune, but simply – the word begs the question – sings it in her crystal voice, shaping the phrases like a saxophone or cello, with a swing always controlled.

Crystal Gayle preserves a rural authenticity even while embracing the blue reality of jazz and this must have been recognized by Tom Waits, that most gravelly and grittily citified of today's singing composers, when in 1980 he chose her as partner for his film *One from the Heart*. Jazz timbre and rhythm now become overt in her singing, even in 'Is there any way out of this dream?', which might be a country waltz, or in a slow nostalgia ballad for 'Old boy friends', or in 'Take me home', accompanied only by Tom's piano, transferred from sleazy bar to the old home's parlour. In Tom Wait's compositions the two worlds designated as town and country prove to have common roots: when Crystal duets with Tom's near-Negro incantation and dialogues with the insidious jazz trumpet, saxophone and piano of Jack Sheldon, Teddy Edwards and Pete Jolly, she can preserve her simplicity while becoming a jazz singer adjusted to the urban eighties, even in Tom Waits's grubbiest downtown bar.

Crystal Gayle's jazz potential provides a link to Bonnie Raitt,[9] who is not so much a country singer embracing jazz, as a modern folk singer who chose the blues. This may have been in reaction to

8 *Crystal Gayle* and *One from the Heart*.
9 *Taking My Time*.

her comfortable milieu and perhaps even an unconscious rejection of her parents, who were show-business musicians on Broadway. In any case her childhood awakening to music was by way of primitive bluesmen like Fred Macdowell and Son House, and of the female classic blues singers from Ma Rainey to Sippie Wallace. During her adolescence in the sixties she got more from early Motown tracks than from the sophistications of modern jazz. Not surprisingly, having turned professional, she became a blues singer nursed in Black traditions, and made herself into a fine guitarist in the savage bottleneck style of Robert Johnson.

In the sixties and seventies she profited from the male blues revival in which old-timers like Muddy Waters and John Lee Hooker figured prominently. Her music was mostly blues-orientated although only exceptionally, as in her version of Fred Macdowell's 'Kokomo blues', did she sing unambiguous blues. In 1976 we find her translating a rousing country stomp, 'Let me in', into barrelhouse music, abetted by Bill Payne's honky-tonk piano, Earl Palmer's aggressive drums, Freebo's tuba bass, and heterophonic blastings on soprano saxophone, flugelhorn and trombone. 'Wah she go do', a Latin American number, acquires jazz dirt to fuel its sunny energy, while Jackson Browne's 'I thought I was a child' intensifies modal line and rock beat with tough timbre and pentatonic arabesques. Mose Allinson's 'Everybody's crying mercy' she begins as late-night bar jazz, but mounts to impassioned blueness.

Still more remarkable is her version of Randy Newman's 'Guilty', a song about whisky and cocaine addiction, and therefore about opting out from a world too troublesome to handle. As singing poet–composer, Randy Newman is a White black comedian comparable with Tom Waits but, coming from New Orleans, mellower. When, as often happens, his own songs are blue, we don't forget that he has become a stranger to the Deep South he sprang from. Bonnie Raitt's thrilling version of 'Guilty' is less alienated than the original, as though she is not singing *about* guilt but has momentarily become it. Much of its emotive charge is due, of course, to the quality of the composition, in which a strong melody is reinforced by a harmonically potent bass.

But the evolution from country music towards jazz is not a common phenomenon and it is hardly valid to think of Bonnie Raitt as initially a country singer. The normal transition is from country music to rock, and the reason for this is not merely because rock rather than jazz was the currently accepted youth music; it is also because country music and rock have similar ends and therefore similar techniques. Both cultivate communality, whereas jazz is a music of individualities and the blues a music of loners. In country music, this communality is with a lost agrarian past; in rock it is with a somewhat desperate urban present, and a potentially sci-fi future. Both country music and rock are 'easier' than jazz and the blues – which may be why few folk–rock compromises have worn well. Linda Ronstadt, however, who came to the fore in the late sixties, has continued to prosper and has deserved to, since although not herself a composer, she has given a personal twist to the country image and, in carrying it into the world of folk–rock, has discovered in it more than nostalgia.

If we take Linda's 1977 disc *Simple Dreams* as representative our immediate response is likely to be that nostalgia for the 'simple dreams' of childhood is the dominant motivation. Yet there is a distinction between these songs as Linda Ronstadt presents them and routine country music in that whereas the routine savours nostalgia complacently, Linda's nostalgia is sad at heart. Her vocal quality is itself childlike and quite often tremulous. Even when in quick numbers she calls on a tougher timbre, she is liable to sudden shifts of gear from middle register to piping treble. She thus achieves a quite complex effect of vulnerability – a quality, as we've noted, also endemic to White urban jazz singers. It's worth bearing in mind that Linda Ronstadt, though she has lived and worked in cities, was born in Arizona, where a vast expanse of desert contains few people. Rural lonesomeness was in her blood and bones, and the country music of Hank Williams and the (vulnerable) jazz of Billie Holiday were more significant in her growth than her brief spell at the University of Arizona.

Linda's first solo LP, pertinently titled *Hand Sown, Home Grown*, was released in 1969, and provides prototypes for the numbers she's still singing on the 1977 disc. Two of them, 'I will never marry' and 'Old paint', are described as 'trad. arr. Ronstadt'. They are not folk songs but old-time country waltzes, which Linda's arrangements render forlorn instead of cosy. Pulse is very slow, texture tenuous, voice frail. In modern country songs, such as 'Simple man, simple dream', her two registers are ambivalent. Her little-girl voice is echoed by the wails of steel guitar; her sinewy timbre is summoned to keep her going when on the point of exhaustion. Sudden leaps into the treble register promote wistfulness, since they might be a hopeful release, or might be a tremor of fear. The extremely slow 'Sorrow lives here' is Linda's quintessential 'heartache song', to use her own phrase. Its composer, Eric Katz, has produced many country standards, but can never have heard a performance more lonesomely lost than this. Linda's success with her *young* public must have been attributable to the honesty they recognized in her response to the country dream. She wasn't kidding them, because she didn't kid herself.

But Linda's songs are not all melancholy. When she hits back it is often by way of a recovery of childhood's Eden, as in her gently Latin-Americanized version of Ray Orbison's 'Blue bayou'. The landscape evoked is somewhere between Louisiana and Arizona, as is that of her version of Warren Zevon's 'Carmelita', a love song winsome rather than sad, since treble choric voices and whining harmonica offer comfort. Occasionally Linda seeks alleviation from 'heartache' in comedy, as in another Zevon song, 'Poor pitiful me', in which, over a driving beat, electrophonic instruments emulate bucolic bagpipes, squeeze-boxes and calliopes. To hold her own, Linda calls on her tougher voice, yet recurrently breaks into yodels, with an effect of jittery hilarity. The only fast tracks on this disc are purloined from sources very different from her own. Buddy Holly's 'It's so easy' lives up (or down) to its title, sounding, in its hypnotic beat and cheery parallel thirds, like infantile regression. Even Mick Jagger's 'Tumbling dice' acquires a playfulness not inappropriate to its gambling theme, though remote from Jagger's savage original.

Although the rock tracks on this disc may be purloined, they hint at the change that occurs in the next year, 1978, as Linda Ronstadt tentatively enters the modern world. *Livin' in the U.S.A.* takes its title from Chuck Berry's rock number of 1959, which Linda presents on its own terms. If one detects ironic overtones in its presentation of the God-given and man-made glories of the USA, the energy of the performance carries all before it. Linda's tougher voice rings triumphantly, without the power of Lacy J. Dalton but with youthful zest; Russell Kunkel's drums blithely bounce, Don Grolnick's barrelhouse piano chatters. Immediately Linda follows this eruption of adolescent hedonism with a classic of the other, nostalgic, pole of pope music – 'When I grow too old to dream' by Oscar Hammerstein and Sigmund Romberg, which carries us back to 1934, long before Linda was born. She takes it as a very slow waltz, at first piping in her little-girl voice, which strengthens to a music-hall bleat when she admits to the truth inherent in the title. We do grow too old to dream, and the admission is positive in that we put away childish things, but negative in that, dismissing dreams, we also surrender some of our human potential. Don Grolnick's sensuously meandering piano is as on the mark as it was in the barrelhouse rowdyism of 'Back in the U.S.A.'

So, having 'placed' both hedonism and nostalgia, Linda can move into the sixties with a rock song, 'Just one look', taken straight and, for her, rather fiercely. Then Elvis Costello's 'Alison', written the year before Linda's album, gives us a modern ballad, a love song in which sentimentality is tempered by irony. The sentiment finds vent through her treble register, lyrically fulfilled; the irony is manifest in her middle register, a bit hard, but not tough. Irony vanishes in the high cadence at the end, in which she doesn't merely tell us, but audibly demonstrates, that 'my aim is true'. She also exploits high-soprano register in Southern's 'White rhythm and blues', a ballad, not a rhythm-and-blues number, which is an appeal for a love that lasts, and is therefore concerned with past, present and future. It may be relevant to note that Linda, double-tracking, provides her own vocal backing. Growing up, she has less need of succour from the outside world, or of rock's communality.

The first song on side 2, 'All that you dream', has a bearing on this. The words of the Barrére–Payne number are about sun and rain as complementary aspects of experience. It's the rain that makes us realize 'just what is true'; only when our eyes are washed out can we see whether the sun is shining. Electrophonics emulate the dream-washing rain, which transforms a hard-rock song into vernal promise. In the final peroration Linda's harder voice jubilates, and the addition of shaker, tambourine and sleighbells to the electric guitars hint at Gospel fervour. Though the communal aspects of rock are evident in this number, in which the backing voices are male, it is Linda's voice, growing in lyrical delight from its hard initiation, that reinvokes 'the land of milk and honey', after time has left its scars. Perhaps because of these scars the next song, William Robinson's 'Oh baby, baby', provides Linda with an opportunity for a (for her) rare jazz performance. It's about a love affair gone wrong, and pain is manifest in Linda's fragmented rhythms and in the blue inflexions her voice assumes, much as does Crystal Gayle when singing with Tom Waits. In dialogue with Linda, David Sanborn's alto saxophone is furiously melancholic;

Don Grolnick proves himself as potent in Modern-Jazz pianism as he was in old barrelhouse idiom and in thirties sentimentality.

'Mohammed's radio', another remarkable number by Warren Zevon, lifts personal jazz experience into a public domain. The restlessness it both jazzily and rockily invokes effects the community at large, and the words hint that Mohammed's radio is offering some kind of religious consolation. Both words and music have Dylan-like echoes, and Linda's performance, rhythmically edgy yet lyrical, is worthy of the composition. Yet the last two numbers return to personal experience. Eric Katz's 'Blowing away' is about 'going down for the last time' because 'love is blind and cannot find me'. Linda's singing is not particularly distraught; it is more as though, growing up, she has learned to accept disillusion. It's significant that she follows this with the 1956 Elvis Presley song, 'Love me tender', sung very slowly, with clear enunciation and in close harmony with Waddy Watchel, suppportive 'to the end of time'. She sings of the ultimate paradox: we need to surrender our dreams, yet cannot live without them. It is impressive that on this disc she has been able to make this quite complex statement through the medium of other people's songs, much as Bonnie Raitt does when she draws on traditional blues or refashions Randy Newman's 'Guilty'.

One might have thought, from this cleverly planned and sensitively executed disc, that Linda Ronstadt was poised for the next step – her metamorphosis into a singing poet–composer making her own songs in an idiom somewhere between folk, country, jazz and rock, with art as catalyst. That did not happen: though she has moved towards art in another sense, in that she became a theatre performer in operetta, using her soprano voice, classically trained. In the 1982 New York production of *The Pirates of Penzanze* she achieved a considerable success, revealing acting as well as vocal abilities previously unsuspected. Such activity is outside the range of this book. Just within it is work Linda has recently done with Nelson Riddle, singing pop standards of the thirties and forties in his expertly syrupy arrangements for theatre orchestra. Having a lovely voice, she does this prettily. But such cocktail-lounge Easy Listening can hardly be, for her and at this date, comparable with the work of a jazz-trained cabaret singer like Peggy Lee. The songs come out as a nostalgia trip of dubious motivation, reminding us that some kinds of self-deception are more pernicious than others. The most that can be said in favour of the exercise is that Linda has spurned the crudest way of keeping up with the times: the transference of country into rock singer.

Suzi Quatro, who performs exclusively with electric instruments, is representative of this latter genre. On her 1974 disc *If You Knew Suzi* she performs rock songs by herself and Len Tuckey (it is not clear who is responsible for what), and by Nick Chinn and others. In her version of Chinn's 'If you can't give me love' we may detect affinity with the jolly communality of country music, though mechanization makes jollification slightly scary. More typical numbers – 'Evie', 'Rock 'n' Roll hoochie coo' – are dead straight, remorseless-metred, totally diatonic. Suzi's vocal production eschews sensitivity as she becomes an undeniably forceful White shouter complementing the 'big Black mamas' who, taking over from men, had carried the blues into tent shows and circuses. That had given communal import to a solitary music. Suzi Quatro, chosen as representative of a norm, becomes a community herself, multitracking *all* the backing voices. The compromise between the self and the world, manifest even in relatively commercial artists like Dolly Parton and Linda Ronstadt, is irrelevant to Suzi. It is slightly sinister that the will of the tribe, so much more powerful than the individual will, should be achieved by so formidable a display of ego.

This is why it is crucial that singing poet–composers should exist who, like Bob Dylan, Randy Newman and Tom Waits, deal courageously with issues that confront young people, admitting to and helping to define matters of conscience and of moral choice. Nor is it surprising that among these singing poet–composers should be many women, who perhaps, as women, tend to set relatively greater store by intuition than by will. Such a genre has been obliquely discussed in commenting on the composed originals of Joan Baez and Judy Collins. They, however, were emulating the model at second hand. The prototype of these modern girl troubadours is Joni Mitchell, whose work seems to me more rewarding, both poetically and musically, than that of any of the male singers except the three mentioned above. The final, and most important, section of this book will be devoted to these women troubadours, concentrating mainly though not exclusively on those who are their own poets and composers.

PART III

NOT FROM NEW ADAM'S RIB: WOMEN AS SINGING POET–COMPOSERS

WHITE SEAGULL, BLACK HIGHWAYWOMAN, RED SQUAW: JONI MITCHELL

Was that very sin – into which Adam precipitated himself and all his race – was it the destined means by which, over a long pathway of toil and sorrow, we are to attain a higher, brighter and profounder happiness, than our lost birthright gave?
Nathaniel Hawthorne: *The Marble Faun* 1860

The first and highest service which Eve renders to Adam is to throw him out of Paradise.
Henry James Snr: *Society and the Redeemed Form of Man*, 1879

Since folk–pop musics have always been concerned with the renewal of instinct, as contrasted with the dominance of intellect and will, it is hardly surprising, as we've noted, that woman should have come into her own in these fields. Even so, she had to wait for social and economic change to make her efflorescence feasible. When once this had happened, the folk–pop scene looked for a woman of genius, as distinct from talent. She appeared in the person of Joni Mitchell, whom Linda Ronstadt sees as 'the first woman to match a man on his own terms as song writer, guitar player and incredibly magnetic human being'.

By birth, Joni Mitchell was an outsider from Vancouver. She embarked on a singing careet in 1963, at a coffee house in the big and then brash city of Toronto. In 1965, the year Dylan 'went electric', Joni was still a novice. Wired neither for amplification in folk–rock nor for protest in folk politics, she 'came to folk music when it was already dying'. Judy Collins, Tom Rush and Buffy Ste Marie sang Joni's songs before she did; only when she began to flit between the relative solitude of Canada and the pulsing energy of Los Angeles was she recognized as a singer in her own right. In Los Angeles and New York, however, she was soon established as priestess of the sixties hip scene. *Time* called her 'a rural neophyte waiting in a subway, a free spirit drinking in the moonlight, an organic Mother Earth dispensing fresh bread and herb tea, and a reticent feminist who by trial and error has charted the male as well as the female ego'. In less lurid prose Joni herself claimed merely that her need for love was a feminine instinct: 'My main interest in life is human relationships and human interaction on a one-to-one basis, or on a larger basis projecting feelings to an audience'; 'I bare intimate feelings because people should know how other people feel.'

This empiricism conditions her approach to versification and to musical structure. All pop lyrics and tunes exist in relation to, sometimes within, 'established' conventions of versification and musical grammar; at the same time they loosen these conventions in ways pertinent to their (usually young) makers' neglect of, or even contempt for, the world they exist in, depend on, but would emotively like to change. Often their verbal and musical laxity is due mainly to insouciance or incompetence; in pop artists of genuine talent, however, the relationship between established forms and empirical behaviour is the heart of the matter – as was noted in the case of the Beatles and, more modestly, Angela Bofill. In the case of a few exceptional artists – Bob Dylan and Joni Mitchell are the most conspicuous instances – this equilibrium between conventionality and spontaneity amounts to genius.

This is evident in Joni Mitchell's first, 1968, album, *To a Seagull*. The verses are comparable, in their corporeally expressive rhythms and instinctive collocations of metaphor and ambiguous syntax, with those of a real folk poet – as is her knack of transforming her verbal felicities into memorable lyricism and harmonic piquancy. As a performing musician she reveals here a natural, untrained voice of some range, vernal in the upper, mysterious in the lower, reaches, and an empirical technique on acoustic guitar capable of magically varied timbre. Before she cut this album, Joni was deprecating about her voice: 'I used to be a breathy little soprano. Then one day I found I could sing low. At first I thought I had lost my voice for ever. I could either sing a breathy high part or a raspy low part. Then the two came together of themselves.' If we recall what we've noted about 'liquid' and 'raspy' vocal timbre in the context of folk musics,[1] we'll recognize that this 'coming together' is the heart of Joni's experience. Joni's breathy and raspy voices represent the contradictory yet complementary aspects of her as Canadian child and Californian woman. The coming together is an approach to maturation.

On the first album 'Sisotowbell Lane' uncovers Joni's roots as she, a big-city girl, sings of her remote country childhood. The remoteness is the point, for through it art qualifies nostalgia. 'We Canadians', said Joni, 'are a bit more nosegay, more old-fashioned bouquet, than the Americans. We're poets because we're such a *reminiscent* sort of people.' In this lovely song the verses, evoking Old Times with rocking chair, muffins and elderberry wine, flow into a tender tune moving mainly by step or by leaps of fourth or fifth, occasionally blossoming into a sixth. Rhythms follow speech, vocal production is folk-like. Yet as a whole the song is a subtle artefact: neither, like Jean Ritchie's 'None but one', a genuine folk tune metamorphosed into art nor, like Dolly Parton's 'Applejack', an artful exploitation of country-music convention, but an original *work* of art that draws on folk and country techniques for subjective ends. Consider the chromatic rise in the melody that appears on the words 'we always know'. Joni sings the chromatics as a microtonal slide which, as the stanzas unfold, balances the resignedly declining cadential phrases, and serves as release from the low repeated notes to which the catalogue of old-time pleasures is recited. A single chromatic note is fraught with feeling since it seems simultaneously to yearn back to, and to seek escape from, the past. This epitomizes Joni Mitchell's position at this time in her life and has perhaps remained a constant.

Another song, 'I had a king', seems to reject nostalgia. It is about a lover – in fact her recently divorced husband Chuck – whose synthetic glamour, in his 'tenement castle', Joni has belatedly seen through. She rejects him for his complacency, for his being 'an actor who fears laughter's sting'. Yet the music, uneasily veering between tonic major, the flattened upper mediant, the flat submediant, and

1 See p. 9.

the minor of the tonic itself, tempers disillusion with regret. Here Joni employs her two voices – folkily treble and jazzily dark – as though they *hadn't* 'come together', and her undulations between them equivocate between dream and reality. But she doesn't identify 'truth' with either. The refrain's rejection of the past ('I can't go back any more') brings in a sharp seventh which, tugging against the tonic pedal on which it belately resolves, sounds anguished, especially after so many modally flat sevenths. Musically, the attempt at resolution brings acute pain – as is appropriate psychologically.

'Song to a seagull' concerns the false values of the city contrasted with the freedom of the bird of the unconscious waters. The musical image is as simple, and as potent, as the verbal image: over a tonic pedal the melody arches up in hopeful syncopation through a tenth, then falls of its own weight, like the gull riding the wind. The sevenths are always flat, floating in air-borne freedom; but the flattening of the habitually major third on the phrase 'out of reach' rings like a knell. Here Joni uses vagaries of pitch like a real folk singer: the E flat on 'reach' sounds dolefully flatter than it would in equal temperament;[2] Joni's dream takes off, with the seagull, only in wish-fufilment. Yet though the fiercely arpeggiated chord at the end sounds dismissive, it cannot destroy the idealized hope that freedom might be possible. This is not so much a song of frustrated aspiration as a song of discovery. Most of the singers previously discussed are recognizable by their distinctive voices and manner of performance. This song is recognizable through its intrinsic poetic and musical qualities. No one else could have created it.

Despite or perhaps because of this subjective flavour, the finest songs of Joni's early period are often those projected into tales or dreams about other people, real or legendary. 'Marcie' is any lonely, lost girl as well as (or rather instead of) Joni Mitchell. The marvellous poem gives her a local habitation as well as a name: 'her faucet needs a plumber, her sorrow needs a man.' At the same time the many-layered metaphors – for instance the shifting permutations of red, yellow and green in the traffic-lights image – are sophistications of techniques typical of a genuine folk ballad and, as in such a ballad, the girl's love loss is both particular and general. The music supports the archetypal imagery. The tune, narrow in compass, stepwise-moving, is lyrically assuaging yet at

2 See Glossary.

the same time lost – not in linear terms, for it is anchored on its 'home' note D, but in its shifting harmonization. The key signature is G major, but the song opens on the triad of B flat and throughout oscillates between G and its upper and lower mediants (B flat and E). Moreover the C sharps that creep into the tune as early as the second bar disturb in being Lydian tritones[3] to the keynote. They also suggest sharpwards modulations that fail to materialize. So the tune, promising but then disappointing movement towards an end, becomes an aural image for the waiting woman. The words' woof of internal rhymes fosters the music's asmymmetries: consider how the mediant shifts in the harmony are inseparable from stressed words in the refrain. The E flat triad makes the 'ocean beaches' open in airy promise, only to close again. Though such harmonic effects may occur empirically – sometimes by the movements of hand over guitar – one must not depreciate their artistry, which is far from the empiricism of folk music proper.

This applies also to another narrative–dramatic ballad, 'The pirate of penance'. If 'Marcie' renders everyday experience mythological, 'The pirate of penance' relates legendary experience to our own lives. The hero is the traditional sailor of folk balladry, who steals not gold and silver but the hearts of women. The narrator, accused of murdering him out of jealousy, sings in her own defence. The story is told in rapid recitative, again harmonized in oscillating mediants, alternating with tonal movement by step. Enharmonic false relations,[4] allied to the use of the leading note as dissonant appoggiatura[5] conflicting with the modal flat sevenths, give the music a nightmarish atmosphere relevant to the tale. The exotic setting – there's a Moorish–Mexican flavour to the refrain – underlines the queasiness. The aura is that of Dylan's (contemporary) psychedelic songs and the plot is not less difficult to unravel: 'I keep watch with my soul. I keep searching for something to come and I am cursed and I don't know.' Yet after a mysterious meeting at 4, on Saturday, near a forest, we have an illuminating line: 'Ask for Penance Grange, she was at the garden, she saw her.' Was Penance, another lover, the murderer? The punning title releases the narrator from guilt.

'Nathan le Franeer', which is comparably scary, strikes deeper because it is closer to hand, as Joni drives in coach or taxi through

3 See Glossary.
4 See Glossary.
5 See Glossary.

the city at night. The song crystallizes the phantasmagoric menace familiar from gangster movies. The regularity of the beat, the repeated notes with which the tune opens, are in tension with the side-stepping modulations. When the refrain expands, vacillating between major and minor third, we are unsure whether the 'ghostly garden' among the 'gangs and girly shows' is solace or deceit. This seems on target, as a comment on the big city, fraught with marvels and terrors, at once a lure and a threat.

'The dawntreader' is another number invoking the sea as an image of freedom. A lover stakes all his worldly wealth on a dream, which the music embodies by teetering between the tonic E flat and the chord of the flat seventh. The flatwards shift hardly suggests that the dream will sprout wings, but in the middle section, in which he 'aches and learns to live', the melodic E flat becomes a suspension[6] in basic B flat harmony and the line momentarily takes off. The return is by way of D flat, which resolves on to the E flat tonic almost apologetically; the lover's 'sea-dreams' come to Joni only vicariously. A more hopeful song, 'Michael from mountains', is also about love and dreams, combined with Joni's childhood motive. Her line, sung in her 'white' voice, envisages the lover as a magician in a child's world of sweets, painted umbrellas, and oil rainbows in puddles. Michael fades into mountain mists, as the music becomes evanescent in side-stepping shifts of tonality. But the tune of the refrain, floating through a fourth, lilting into an unexpected upward sixth, convinces us that 'some day' she will know the elusive lover 'very well'.

In all these songs the harmonic and tonal subtleties sound as though they've been arrived at empirically, though not fortuitously, through improvisation on guitar; they are, however, improvisations that having been notated, remain constant for each performance. The melodic shapes, on the other hand, cannot be adequately notated, since rhythms and durations change according to the stress given to particular word. Thus Joni Mitchell's songs are at once artless and artful: conceived in the spirit of folk music, yet sophisticated in execution.

The other albums that comprise Joni's early period are perhaps less consistently inspired, though all include numbers of typical poignancy. Many of the songs in the 1969 album *Clouds* take up the equivocation between illusion and disillusion that haunts 'Michael

6   See Glossary.

from mountains'. 'Both sides, now' admits that she is unsure both
of the shape of clouds, of their nature amorphous, and of the
difference between past and present, not to mention the future,
which dreams may presage. As a child she used to look at clouds as

. . . blows and flows of angel hair,
And ice-cream castles in the air,
But now
. . . they only block the sun, and rain and snow on everyone.

The music, however, tells us that so sharp a dichotomy betwen
illusion and reality is oversimple, for the diatonic-major melody,
climbing up a seventh only to droop *through* a seventh from its
highest point, creates a small affirmation out of dubiety itself.
Though she may 'not know life at all', she gets by on a knack for
living.

Something similar happens in the delightful 'Chelsea morning',
which opposes the passions and maybe terrors of the night to the
childlike pleasures of the pin-bright morning. She's trying to
persuade her lover to stay for breakfast, when they can 'put on the day'
instead of clothes, and when there's a (free) 'sun-show every second'.
The tune is Mixolydian,[7] occasionally agitated by a sharp seventh of
Lydian fourth. Joni sings it jubilantly, as though she momently
believes in the moment, though whether her man does is unclear.

'I don't know where I stand' triumphs less, as its title indicates,
over dubiety. A pentatonic phrase evokes the 'sunny day, braiding
fall flowers and leaves in my hair' – until the illusory nature of
happiness is revealed in a sudden enharmonic shift and a loonily
scatting refrain. Joni is safeguarded from despair by an ironic
insouciance that doesn't undermine pathos. Tonality in this song is
appositely precarious; even the pentatonicism is riddled with Lydian
incertitudes. 'Roses blue' sounds tonally even more vulnerable,
perhaps because the tune is less defined. Since it is about a
fortune-teller, who by occupation propagates illusions, it's not
surprising that the music, shivering between chromatically and
enharmonically related triads, should defy conventional grammar.
Again a scatting refrain adds a further ambiguity, for in mocking
those who would hand over their destinies to Zodiac or Tarot, it
hymns the pathos of human hopes. As often with Joni's songs, one
doesn't know whether to laugh or cry.

7   See Glossary.

'Tin angel' is concerned with hope in a more positive sense. Here Joni, so often a slave to memory, dismisses the past to take a chance on a new love that might be the real right thing, and convinces us as well as herself when the meandering pentatonic line becomes hope incarnate in a *tierce de Picardie*.[8] But the E major triad isn't approached by way of a conventional dominant but from a seventh on the flat seventh – a dominant seventh in G major. This makes the E major triad sound not less warm, but less final; in the nature of things the new guy will probably end up among the memories from which the song started.

Similarly, 'The fiddle and the drum' is a song about the uneasy relationship between hope and betrayal, manifest both in a lover and in America. Joni sings it monodically, with a rhythmic freedom stemming from the words, but with a latent harmonic dimension in that the thirds are often ambiguously – 'falsely' – related. Given its minimal means, the song is powerful, an artful art song calling on folk techniques. It's worth noting that in this unaccompanied song Joni's approach to rhythm by way of verbal inflexion doesn't differ from that in her accompanied songs. The melodic line divides the four crotchets a bar into every possible permutation of eight quavers, independent of metrical beat or harmonic rhythm.

The next album, *Ladies of the Canyon* (1970), marks a turning point because Joni plays piano as well as acoustic guitar, and because obbligato instruments – flute, clarinet, saxophone and cello – are intermittently employed. The cycle is concerned with the state of Eden and its loss, the title song presenting, in a lilting Tex-Mex rhythm, a group of canyon women in vegetative content:

Cats and babies round her feet
And all are fat and none are thin.

Joni's familiar side-stepping modulations make contentment mirth-provoking rather than complacent: it's a small victory when the doo-doo-doo tra-la-la' refrain purrs in parallel thirds. In this song Joni's voice is as bell-like as Jean Richie's: as it is in 'Morning Morgantown', a picture of an American small town on a sunlit morning when

Merchants roll their awnings down
And milk trucks make their morning rounds.

8 See Glossary.

The tune rocks through thirds, the accompaniment babbles in an A major traditionally associated with childhood and youth; yet again the happiness is neither mindless nor escapist. The familiar mediant modulations, and even a shift from A to the dominant seventh of B flat, liberate as they disturb.

The key song in the album is 'Woodstock', celebrating 'the most famous ever' pop music festival, though Joni wasn't at it. She meets 'a child of God' on the road to join a rock-and-roll band, hoping to 'get my soul free'. The song, typical of the psychedelic sixties and the dreaming Age of Aquarius, is an ecological protest against smog, a political protest against Vietnam, and a general protest against apathy. The young, 'half a million strong' by the time they reach Woodstock, recognize that although they are 'stardust' they too are

. . . caught in the Devil's bargain.
We must get ourselves back to the garden.

So this is another Eden song, and in that crucial refrain the chromatic alteration in the descending minims melts the heart the more because thus far the pentatonic tune has been undisturbed by Joni's tonal ambiguities. Her voice acquires an added depth, reminiscent of folk blues, and the melody owes its emotional fervour to its wide range. Hovering below and around the low E that is the tonic, the line stretches up to the flat seventh; when the upper tonic is finally achieved it sounds, in Joni's suddenly unclouded vocal production, remote, even alien. Rhythm too is ambiguous, for the continuously shifting permutations of the eight quavers a bar in the vocal line are poised over the steady, walking rhythm of the electric bass, which emulates, with eerie inevitability, the boy's trudging along the dusty road.

When Joni Mitchell attempts to face Experience *contrasted* with Innocence, her music, if not her words, convinces less. 'Rainy night house' presents two conventional goodies opting out from 'sunday school and the golden factories' of a wealthy family to discover 'who in the world' each might be. The disorientated tonality and the false relations express their perturbation accurately enough, but the lack of a coherently shaped melody leaves us as well as them stranded; the number comes out as bemused rather than compassionate.

But two songs in the cycle, though not entirely convincing, make a bid for a deeper sense of responsibility, thereby initiating her second phase. In 'The arrangement' Joni uses the deeper, bluesy voice she'd given intimation of in 'Woodstock' to deflate a man who

> . . . could have been more
> Than a name on the door
> on the thirty-third floor
> . . . more than a credit card. . .
> More than a consumer
> lying in some room trying to die.

While the low voice encourages change, Joni uses her high voice, squeakily, for the wife who 'holds the keys'. The nagging persistence of the wife induces nightmare ('no one really cares who you are') – which undermines Joni's search for identity, her own as well as the man's. The flattened leading note, lunging downwards at 'the arrangement', shocks us (and him?) into an awareness of the reality of the situation.

Particularly touching is the brief modulation whereby the wife momentarily becomes a suffering human rather than a cypher; while the transition from *parlando* recitative to speech at the end highlights responsibility and awareness: here is the nitty-gritty of life-as-it-is. On the other hand the piano prelude approaches portentousness, which doesn't fit with the 'medium folk style', let along the 'much feeling', which is asked for in the song itself. This hints at dangers that Joni, in later, more self-consciously 'serious' songs, doesn't entirely escape, though self-consciousness may have been necessary to growing awareness. But another number, 'He played real good for free', indicates that Joni can deal with moral responsibility without suspicion of pretentiousness, as she contrasts her own success in the music industry with the one-man band by the quick-lunch stand on a noisy street corner. She doesn't merely admit that she had played for 'velvet curtain calls', but involves us too:

> Nobody stopped to hear him
> Though he played so sweet and high.

The concluding song, 'The circle game', adapts the folk convention of the seasonal rune, viewing life from childhood to adolescence to age as a merry-go-round. The rhythm jogs, the tune circumambulates in straight diatonic major except for an evanescent flat seventh. If the melody is hardly inspired one wouldn't, given its burden, expect it to be; acceptance of the circle game was necessary if Joni were to progress beyond the seagull-soaring visions of her early youth.

The disc includes one number, 'Big yellow taxi', that transmutes a folky idiom – the refrain is a primitive tumbling strain – into city rockabilly, with aggressive percussion and electric guitars. These are prompted by the theme, for this is an anti-city song about turning paradise into parking lots and putting trees into museums. Yet lyricism survives, and hints at an evolution for Joni's songs as she enters the seventies.

Up to this point any Black tinge from the blues has been precipitated from White folk sources; from here onwards the impact of the urban blues, modifying the country heritage, is direct. The melodies tend to be more chromatically coloured, the harmonies tougher, the rhythms more nervous. Strumming, a technique seldom previously encountered in her work, now creates a continuum of sound to encourage twitching feet; while the *dis*-continuity of the line promotes fluidity, loosening the bonds by increased syncopation and more flexible alternations of duple and triple metres. Lyrical arabesques roam more widely, though jazz freedom is counteracted by the tighter rhythms Joni had picked up from rock and roll. This tension between freedom and discipline cannot – as Joni's later career demonstrates – have been easy to sustain. Both passion and pain are manifest in what Joni does with her voice, which now moves over a range of one and a half octaves, the timbre varying from that of Whitest folk to Blackest blues singer, with hints of other ethnic cultures thrown in for good measure.

The 1971 album that marks the turning point in Joni's career is in fact called *Blue*. Clearly she was conscious of the change in her verse and music, and it cannot be fortuitous that the songs tend to be more autobiographical than those on previous albums. Most of them she wrote while touring Europe. In this sense they are songs of separation – from lovers, from California, and from Canada, her first home. The California scene, which had brought her fame, is rejected in verses less 'poetic', more colloquially vernacular than was her wont; the vocal line is gutsier, the harmonies bluer in more than one sense. She still gives us a comic-nostalgic song about childhood, 'Little green'. But the child is an unmarried mother's and the father is 'afar' – so the balance between spring-like grace and wintry desuetude is delicate, the lyricism waverily air-borne, the percussive beat jittery. Little Green, the baby, is encouraged to become a 'non-conformer', and the song is lovely enough to suggest that she may make it. At the same time the music tells us that the non-conformer's path cannot be smooth.

The title song, 'Blue', is a 'foggy lullaby' dealing with the pressures to which the young are submitted in a commercially manipulated world. Again Joni teeters on a tightrope between hope and self-indulgent submission. She seems to dismiss

Acid, booze and ass,
Needles, guns and glass

while at the same time admitting that

I'm going to take a look around it though.

The words' indecision is mirrored in the melody, which hovers around the fifth and aspires to the ninth, and in the tonality, which once more oscillates between upper and lower mediants. Yet the song is tightly constructed. Joni varies the length of the lines without disrupting the flow. The first eight, in the Dorian mode[9] on B, is repeated, melodically varied; the next four bars are thematically contracted though structurally similar, ending in hiatus. After a reminiscence of the introduction there's a 'middle' in D major as relative to the Dorian B; and a *da capo* of the first theme, again varied, ending on a very blue third with flattened seventh. All the phrases droop, apart from the aerial motif that expresses her momentary indulgence in the phrase 'Blue, I love you'. In this song Joni finds her 'high' mostly in illicit panaceas.

But the theme of this album as a whole is not the difficult relationship between loving and fleeing into whatever atemporal realms drugs or freak-out may lead one. It is rather the lost lot of the highwaywoman who takes to the roads – as is evident in 'All I want', which turns out to be quite a lot. Though the language is plain, compared with the metaphorical flights of her early numbers, this song does fly, being a late flutter of her once-soaring seabird. We can believe that she wants to dance with, take a chance with, her man, making them both better and freer in the process. Though the electric guitar's ostinati are often harsh, the vocal line sings and dances within its rhythmic complications: consider the lilt on the repeated 'do you sees' and the lovely lift that makes them 'feel free'. Verbal comedy ('I want to renew you, shampoo you') combines with

9   See Glossary.

elliptical rhythms to create an uneasy joy. Happiness, though possible, is elusive, and Joni's 'vernal' voice sounds the more touching in association with her now habitually jazz-tinged idiom. There's a similarly positive nervosity in 'My old man'. The asymmetrical melody makes her lover sing in the park, dance in the dark, while the blue harmony that happens when he's 'away' makes audible the fact that without him 'the bed's too big, the frying pan too wide'. The tonal shifts here are sophisticated, and the vocal melismata are as wild as the modulations, enacting the fact that 'we don't need no piece of paper from the city hall to keep us tied and true.' Vulnerability is the essence of Joni Mitchell's art, which can make a song like this at once happily hilarious and tremulously sad.

The key song in the album is 'California', which recounts Joni's bumming around Europe, picking up experience and men, sensible of wars and of the disintegration of the Old World. Homeless and 'travelling', she dreams of California, from which she'd intentionally escaped, as an Ideal Home, to be built in the mind's eye and the heart's core, if not in stocks and stones. The fastish beat and nervous rhythm are both literally and metaphorically electric; the interlocking structure of the phrases is complex; the 'coming home' refrain, with its lift through an octave and pentatonic descent, is half sentimentally indulgent, half comic. Here Joni's vulnerability comes close to desperation, but is salvaged by her sense of humour. Sometimes, however, the strain is too much. 'The river' gives way to passive nostalgia, as Christmas festivities remind her of her Canadian childhood. The melody, at first rooted in middle register, floats upwards when she hopes that the river might teach her to fly, but Joni's seagull, distantly evoked, doesn't manage to spread its wings. A descending phrase suggests the hurt she had caused her lover, and the second stanza's second flight is counteracted by a stepwise descending bass. Nostalgia tends to induce moroseness. Subdominant-tending harmonies create a low-ebbed mood.

The final song, 'The last time I saw Richard', is also deflating. An ex-lover tells her that

. . . all romantics meet the same fate some day
cynical and drunk and boring someone in some dark café.

She thinks she is immune but her

. . . eyes are full of moon,
you like roses and kisses and pretty men
to tell you all those pretty lies.

Though she thinks she leaves him defeated, with a little wife, the coffee percolator and the flickering television, she has no answer to her own pain except to

> . . . blow this damn candle out.
> I don't want nobody coming over to my table,
> I got nothing to talk to anyone about.

Though the melody is, perhaps appropriately, unmemorable, the glum honesty of the song was necessary to Joni. The album ends on a question mark. Her sad café days may be

> a dark cocoon
> before I get my gorgeous wings and fly away.

On the other hand, her flight might be mere escapism.

The best songs in this album are like the proverbial cat on hot bricks – from which Joni sometimes, understandably enough, wants to jumps off. That she was uncertain of her direction is suggested by her 1972 album *For the Roses*, which is less jazz-orientated than *Blue*, though it moves into folk–rock idiom, consistently using electric bass. 'My music is now becoming more rhythmic', said Joni. 'It's because I'm in Los Angeles and my friends are mostly rock-and-roll people.' All these songs are moderate in tempo and countryish in flavour, though electrophonic techniques render them nervously urban. Verbal metaphors of fire, electricity and static pervade the verses, sometimes with positive effect, as in 'You turn me on, I'm a radio', in which she admits to being 'a country station, a little bit corny', though the beat quivers and the melody asymmetrically unfurls to present her as 'a wildwood flower'.

More commonly, mechanistic metaphors are used dangerously, as in 'Electricity', in which failed human contacts are equated with broken electrical connections. Still more savage is 'cold blue steel and sweet fire', perhaps the best song on heroin addiction since 'Sister Morphine' by the Rolling Stones. A hell is precisely delineated as Cold Blue Steel looks for the sweet fire. Lady Release taunts, 'come with me . . . down, down, down the dark ladder.' The metre is jagged; harsh false relations cavort in instrumental *breaks* – a technical convention allegoricaly appropriate. The instrumental coda is the nearest Joni had yet come to re-creating Black jazz–blues. The 'red water in the bathroom sink' hisses. Musical ambiguities parallel the verbal pun that speaks of 'bashing in veins for peace'.

The Darker Shade on this song is patent and potent. More characteristic of this disc are confessional songs, which, from the nervous present hark back to youth and childhood. 'Lessons in childhood' offers precisely that, and she doesn't know whether the lessons are 'paranoia or sensitivity'. The line is conversational, the rhythm nagging; in the context the melisma that creates 'my sweet tumbleweed' seems the more frailly childlike. The title song, 'For the roses', echoes 'He played real good for free' in being about the perils of success. The poem is complex and moving: strong enough to carry a *parlando* line that doesn't need to flower into song. She used to sit and make up tunes 'for love'; now they

> . . . toss around your latest golden egg Speculation –
> Well who's to know if the next one in the nest will glitter for
> them so.

Joni has seldom sung an arabesque more heart-rending than that with which she embroiders the word 'glitter'. It sounds tarnished, yet at the same time encompasses the hopeful dreams she'd lived by. She pipes the verse from her roses and Canadian mountains, but the sharp fourth in the tune, summoning 'applause', is dampened by the E flat minor triad in the answering clause. In the previous, also autobiographical, song, 'Let the wind carry me', she opposes the cliché image her mother (who is 'always cleaning') wanted her to be to the 'wild seed' her father (whose 'faith is people') accepted her as. Though she's had undefined longings to settle down and raise a child, she remains her father's daughter. The need for stability 'passes like the summer' and she's a 'wild seed again, let the wind carry me'. The message looks back to Joni as she was in her Seagull days, though the 'innocent' voice is breathier, the instrumental parts jazzily on edge.

For the Roses is a marking-time album. It is the last disc directly to revoke childhood, and in the next year, 1973, *Court and Spark*, attempting to put away childish things, gives to the blue moods of *Blue* a more overtly autobiographical slant. The songs, forming a whole, tell a story of nervous collapse. The crisis involves tension between personal sensibility and modern technocracy, but whereas in *For the Roses* songs such a 'You turn me on' had used mechanistic metaphors positively, in *Court and Spark* such metaphors are minatory. The album is given the full electrophonic treatment.

In the title song the girl – perhaps we should resist a *too* straightforward identification of her with Joni – casually meets a 'madman' who casually wants to 'court and spark' her off. She is impressed, and presumably seduced, by his talk, but won't relinquish her freedom or Los Angeles, city of fallen angels. The second number, admitting that she may be falling in love again, finds the prospect scary. It's a cry for 'help', in which beat is agitated, line broken, harmony chippy with hard major sevenths, vocal tone pinched. She and her 'sweet-talking ladies man' love their loving, but not so much as they love their freedom.

The next number, 'Free man in Paris', debunks the man's Parisian freedom (which carries him blithely to the submediant), opposing it to the prison of the pop-music industry in which he works, 'stoking the star-maker machine'. 'People's parties' maroons the girl in idiot sociabilities, living on her nerves, squeaking in high register, 'fumbling deaf, dumb and blind'. Like most people on the verge of breakdown, she is no longer rescued by a sense of humour. The language is flat, 'ornery', even when, in 'the same situation', she is sending up a prayer 'wondering who there was to hear'. Complementarily, the line doesn't attain lyricism, though it has its own pliant strength and hints, in the coda, at lost modes of feeling by way of pentatonically folky music for strings.

In the next song the girl is waiting, listening to sirens and radio, for 'A car on the hill' that will bring another lover. Though the climbing melody sounds hopeful, no car comes, and after the glum 'Down to you', with its woozy instrumental interlude, 'Just like this train' substitutes railway train for car and malice for regret. The rock beat is powerful, the chromatically sliding harmony both ferocious and melancholy, the vocal line spastically fragmented. Not only has she no one to love, she has 'lost her heart', forgotten how to feel. Animated by 'sour grapes', she relishingly watches her vain lover's hairline recede:

Lately I can't count on nothing,
I just let things slide.

She presents herself as a strong cat without claws, a thin man smoking a fat cigar, an empty seat in a crowded waiting room. Negation seems at least to have promoted energy, which proves to be a step towards collapse.

'Raised on robbery' sidesteps the personal issue: the woman is a hooker failing to make a pickup in a hotel lounge. The honky-tonk beat is fierce, poles apart from the tender flexibilities of Joni's early songs. Throbbing quavers grow desperate, with D sharps grinding against the tonic E naturals, and B flats searing through the B naturals of the dominant. With 'Trouble child' Joni, returning to her own situation, admits to breakdown. Each stanza pushes her further beneath the encroaching waters, 'breaking like the waves at Malibu'. 'Advice and religion' fail her, and she's left with

>   . . . a river of changing faces,
>   up in a sterilized room
>   where they let you be lazy.

Uncertainty is again manifest in a plethora of seventh chords, often with the seventh as bass. Rhythms are offbeat, metre shifts between 4/4 and 3/4. The pentatonic phrase for 'the waves at Malibu' recalls Joni's childhood dreams, floating through the haze of drugs the hospital has submitted her to. As dreams float away, she feels that her 'right to be human is going over too'.

But this sad song is not total renunciation, for it leads without break into a vigorous jazz interlude, out of which grows the epologic number, 'Twisted'. This is nearly a comeback, though significantly it was composed not by Joni but by Annie Ross and Wardell Grey. Not since her student days had Joni sung songs by other people. It's as though she were admitting that at this stage she cannot effect recovery herself, but needs the prop of other composers as well as of her psychiatrist. The comeback is both musical, in that the nervous line – in a jazz idiom related not only to Annie Ross but also to the great Billie Holiday – points in a direction where Joni might reconcile her dreams with the corruptions of a mechanized world; and also poetic, in that the verses deal with nervous collapse honestly, with a wit that is more than defensive. Her analyst told her that she was 'right out of her head'; she retorts that, although her father's 'wildseed', she always 'knew what was happening, I knew I was a genius'. The Trouble Child justifiably preserves that fundamental self-confidence, though at the moment she is too low to produce a jazz song such as this unaided. In her next few discs she has to plummet depths to work through psychological crisis. When she re-emerges, heart-whole if not fancy-free, it will be to create a music more jazz orientated in lyrical and rhythmic vivacity, and a poetry once more capable of wit and irony.

The album *For the Roses* was issued after *Court and Spark*, though its songs had been written at least four years earlier. This suggests both that Joni didn't know where to turn as a result of her psychotic disturbance, and also that she wanted to let her fans down lightly.

By the time she releases another album, however, she had decided that a new image is unavoidable, and achieves it, in *The Hissing of Summer Lawns* (1976), by standing back from herself and substituting for autobiography a consciously planned, carefully constructed 'work' of art. To this album the word 'folk' is hardly relevant. Joni herself describes it as a 'total work conceived graphically, musically and accidentally – as a whole'. Though the title itself indicates that Joni is still a poet, it has also a pretentiousness atypical of her earlier work. The obliquity of the poems seems a deliberate mystification rather than, as in Dylan's later verses, a reflection of valid compromises and ambiguities. Disillusion leads to cynicism, even sarcasm, for Joni has no empathy with her dramatis personae. While we may understand the motives that prompted Joni to withdraw from herself, her liner notes are an apologia that embarrasses more than it convinces.

Nor does the sophistication of the electrophonics help. *The Hissing of Summer Lawns* is verbally arresting and electrophonically atmospheric, yet in inverting her youthful aspirations it leaves only 'darkness, darkness, no colour, no contrast'. The most convincing songs are centred in the Big City, like 'In France they kiss on Main Street', in which melody and harmony are subservient to rollicking rhythm and rocking beat. The young are dancing, necking and rebelling against parental authority in the spirit of the liberated sixties; but such virility belongs to a past era and gets submerged in peevish grousing about the wickedness of social convention:

> They've been broken in churches and schools
> And moulded to middle-class circumstances.

Malaise is too easy a way out of trauma – as is evident too in the money-grubbing death dance celebrated in 'The Bohu dance', or still more in 'The jungle line' in which Joni, feigning a dark 'Black' voice, reaches back to the barbarous jungle, with references to Rousseau's sleeping gypsy and predatory lion. It must be because the message is negative and nugatory that Joni Mitchell's 'feigning' sound so different from that of Duke Ellington in *his* jungle pieces. He was reinvoking a dream world that was also 'the beauty of his wild forebears' and a mythology relevant to us all. Joni's 'Blackness' is a parodistic act, inspired by dislike, if not by active hatred.

Interestingly enough, the best music in *The Hissing of Summer Lawns*, as in *Court and Spark*, is not by Joni herself. In 'Harry's house – Centerpiece' Joni with tiresome arrogance slings mud at

Battalions of paper-minded males
taking commodities and sales
while at home their paper wives and their paper kids
paper the walls to keep their gut reactions hid.

This is a later, more malign version of 'The arrangement', in which a man successful in business fails in human terms. He is allowed to daydream of his courting days, and his dream-song is a Johnny Mandel–Jon Hendricks number, brilliantly sung in fifties jazz idiom. This recollection of 'happy' love is dismissed in the final stanza, in which the wife, shattering the dream, tells him

just what he could do with Harry's house,
And Harry's take-home pay.

It would be good to think that this 'Centerpiece' is saying something on behalf of common humanity, though one suspects that it is intended satirically. The assumption that Joni's music is here better, truer, than Hendricks's is unvalidated. Her jazz singing in the 'Centerpiece', however, in combination with Joe Sample's splendid post-barrelhouse piano playing, gives intimation of things to come.

In an earlier song, 'The last time I saw Richard', Joni had uttered glum words about the fate of 'all romantics, cynical and drunk', boring one another in some sad café. In reference to *Hejira* (1976) these words seem all too relevant to Joni herself. The magic of her early songs lay in the wonder they generated: the sense of possibilities, however fragile our dreams. The *Hejira* songs are less accessible and less tuneful than earlier numbers, but this doesn't make them, as sleeve notes and some reviewers suggested, folk–pop's equivalent to third-period Beethoven. (Joni herself didn't quite make this association, though she did suggest a parallel with Picasso in remarking that no one would would expect the painter to repeat his Blue Period simply because it had been approved of!) Here the verses are slack compared with the artful assonances and metaphorical illuminations of earlier songs, even the relatively deadpan, jazzy ones on *Court and Spark*. The voice has lost its bloom and the melodies hardly seek to transmute speech into lyricism, such refrains as survive being self-consciously bathetic ('He's a strange, strange boy'). Perhaps the songs epitomize a generation, but it's a cheat to imply that this freedom of 'the fine white lines of the freeway' is more honest, because more grim, than the flight of that aspiring seagull. It isn't the gull that is gulled.

Most of the songs in *Hejira* are about being on the road and in the title number Joni offers explanation and perhaps excuse:

I'm travelling in some vehicle
I'm sitting in some café
a defector from the petty wars
until love sucks me back that way.

Discounting lovers, she seeks self-reliance; yet in one number, 'Song for Sharon', she still admits to dichotomy. Travels between 'land and sky' mean little unless one has someone to share them with; on the other hand 'white lace wedding gown' romanticism is a deceit. Reminiscing to her old school friend Sharon, Joni confesses that she is balked of love because she doesn't know how to love herself. The dismal self-communing of this long song is alleviated when, in 'Blue motel room', she allows herself a measure of queasy irony, becoming a little girl again, but also a failed frail crooning a slip of a tune cushioned on jazzy, fortyish harmonies. This is the only number in which Joni makes even ephemeral contact with a man. She ends by leaving him with his 'pretty girls', she with her freedom down the highway.

The most convincing songs on this album are the nastiest, notably 'Black crow', a fast boogie number in which vocal gutturals and rancid electrophonics oppose the black crow she's become to the blue skies she had once hoped, like her white seagull, to soar through. In 'Coyote' she sees her travelling as escape from wolfmen who want to gobble her up. Flight down the highway paradoxically parallels sexual flight through the blue heavens, a fantasy admitted to in 'Song for Sharon'. In 'Amelia' she basically confesses:

Maybe I've never loved.
I guess that is the truth.

The same point is more movingly made in the best song in the cycle, 'Furry sings the blues', which describes Joni's trip to Memphis's famous Beale Street to meet the ancient bluesman Furry Lewis. Between grunts and growls, spiels and snatches of song, Furry rasped out 'Ah doan't laike yew' – and meant it, Joni opines. He had the right to mean it. Old and ill, on his last legs in the last ditch of a moribund world, he can still tell a tale and chirp a chune. Joni's elegy evokes 'such strong impression of your heyday', but there is little left of her day, hey or high. In indigence of body and spirit, Furry has his triumph, whereas Joni, 'rich and fey in my limo', is defeated. Her authenticity, unlike his, is suspect. The best lines on this disc are

We all come and go unknown,
each so deep and superficial,
between the forceps and the stone

which, though cleverer than it seems, is comfort as corny as it is cold.

Hejira is the nadir of Joni's post-psychotic disturbance. The next year's double album, *Don Juan's Reckless Daughter* (1977), shows signs of renewal, though the effect is weakend by the cycle's unjustified length. The sleeve suggests that, after her debunking of primitivism in the jungle songs in *The Hissing of Summer Lawns*, Joni is confronting head on the Black and Red stains on the American consciousness. She is depicted in the garb of a Black minstrel-show entertainer against a South Western landscape peopled by Black Afroamericans and Red Amerindians as well as straight American Whites. Verbal rhythms are still conversational, tunes seldom defined; vocal production is still bleak, presumably in keeping with Arizonan deserts. On the other hand verbal imagery is high-flown, with references to Jericho, Jesus and Judas, Hitler, Shakespeare, Raleigh and Columbus, tossed into hallucinatory landscapes of cotton fields, adobe houses, music- and tequila-filled streets, torrential rains and blistering sunlight.

The cycle climaxes in a dream of the Plains Indians – a snaking turquoise river, wind-swept mesas, the empty ashes of their desolate land – which are also the emptiness of Joni's heart. This long song, 'Paprika plains', embraces within its vision of aboriginal America a retrospect of Joni's small-town Canadian childhood. Like 'late' Dylan, she now senses Amerindian culture shallowly buried beneath the glossy surface of her American life. The number fascinates but does not entirely convince, since it degenerates into a long quasi-Indian Tex-Mex instrumental that is aboriginally piffling rather than basic. Wayne Shorter's fine postlude on soprano saxophone does much to redeem it, however, transporting aboriginal America into the modern city.

Joni Mitchell's delving into America's ancestral past is itself an attempt at redemption, for herself rather than the world at large. In the title song she talks to 'the split-tongued spirit of the ancient world, Mother Earth to Father sky'. We have to learn to accept the duality of the eagle of clarity and the serpent of blind desire. The motif is familiar in much twentieth-century art, including pop music, but Joni has won the right to 'renewed identity', since her 'restless multiplicity' reanimates 'good-old-God-Save-America, the home of the brave and free'.

This is why she can end the cycle with a song simply for her voice and acoustic guitar, the poem of which has the rhythmic subtlety and lyricism of her early years. In the first stanza Joni warns tender schoolgirls of the inconstancy of brutish men, yet advises them not to evade toil and danger. In the second stanza she regrets her hypersensitivity, since if she had seen through 'the silky veils of ardor' she would have locked up her heart in 'a golden sheath of armor.' But Joni now sees beyond the falsehood of her dreams. Flight down the highway is no less an illusion than flight with her heaven-seeking gull, or on the wings of the high life of fame. Though a 'poor wayfaring stranger', a White Amerindian without a home, Joni can again write touching verses in traditional folk vein:

I wish I had the wings
of Noah's pretty little white dove
I would fly the raging river
to reach the one I love

But I have no wings
and the water is so wide
we'll have to row a little harder
    It's just in dreams we fly!

Though fragmented, the melody to these words recalls the folk-like manner of Joni's early days. Now, as she rows rather than flies, the pulse is wearier, the vocal timbre more pallid, the mood bluesily autumnal rather than folksy spring-like. Even so, Joni's spirit, if not melodic line, survives. The white dove broodily returns, ousting the black crow, for you can't keep a good girl down — certainly not one blessed with genius as well as talent. Joni Mitchell's next disc suggests that the new direction latent in *Blue*, but submerged in her nervous disintegration, may reach fruition.

Perhaps the ethnic elements in *Don Juan's Reckless Daughter* — the Amerindian and Tex-Mex elements — encouraged her again to embrace the tensions of the big city, as incarnate in the ethnic world of jazz. On the 1979 album *Mingus* that reference becomes explicit, for the disc is a collaboration with the Black modern-jazz man Charlie Mingus, and became a memorial to him after his sudden death at the age of 56. All the verses are Joni's, but she wrote music for only two of the songs, the others being by Mingus himself. With one exception, all the songs are slow, moodily retrospective over lost loves and dead musicians. Yet the affiliation with the Black blues denies any lapse into enervating self-indulgence. The beat, however slow, never loses jazz's nervous resilence; the melodic phrases, however shattered, are emotive with the lyricism of the blues; the post-Ellingtonian harmony maintains momentum through the nocturnal elegiacs. This is not surprising when the instrumentalists include jazzmen of the calibre of Wayne Shorter, Herbie Hancock and Peter Erskine, not to mention Joni's vote of thanks to Eddie Gomez, Gerry Mulligan, John Mclaughlin and John Guerin for help in rehearsal!

The effect of this jazz liaison on Joni is remarkable. The poems have done with the mumbling mystifications of the previous few discs; they are tightly contructed and, in their sleazier way, are as poetically evocative as the lyricisms of her early youth. The refrains are haunting, and move us the more deeply because Joni is concerned with people other than herself. 'Goodbye pork pie hat' – an elegy for the tenor saxophonist Lester Young – wistfully celebrates the (partial) passing of racial prejudice: things have changed since Lester's day to the extent that it's unlikely that Joni and Charlie will be 'driven out of town or hung in a tree'. Here the rhythmic freedom, far from being lax in the manner of *Hejira*, is jazzily elastic: consider the treatment of the street-dancing children and the 'summer serenade of taxi horns and fun arcades', or the last stanza's caper of Black babies outside the bar. 'Sweet sucker dance' is especially memorable melodically; Joni's flexibilities of phrase manage to be both humorously compassionate and un- rather than dis-illusioned. Wit balances insouciance in the only quick number, 'The dry cleaner from de Moines' – a guy with a job that lacks sparkle, who compensates by making money on the pin-balls and one-armed bandits. Jaco Pastorious, now Joni's regular bass player, scored this fetching number with Basie-like precision, and seems to have had considerable influence on the album as a whole.

Throughout, Joni's singing is worthy of her poetry and of the instrumental playing. She has become a fine jazz singer, true to her White self even while reminding us now of an old-style Black 'mama' like Ma Thornton (consider her sultry tone on the words 'generation on generation' in 'Pork pie hat'), now, in middle register, of the sadly searing Billie Holiday, and now, in the upper reaches, of the vibratoless waif voice of Blossom Dearie. Some such mating of innocence and experience was just what was needed if Joni were to escape escapism, whether in dream or despair.

These comments refer only to Joni's verses and to her singing, since we have seen that for the music of these four numbers she turned to another creator, as she had earlier had resort to Annie Ross and Jon Hendricks. But the two completely original songs on *Mingus* suggest that her own song-writing may move in a similar direction. 'God must be a boogie man', though more fragmented than the Mingus-composed numbers, is no less blue in spirit, the disintegration being ballasted by the wit that, in the refrain, is musical as well as verbal. 'The wolf that lives in Lindsey' — surely the best song Joni has composed for years — concerns the baddies of today's mechanized society (the tycoon wolf, the murderer, the slanderer) in relation to 'derelicts and ladies of the night'. Unlike the anti-society songs on *The Hissing of Summer Lawns* it doesn't preach, but allows the wayward lyricism of the melody to pay homage to 'the inner laws of spirit' as opposed to the fallible laws of man. The refrain — 'The stab and glare and buckshot of the heavy heavy snow, it comes and goes' — sung with the subtlest variations of timbre and nuance, carries an explosive emotional charge. It sounds as inevitable as the eternal snow: the weeping *of* us and nature, *for* nature and other people. This means that the real wolves who bay as aural background are no mere elec-trophonic gimmick: they howl what the human music wails. Joni's vocal quality is halfway between her early folk lyricism (her tremor on the word 'heavy', and the suddenly white-toned lift on the words 'snow' and 'go') and the blue intensity she's developed for this disc (her sepulchral evocation of the wolf in the last stanza).

Though this album is exploratory rather than consummatory, its 'difficulty' is the consequence of real tensions, not of self-regarding defeatism. Mingus wanted to make music for Joni's poems; she learned from him, as composer, in singing them. 'Next time', she sang in 'A chair in the sky',

I'll be bigger!
I'll be better than ever!
I'll be resurrected royal!
I'll be Standard Oil!

After a three years' silence she has come near, in *Wild things Run Fast* (1982), to fulfilling this prognostication. This album takes off from the jazz orientation of *Mingus*, but relates it to her own idiom as exemplified in *Blue* and *Court and Spark*. Although these love songs are disturbed rather than happy, they balance between weariness and spryness. Such an evolution is endemic in growing older. On the brink of 40, having experienced illusion and disillusion, Joni cannot expect to revive the ecstasy of her adolescent seagull; she does well to create this tenuous lyricism out of fragmentation. The tunes are not all intrinsically memorable, though all are intermittently moving, and it's interesting that the most lyrical moments spring from her variety of *spoken* inflexion. Whereas in *Hejira* speech degenerated to a mumble, here it soars and sings, opening horizons over the shifty sands of love's deceptions and desperations.

This happens even in the first number, 'Chinese café', which is specifically about growing middle-aged, admitting that 'we were wild in the old days'. 'Nothing lasts for long', runs the refrain; yet memories of love surface from time's impervious flood. The break into speech on 'I need your love' oddly becomes climax to the song's lyrical yearning, balancing the melisma on the word 'wild'. The vocal line parallels the flickering of Steve Lukather's electric guitar and Larry Williams's Prophet synthesizer. The tight rhythms and wiry sonority are close to those of the *Mingus* album though the mood is less bleak; the harmony acquires a scrunchy vigour through its piling up of thirds. A comparable tautness characterizes 'Wild things run fast' and 'Ladies man', two perkier numbers which display contempt for uncaring man as distinct from caring woman, while at the same time longing (not lusting) for the delights love can offer. That 'wild things' happen in bad dreams is manifest in the nervous agility of the music, in the near-spoken rhythm of the words and in their varied coloration. Listening to these songs one understands why 'poetry and jazz' became a distinctive medium, springing from the immediate texture of living.

'You're so square' appropriately uses square rock rhythms and harmonic clichés to represent the guy's conventionality, yet Joni's response to him is both flip and caring. She pipes 'I don't care' because, *although* caring, she won't be subservient. In 'Underneath the streetlight', bouncing in Latin-American rhythm, she creates through her bubbly vocal production a nocturnal street scene that, despite its mechanization, succours a simple-hearted love. Scene and emotion are identified, as they are in the songs of Rickie Lee Jones.[10] One recalls Rickie Lee in the finest, jazziest and most ambivalent songs on the album, all three of which feature Wayne Shorter on soprano saxophone. The dialogue between his whimpering horn and Joni's voice reveals depths in the metaphorically rich and rhymically sensitive verses. 'Moon at the window', a song of loss, tells us in its refrain that the thieves at least left behind the moon at the window – which musically becomes a reminder of love's potential. Joni's melismata on the words 'care', 'hope and despair' and 'fear' are deeply touching, and Wayne Shorter's echoes relate the experience to us as well as Joni.

'Be cool', an apparently slighter song, is about the evasion of hurt:

> you're a fool
> if you can't keep cool,
> charm 'em,
> don't alarm 'em.

The rhymes and half-rhymes are comic, yet the musical resonance of Joni's 'cools' and 'fools' makes for pathos, telling us that she knows that evasion conceals distress. In the last stanza her tense vulnerability again suggests Blossom Dearie. The childhood theme becomes overt in the final song 'Love', which weaves variations on St Paul's words in 1 Corinthians 13: true love

> . . . sees like a child sees. As a child I spoke as a child, I thought and I understood as a child, but when I became a woman I put away childish things and began to see through a glass darkly . . .
> Fractions in me of faith and hope and love
> and of these great three Love's the greatest.

The love Joni speaks of is not St Paul's, nor does it imply a Dylan-style conversion. Yet the mystery of this most beautiful song does involve a spiritual dimension, so there may be some (affinity) between the evolution of the finest woman folk–pop–jazz singer and the finest male exponent of the genre. Dylan discovered through his Gospel message that unless we become as little children we cannot enter the Kingdom of Heaven. Joni returns, in her fortieth year, to the celebration of the childhood she'd effected in her earliest songs,

10   See p. 216–28.

with the difference that she no longer needs recourse to nostalgia. The song she calls 'Love' entails, in a manner more intimate than Dylan's, its own New Birth.

In 1985, after a gap of another three years – she can now take her time – Joni Mitchell has produced another disc, bleakly entitled *Dog Eats Dog*. This is a logical evolution from *Wild Things Run Fast*, in the same toughly urban jazz–rock idiom. Of the ten numbers only the first and last – and possibly the penultimate – are 'personal'. The others deal dispassionately with the criminal imbecilities among which we live, but evade preachiness precisely because they play down personal involvement. One could put it another way by saying that the verses convince, inducing passion and compassion out of dis-passion, because of their exceptional intelligence. Joni's analysis of the 'fictions' the media encourage us to batten on; her dismissal of ('taxfree') sanctimonious evangelists who are merely tycoons in skunks' clothing; her sharply astute citation of 'artifice, brutality *and innocence*' as the 'three great stimulants' through which we hope to escape the horror deduced from our phoney social and political values – all these are so live on the mark that they surprise and enliven in the same way as (if they aren't quite) poetry. Routine wailing about the ills of capitalist society becomes illumination when Joni tells us that we live in 'a land of snap decisions/Land of short attention spans/Nothing is savoured/Long enough to really understand'. A song about flash girls and boys who love their Porsches and other 'shiny toys' reveals the pathos within their vacuity: the more so because the song is juxtaposed with a straight number about Ethiopia considered not merely or mainly as military and political massacre but as a despoilation of the earth. Here the hauntingly 'ethnic' stylization is musically more rewarding than the chippy jazz–rock so far referred to, though that is precisely appropriate to its impersonally social function.

The essence of this disc is that, however bleak, it is honest: so it is not surprising that the first number, 'Good friends', which says what is to be said for personal relationships, sets its sights low. Joni whispers and whimpers, occasionally shouts that it's a matter of walking on eggshells; we can't expect to find 'hearts of gold or nerves of steel'; we must 'accept no blame for what we can and cannot feel', much less control. Yet if we must be satisfied with small mercies, those mercies are audible in the song which, without sustained lyrical tune or compulsive rhythm, carries us along, generating modest well-being. This links up with the penultimate song, 'Impossible dreamer', which envisages, in our dark, shark-infested society, a dreamer who might irradiate reality like the bright moon in a black night, or even like the clear day. The lyricism fails to soar, for the dreamer is, after all, 'impossible'. Even so, he makes feasible the last song: in which Joni, calling herself 'Lucky girl', seems at last to be such. The song is about a real man 'at the rainbow's end' (her varied timbre and inflexion on the rainbow are deeply touching). He proves stronger than the 'wise guys and shy guys and sly lover boys with big bad bedroom eyes' whom she'd never trusted 'as far as I could pitch my shoe'. The insouciance of the metaphor makes a point, and the rhythm remains nervy, the sonority hard and sharp. Yet there is a bouncily resilient tune, which Joni now *sings*, perkily and happily, if without obvious emotional involvement. Moreover, as in *Wild Things* she is again ballasted by a superbly taut tenor saxophone solo from Wayne Shorter — who had more tentatively appeared in that previously 'impossible' dreamer. The re-creative power of the jazz experience seems again relevant; though the voice's tenderly whispered final cadential fall and the saxophone's broken fade-out remind us that what's to come is still unsure. This is an impressive enough climax to so remorselessly intelligent and unhoodwinked an album. Perhaps Joni's forty odd years, as well as her innate abilities, have been needed in order to arrive at it.

Chapter Nine

THE MIDNIGHT BABY AND THE HOLLYWOODEN DREAM: DORY PREVIN

Dat little man he say woman
can't have as much rights as man
'cause Christ wasn't a woman.
What did your Christ come from? Whar?
From God and a woman.
Man had nothing to do with him.

Carl Sandburg

We're children of coincidence and Harpo Marx.

Dory Previn

The evolution of Joni Mitchell's songs is the story of her life. She began as a modern, because highly subjective, type of folk singer whose words and music gave a personal slant to folk themes; she became obsessed with her perplexities; sought a way out through a return to America's roots. There is a parallel with the evolution of Bob Dylan, though whereas he unearthed Red Amerindian prehistory unconsciously, her rediscovery was conscious, and perhaps for that reason less convincing. For both, however, the fusion of White with Black wellsprings was basic. It is evident throughout Dylan's career and was germane to *Blue*, the turning point in Joni Mitchell's development. Partially submerged during her 'post-psychotic' phase, Black jazz has surfaced again in Joni's recent work, leaving her poised on a question mark.

Dory Previn, who like Joni writes all her own words and music, has also used her art as personal therapy and has done so more fanatically. This brings both advantages — she is very clever, aware of what she's doing — and disadvantages — being more obsessive, she is less open to experience and to growth and change. She states her case, and it moves and amuses us. Her art doesn't, however, develop from one album to the next; one might even say that her most recent disc is the least satisfying and that *Mythical Kings and Iguanas*, the 1971 album that made her famous, remains her definitive statement.

Something of a child prodigy, Dory Previn has created words and music that, even more than Joni Mitchell's, are rooted in (mostly painful) childhood experience. In her autobiography[1] Dory reveals that she was born on the stroke of midnight, and accepts the superstition that such babies go through life divided, unsure whether they want to go back to the day before or forward to the day after. She wrote her book out of a schizophrenic division of herself into woman and child: the child demanded that her story be told, and the woman agreed, knowing that she needed to extricate herself from the child's grip. The book, told in the child's voice since it is 'her say', shows a childlike freshness of imagination, as well as a precocious fascination with words relevant to her adult verses. She jokily points out that her initials, D.V.L., need only an E and an I to spell devil, and that Heaven/Hell, Eternity, Limbo, Purgatory spell help. The child Dory's sense of humour has a clownish quality prophetic of the adult poet: at her confirmation, she feels guilty about her fascination with Jesus's loins, disgusted with the priest's fingertip, wet from the neighbouring confirmant's saliva. Visiting her father in a mental hospital she was more concerned about the possibility of cutting her windpipe open on a lifesaver than with waving to him.

Dory's mad father dominated her childhood, the more so since her mother had been driven to drink. It took eighteen years for the fury and agony of those scars to erupt when Dory, sitting in a plane about to take off for London, heard a woman screaming. Only when air-borne did she realize that the woman was herself. Such detachment is the secret of her art, saving her from the confessional

---

1   *Midnight Baby*, London, Hamish Hamilton, 1977.

perils that Joni Mitchell cannot always circumnavigate, yet also limiting her scope. Nearly though not quite all her verses mingle pathos with mockery and so safeguard her from indulgence – and protect her from her mental instability. The music almost, though again not quite, always involves satire and a basic paradox: whereas the words react against a Hollywooden life-style, the music parodies obsolete commercial genres of the twenties, thirties and forties – the era through which her parents lived but didn't flourish. The tunes are usually plain diatonic rather than modal; rhythms are square; modulations have the conventional sophistications of her prototypes. Even so, she created from cliché a unique language, partly because she uses the corny conventions brilliantly on their own terms, partly because she modifies them through texture and timbre.

Mythical Kings and Iguanas had been preceded by a 1969 disc with the pertinent title of *On My Way to Where*. This didn't make a decisive impact and perhaps didn't deserve to; it none the less formulates Dory's essential themes and the techniques appropriate to them. 'Scared to be alone' is about loneliness and fear, and already turns on the disparity between 'real' life within the heart and the plastic deceits of the Hollywooden Dream. Basically, this is a countrified music with a gentle lilt, but with satirical refrains in the manner of forties and thirties dance-band music. 'Veterans' big parade' also anticipates later songs in trite military idiom: the self-confident White American march becomes clownishly pathetic. 'Beware of young girls' evokes adolescence in illusory lyricism: a mode Dory is more bitterly to explore in later, more autobiographical songs. 'With my daddy in the attic', though not musically distinguished, also anticipates a later obsession.

Although this album is enjoyable, it hardly prepares us for the maturity of *Mythical Kings and Iguanas*. The title song defines Dory's basic theme at its deepest level. The verses are beautifully composed and, like the best of Dylan, read well as poems while suggesting that their verbal felicities are of the kind that can find consummation only in song. The theme is the sundered wholeness of human experience. We are heirs to the post-Renaissance civilization that has severed Orpheus's head from his body: intellect, soul, spirit, aspiring up, are considered 'good', whereas the body and 'subconscious' feeling, delving down, are 'bad'. Much twentieth-century art, at all levels, has been an intuitive protest against this separation of Ariel from Caliban. Dory, on the crest of

Women's Lib, presents the theme with touching lucidity. She has been flying

> . . . on bent and battered wings
> in search of mythical kings,
> sure that everything of worth
> is in the sky and not the earth.

'Singing scraps of angel song' she has accepted that 'high is right and low is wrong'. Now she is rejecting

> . . . mystical things
> That cry for the soul but will not face
> the body as an equal place

and she sings to the iguanas in their lowly mud, symbols of the pre-human who, assisting her rebirth *ab ovo*, may help her to 'touch for real'.

Musically, this artfulness is artfully achieved. The instrumental prelude creates a dreamily arpeggiated texture, like a surreal country music, from piano and electric guitars. Dory's voice is folk-like in lacking vibrato, yet velvety and more mellow than the 'embryonic' timbres of Joni Mitchell in her early numbers. The tune that emerges through the dream-like accompaniment mostly moves by step, yet its simplicity is compromised by the fact that its caressing contours are effected, in a manner alien to real folk music, by its harmonization. In the middle section the disembodied modulations that reflect Dory's tinkering with Tarot and I Ching are both comic and scary, as are the iguana gollopings at the end. Characteristically, Dory walks a tightrope between passionate commitment and ironic detachment. Her voice is childlike yet voluptuous; her melody lyrically enchanting, yet diatonic rather than modal; her harmonies and modulations, though sophisticated, are direct in relationship to the words. Similarly she uses technology's electrophonic resources to remind us of values that are technocracy's denial. Her appeal to the iguanas to 'teach' her how to feel the inchoate things they feel again synthesizes pathos and wit.

This preludial song is a general statement of the theme. It is succeeded by numbers that deal with particular, usually personal, instances of our failure of nerve and sensibility. 'Yada yada la scala', is a raggily satirical song about our substitution of talk – the yapping of disconnected minds – for feeling. The twentyish idiom is banal, as is appropriate, though unconventional modulations reflect the lovers' insecurity. Verbal rhyme and musical hiatus are alertly exploited:

> We sit at a restuarant table
> discussing reasons we're not able
> to commit;
> that's not it.

The final stanza dismisses the

> . . . chipmunks' chatter
> and we go mad as a hatter
> and nothing at all gets said.
> Talk to me please in bed
> where it matters.

The 'yada yada' postlude suggests that this appeal to the iguana in her lover won't have much effect. The satire is bitter, though still insouciant. In satirical numbers Dory often has the edge over Joni in that her verses, debunking social pretence, are very funny whereas Joni's descend to peevishness.

What Dory called her 'funny sense of humour' may, however, be disturbing, as in 'Lady with the braid'. The girl – and this is a confessional song whether or not we identify the woman with the poet–composer – invites a man to 'stay till sunrise' because 'going home is such a long and lonely ride'. She really wants him to stay to save *her* life, since 'the night cuts through me like a knife'. Her terror is revealed by way of bare description of objects in her apartment, desperately used to bolster insecurity:

> I papered that wall myself.
> When you leave
> will you come back?
> You don't have to answer that at all . . .
> The bathrom door is just across the hall.

Musically, both tune and accompaniment are countryish, moderate paced, with a wistful arch through a fourth that then limply declines. The near inanity of the rocking tune and rhythm carry a burden of heartbreak; trite musical conventions are imbued, by response to particular words and phrases, with disturbing reality.

Another confessional song is 'Lemon haired ladies', about a woman with a lover younger than herself. It is difficult to resist the suspicion that he is André Previn and that one lemon-haired lady is

Mia Farrow, and although Dory says that she will eschew self-pity and accept him for what he is, that is patently what she is not doing. The music is a corny diatonic waltz, rendered painful, after a deadpan start, by the intensity of Dory's vocal production. The middle section's modulations express the man's physical and moral vagrancy yet also prepare us for the shilly-shallying within the woman herself as she orders her faithless lover to take himself off, only in the next breath to appeal for his return. The declining scale of the refrain leaves no hope for the woman, in face of the yellow-haired hussies; yet its very simplicity, in its waltzing lilt, carries an irony. Dory's final recognition that she is supposed to be, but isn't, wiser than he results from her detached observation of herself. She can thus take failure as Joni Mitchell, in her *Hejira* phase, couldn't.

'Angels and devils', also confessional, is not exactly about failure, though it is perplexed. It opposes two lovers, an artist and a truck driver, and two kinds of truth. Bodily bruises from the tough guy weigh lightly against the psychological hurts occasioned by the sensitive artist, but while the husky voice at the end convinces us that 'love on the floor was fun', the brash, metrically rigid diatonic tune tells us that the dichotomy between Art and Entertainment isn't as simple as that! The muddy iguanas whispered of more than a brutish fuck.

'Her mother's daughter' could be a story song about any girl dominated and destroyed by a vampire mother, but is probably autobiographical also, being the first of many (often vitriolic) anti-parent songs. Even here the bland tune that evokes the 'sweet and genteel lady' grows rancorous in the middle section that deals with time's oblivious fleeting. The end juxtaposes rhythmically aggressive hate for the mother with tonal insubstantiality as the woman

> . . . listens in on other's people's joys
> and looks longingly at all the passing young boys.

An abrupt mediant shift yanks her back to the pretence which is all she has left to live with:

> Yes, of course I love you, Mother,
> I'll never leave you, dear.

Another story song – the more impressive because detached from Dory herself – is 'A stone for Bessie Smith', a threnody for Janis

Joplin who died in Hollywood in 1970. A 'smashed woman' on
drink and drugs, Janis was a jazz–soul singer who, having bought a
stone in memory of Bessie Smith, had no money left to bury herself.
Though Dory is more 'civilized' than Janis or Bessie her tribute to
their veracity is heartfelt. For this powerful song she calls on a
bluesy voice and blue-inflected melody and harmony. We respond to
its truth against the façade of the Hollywooden Dream.

   This is patent when we listen to 'Mary C. Brown and the
Hollywood sign', the key song on the B-side of the disc. It's about
the celluloid world we've made in our forgetfulness of iguanas: a
Miss Average Starlet, having failed to make it, kills herself by
leaping off the immense Hollywood sign that glares over Beverly
Hills. The verses are casual, almost facetious, in their account of
Mary C. Brown's trip on a Malibu bus and the plunge, 'with the
smallest possible fuss', from the fatal letter. Dory says that her
dream, also facetious if bitter, is to hang herself from the second or
third letter O. Not even the Statue of Liberty has welcomed more
refugees than Hollywood, that haven for outcasts – starlets,
carhops, midgets, chimps, chumps, freaks, whores, flunkies,
junkies. The refrain becomes a lament for and a celebration of them.
Though the musical idiom cannot be the real Black jazz of 'A stone
for Bessie Smith', the tune, within the commercialized conventions
of Hollywood, haunts us insidiously. Dory's voice sounds like a
child who is as old as the pre-Hollywooden hills. In the refrain
saxophones wail in thirtyish dance-band chromatics, against the
deadpan inexpressivity of the narrative sections.

   Although the song hovers between farce and pathos, there is
nothing funny about the girl's fate – or for that matter about what is
happening to Dory and us, in our plastic cocoon. And the last song
of the cycle accepts fakery as our lot, equating our lives with a game
of chance in which all the dice are loaded. The instrumental ostinati
in 'The game' emulate the gyration of the roulette wheel, on which
we ride willy-nilly. The melody winds on top, drawing us into its
stepwise convolutions; Dory's voice is paradoxically both bleak and
voluptuous. As the music swings into the minor the scene – with
tinnily guffawing croupier, jovially cheated 'sport', neon lights and
gilded walls – is vividly presented. A stomping middle section
parallels this trumpery trickery with Pilate's soldiers gambling at
the foot of Christ's Cross, though the clatter of honky-tonk piano
forbids escape from the low dive in twentieth-century California.
The end is powerful, if melodramatic. Although Dory knows the

game is fixed, she submits to the dealer's 'taunting, toothless grin' and, after a ferocious, unaccompanied 'God damn it', orders him to 'deal me in'. Unless we opt out like Mary C. Brown, we have little choice in the matter. Dory's voice is searing, yet also tremulous.

This grim song is not quite the end of the cycle, for it merges into what begins as a *da capo* of the first song, 'Mythical kings and iguanas'. 'Hollywood' seems to have rendered the antediluvian creatures obsolete – though the irony is more complex than that, since after its initial statement the 'mythical kings' tune is combined with the 'going home' motif from 'The lady with the braid'. Whereas in that song going home had been a 'long and lonely road', yoked to a plea for compassion, here it turns into a communally choric refrain in gospel style, growing progressively louder. There's a further irony in this, if we think of the vocal backing in terms of the angelic choruses of old-time Hollywood movies. Musically, however, the gospel song's exuberance, being positive, leaves the possibility of iguana-like rebirth open. Old-fashioned Evangelical enthusiasm merges into showbiz euphoria: an equivocation apposite to this ingenious, moving sequence of songs, each of which is an entity in itelf, while contributing to a whole.

With the exception of the title song the numbers in *Mythical Kings and Iguanas* have not the musical inspiration of the best songs of Joni Mitchell. Whereas Joni creates her idiom empirically, Dory *exploits* conventions from a ragbag of pop musics current in her childhood, usually for satirical ends. Joni is inclined to hit or miss; Dory polishes nails before hitting them squarely on the head. Nail-bashing is dominant in the next album, *Reflections in a Mud Puddle*, the B-side of which is a 13 minute sequence in which Dory attempts to exorcize ghosts. Cunningly using a technique of time-travelling, 'Taps, tremors and time steps (one last dance for my father)' interweaves a 1971 telephone call from her sister in Los Angeles, reporting her father's death in an earthquake, with memories of childhood and adolescence.

The first section, over country guitar arpeggios, recounts the death in diatonic narrative, apparently uninvolved, but grows fraught when narration merges into memories of Dad playing the jew's harp until he broke a tooth. In a flashback, Dad's world takes over as Dory recalls watching, with him, the final 1937 flight of the Zeppelin *Hindenburg*. Dad's thirties dance-band music is parodied by wah-wah- saxophones, yet parody doesn't preclude emotion. The cliché-ridden tune is oddly affecting, springing from Dory's

ambivalent attitude to her lunatic parent, who fosters her dream of
flying ('it's the safest way') yet deceives her with broken promises,
scares her with his 'terrible eye'. The childhood retrospect incorporates a separate song about Dory herself, who 'danced and smiled'
to please her father, to make her mother proud, 'to gain some small
attention'. This, naturally enough, is in Dory's own idiom, in so far
as she has one: a moderate rocking beat, an arching, sighful tune,
jazzy, fortyish harmony. This song of introversion fades back into
the childhood memory of disaster, and that into a recapitulation of
the original telephone call from California.

   So the piece is structured around Dory's introspection, in mirror
formation:

A   narration in the present moment
B   lyrical retrospection on a childhood past
C   introversion in past and present simultaneously
B   lyrical retrospection, intensified
A   narration is the present moment, ending in silence, after
    the ironically spoken words 'God is kind.'

The centrepiece in both past and present begins with a pun in the
form of a quotation from the *Los Angeles Times*: 'After an initial deep
split the tremors can go on indefinitely.' So Dory links the
earthquake to her relationship with her father, and perhaps to
breakdown in her divided self. When she sings 'If I could love me
more I could love you less' she is belatedly on the way to
self-knowledge. This is paradoxically dependent on the variety of
musical styles; yet so deep is the interlacing of past and present that
throughout the parodies the same tune is employed until the
consummatory third song. Considering that its musical materials
are synthetic, the sequence has remarkable power. Dory's art hits
back at the Plastic Age she was born into and ambivalently
celebrates.

   The separate songs on the other side of the disc are related to the
same theme. 'The new enzyme detergent demise of ali macgraw' is
about a woman with a 'handy disposable heart that marks time in a
plastic breast'. Though her friends were 'fooled by the fact that I
still breathed and I spoke', it was 'an imitation life-disguise kit, I
sent away for it'. Nobody cottoned on to the fact that she was
'non-biodegradable'. The wit of the words combines with the
cumulative repetitions and odd ellipses in the music to send up the

Hollywooden prototype. Something similar happens in a sombre rather than cynical permutation of this *alter ego* motif. 'Doppelgänger' is the dark stranger who 'hides inside the shadows watching children in the park', who was 'in the crowd at Dallas', who was 'hanging out with soldiers trading heroin for pot, and he was smiling, smiling'. Here the technique is narrative, though the repeated notes build up lyrically as Dory identifies the enemy as within herself. The obscene writing on the wall is in her own hand. We are all responsible for the world we live in.

In most of these songs music is merely supportive of words. In 'The altruist and the needy man' the two elements are more closely knit. It's about a Modern Man who has 'a passion for ecology, compassion for minorities', but is incapable of an individual act of love: 'he can love the whole damned human race, oh then why is he so afraid to be in love with me?' In this case Dory imbues a familiar moderate-gaited country convention with surprise through the music's response to particular words – for instance the harmonic shift on 'collective guilt' or 'could ever be alone'.

More mysterious is the final number, 'Play it again sam', a bit of nostalgia for the good old days of World War II when goodies were goodies and baddies baddies, and hearts were as brave as love was true. The mystery lies in the fact that the music appears to be merely a revocation of a forties pop song, and the ironic reversals of the words –

. . . a war
proud as trumpet horns
but a rose by any other name still has thorns

– don't obviously communicate themselves to the music. It seems that the tune is so good within its moribund genre that we accept retrospection as re-creation. The song, affecting as well as amusing, sets the scene for the remade autobiography on the disc's other side. Sam must be a crony of Dad's, if not Dad himself.

The album Dory produced in 1972, though not better than the two previous discs, is in no way regressive. Called *Mary C. Brown and the Hollywood Sign*, it takes that song from *Mythical Kings* as jumping-off ground. One of the themes of that number had been contrast between the illusion and disillusion of the Hollywooden Dream and the stark veracity of

your poor, your maladjusted,
your sick and your beat,
your sad and your busted,
Your has-beens, your twisted,
your loners, your losers,
your black-listed.

The most searching songs on the new album deal with these
outcasts, with whom Dory, crippled by her childhood history,
aligns herself. 'Cully Surroga' is a youth literally blinded by his
mother's suffocating care. The narrative is told in folksy country
style, representing Ma's cosiness, while the boy's inane OKs are in
mindless rock idiom. Again, though the musical material is corny
per se, it acquires poignancy through Dory's response to particular
phrases: the babyish whine on 'mother's son', or the weird
modulation when 'the day went dim' as Cully, urged on by Mum,
stared at the sun in the hope of absorbing its vital rays.

Verbally brilliant is 'The midget's lament', an appeal that we
shouldn't dismiss even midgets generically –

. . . I mean
y'seen one midget
y'seen them all,
Oh yeah midget,
Oh yeah small

– but should recognize that there are

skinny midgets, fat midgets,
gay midgets, flat midgets,
even midgets in deep despair.

Sure they're cute
and they're a lot of fun
but would you want your sister
to marry one?

Again it is difficult to say why the ragtimey tune proves so
irresistible since it conforms, as Joni Mitchell's tunes never do, to
an obsolete pop pattern. As with 'Play it again Sam', the pattern
must be one in which good tunes may still be composed. The wit of
the words gives an ironic gloss to music that is lyrically positive
enough to temper merriment with compassion. The middle section
admits to an inner agitation, while the coda, in which the midget

yearns to be Black and therefore a minority within a minority, is at once ludicrous and heart-breaking.

Some relatively slight songs debunk Hollywooden dreams. 'Starlet, starlet, on the screen, who will follow Norma Jean?' refers to the rivalry between youth and age in the fairy-tale: mirror, mirror on the wall, who is the fairest one of all? The music is briskly raggy in dealing with the savage words, which concern various types of prostitution. 'King Kong', an equally jolly but fierce rock number, is also savage in total effect because it takes the side of Hollywood's mythic monster against civilization, turning him into one of Dory's outcasts:

> Once I roamed a handsome thing
> in my Natural place
> here I am repulsive
> 'cause I'm different from your race.
> But who decides who's ugly?
> Who decides who's right?
> I tell you in my jungle
> you would be a sorry sight.

More musically rewarding are two more intimate songs dealing with the paradoxes of our culture, an anti-man song, 'When a woman wants a man', being balanced by a number, 'Don't put him down', that mocks man while taking pity on his insecurity. Both these numbers eschew Dory's parodistic techniques in favour of a straight jazz idiom. The two stanzas of 'When a man wants a woman' contrast the social and psychological consequences of a man's desire for a woman with what happens when the process is reversed. Though the stanzas are set to the same music, Dory's performance transforms it. She proves herself a fine jazz singer, of an earlier vintage than Joni Mitchell on *Mingus*. Her voice is sultry as she tells us that a man's wanting a woman is construed as a compliment. The melody arches up to express yearning, balancing its sustained opening phrase with short antithetical phrases that prick the bubbles of pretence without destroying lyricism. Although her voice is accompanied only by guitar, the Ellingtonian ripeness of the harmony, pinpointing the crests of the melody, has a quasi-orchestral luxuriance. In the second stanza the same antitheses demostrate how when a woman wants a man she is accused of threatening, trapping and chaining him. Dory's darker timbre makes the music more bitter, but more rather than less erotic. The sheer musical quality of this song lifts it beyond the category of a feminist number dedicated to a cause; we simply find ourselves assenting to its truth – as we do with the companion piece, 'Don't put him down', the title of which is a bawdy pun. The number is basically comic (a girl ought to commiserate with a guy since *she* doesn't have to 'get herself up on cue like a performing seal, in a zoo'), but is also aware of fear-ful pain. The fast middle section is a frantic honky-tonk that doesn't obliterate the lyricism of the love-seeking verses.

The two most crucial songs on the album once more relate these themes to Dory's own childhood. 'The holy man on the Malibu bus no. 3' is a mythic–narrative number about a holy man who blessed Dory, age 2, for being 'different, a child destined for pain'. She's looked for him ever since, unavailingly – until she comes to identify him with her own and everybody's search *for* identity:

Would you laugh if I should mention
Sometimes I think he was me.

The song is in Dory's moderate-paced country style, diatonic rather than modal, but insecure, because unexpectedly rapid, in harmonic movement. She remembers the holy man identifying 'normal', right-thinking social behaviour with right-handedness, and linking mystical and 'subconscious' illumination with the left-handedness that is her own lot. She makes a song, 'Left hand lost', in one sense to confirm and in another sense to repudiate the superstition current until the early years of the century:

Right is the angel's side,
Left is you-know-what's.

In her autobiography Dory recalls her mother's refusal to pass a teacup with her left hand and tells us that she had a mysterious – in the strict sense sinister – uncle with a withered left arm. Though her right hand 'fills the china teacups and needlepoints with old maid aunts', it 'never painted a picture nor run for president'

This version of the *alter ego* theme gives Dory's parodistic bent a new outlet. A plainchant-like modal incantation represents her left-handed alienated Self, sounding weird as, in the context of the streamlined Nashville waltz that represents her right-handed social being, it is. Yet neither left nor right hand is what it seems. The plainsong-like theme sounds forlorn, rather than undivided in its wholeness, as was real plainsong, while the country waltz is compromised by harmonic sophistications. The quick, raggy middle pays tribute to the right hand's mundane triumphs, but the song ends with the left hand's reassertion, in a rock music fiercely honest but unfulfilled.

Dory as Outsider is thus affiliated with the midgets, chimps, starlets and junkies she pays homage to in other songs. The theme returns in the two final songs, sung without break. 'Jesus was an androgyne' presents him as man–woman, pagan–priest, beauty–beast, yet also god; 'Anima/animus' then relates this androgynous state to the beauties and beasts, the freaks and dropouts she's previously sung of, as well as to all mothers and fathers, sons and daughters who are freakish in being tied in human relationships! Concerned with truth in the Hollywood world of pretence, she habitually asks questions about identity, using 'artificial' (technically sophisticated) means for instinctive ends. Her eclecticism bears on this. We can recognize a Joni Mitchell song through its intrinsic musical and poetic qualities and she has told us that she writes music more easily than words. We can recognize a Dory Previn song not so much through its usually borrowed musical idiom as through its witty and/or touching verses, which come first. If her simplicity promotes the countrified aspects of her style, her country manners are not a folk utterance but are those of the country-music industry which, through Dory, acquires light to illuminate darkness. Similarly her nostalgic revocations of twenties dance-band and thirties and forties ballads reveal the hopeful heart beneath hedonism and escape. In physical appearance Dory, with her golliwog mop, immense round spectacles and long, loose-limbed body, resembles a clown. Her songs pun, like a clown, on appearance and reality.

In the 1974 album, called simply *Dory Previn*, there is no extension of range and a less clearly defined interrelationship of parts to whole; a few numbers, however, explore their by now established types with greater complexity. 'Coldwater canyon' and 'Atlantis' are complimentary man–woman songs, one comic, the other pathetic. The former is a story song about a would-be seducer who takes a girl to his little place in the canyon, where he had

> a bed that was covered with tiger skin
> it was a non-ecological scene
> and she felt so scared
> 'cause its teeth were bared
> and its smile was righteously mean.

What seems like description proves to be sharp social and
psychological criticism. The jokes are so good and the boogie
rhythm so infectious that we accept the song as high comedy
though it ends with the girl running wild, 'like a paranoid child',
into the empty night. The coda stanza is far from comic:

> coldwater canyon,
> you got no grace
> if you got no place
> to be alone.

That was not what the smart guy meant by inviting the girl to his
weekend retreat. What is remarkable is that Dory can imbue such
clownish music with the implicitly religious 'grace' she refers to in
the final stanza. Her melisma on the last 'alone' induces a laugh on
the brink of tears.

In 'Atlantis' Dory lies in bed with her man, dreaming of paradise
lost. The manner is that of a folk ballad, with a flowing tune over
guitar arpeggios. Mostly, she is seeing through the pretences of
mankind as opposed to womankind; the occasional pinprick –

> I've learned his body's
> line and length
> and memorized his grin

– promotes musical as well as verbal surprise. Watching him sleep
and dream, she envisages a celestial Atlantis 'Off the Spanish coast'.
Folksy lyricism is animated by exotic tango and habanera rhythms,
and sonorities are string-enriched, for Hollywooden dreams call for
Hollywooden resources. Yet it's no mere opposition of phoney
dream to glum reality, for the Hollywood music is lovely, the
dreams not merely a sham. Such might be the potential of sexual
love. That for Dory it hasn't been and probably won't be, makes her
blue notes on 'his lies' and her wails on 'the region of his dreams' the
more affecting. The wails float *upwards*, in piteous hope. Only the
extended moan at the end, after his threefold asseveration that he'll
never leave her, sounds final. We cannot say that this song is
disillusioned since its illusions, however undermined, remain
potent.

The two best songs on this disc are the funniest. In 'The obscene
telephone call' Dory has received one. She complains about this
plastic-age threat to her identity and truth, ringing up a series of
Authorities, each more august than the last, each reluctant to do

anything except pass the buck. Having assayed the PED, the FBI, and the CIA, she gets on to GOD, telling him that

> I've tried them all
> tried the big and small
> I called the whole inoperative lot.

God brings the wheel full circle, saying he's 'inclined to find this call obscene', and disconnects her, or is himself disconnected. (By Whom?) The music for this clever joke is unashamedly jolly, casual rather than causal. That it seems heartlessly commercial is the point, for the im-personality of bureaucracy and technocracy is the reason for Dory's divine disconnection. Again Dory demonstrates that a commercial idiom may be used, as Cole Porter used it, to hit back, if tune and rhythm are strong enough.

'Did Jesus have a baby sister?' is even more risible, and the mirth turns a feminist tract into a celebration of life.

> Did Jesus have a baby sister?
> Could she speak out, by and large?
> Or was she told by mary mother
> ask your brother He's in charge?

The style is ragged White Gospel music, with backing girlie chorus. Again the tune is irresistible, and as the jokes accumulate, so the music reflects them – for instance in the impudent modulation at the reference to the fact that little sister, unlike big brother, gets 'precious little notice in the local press'. The verbal punch-line is brilliant:

> Did she long to be a saviour
> saving everyone she met?
> and in private to her mirror
> did she whisper Saviourette?
> Saviourwoman? Saviourperson?
> Save your breath!

Yet this high-camp comedy embraces pathos, as in the unaccompanied singing of the words 'what was her name?' and the last stanza proves that the heart of the song is concerned not with Women's Rights but with a fundamentally feminine, iguana-like belief in feeling rather than in will:

And did she cry for mary's comfort?
as she watched him on the cross
and was mary too despairing?
ask your brother He's the boss.

When Dory cries, with a wobbly roulade, 'he's the *man*, he's the *show*', the Christ legend has itself become part of the plastic pretence, and it's the mythical little sister who might salvage god for good. Dory is telling Christians and pseudo-Christians to come off their high horses and to see themselves as well as us for the freaks they are. The music, underlining the verbal wit, ensures that irony is not negation but affirmation.

Though the jazz element in Dory's music seems to represent 'truth' as against the Californian dream, it is not integrated into Dory's idiom, as Joni Mitchell integrated Black jazz into *Mingus*. This is not surprising, for since Dory's manners must be eclectic to deal with her habitual themes, she has no clearly defined idiom for anything to be integrated into. 'Did Jesus have a baby sister?', which musically is pastiche White gospel music of fairly recent vintage, turns out to be Dory's quintessence. Hilariously funny at the start, it becomes *wonderfully* so as the child voice darkens to woman in the final stanza. The girlie chorus fade-out takes us back to the ironic end of *Mythical Kings and Iguanas*, in which 'going home' becomes a promise of rebirth and even, *in potentia*, a benediction.

Joni Mitchell came from Western Canada and spent her early youth in the hippiest areas of California. Throughout, she has 'charted the map of the heart', embracing sociological issues only in so far as they effect her personal destiny. As a basic woman of Instinct, she is more intimately in tune with music than with poetry: 'What I like best is making new music. It's like going into a trance. I sit down with a melody and reminisce.' Dory Previn is hardly less dedicated to her personal history, but is more intelligent about it, more concerned with the context of the world she lives in. She too had small-town origins, spending her childhood and adolescence entertaining as singer and tapdancer in parish minstrel shows. When she entered the big world she did so at the centre rather than, like Joni, on the hippy periphery. These facts condition the differences between the two women's music. Joni's usually has affinities with the 'instinctive' world of folk music, however radically metamorphosed; her tunes tend to modality, her rhythms are malleable. Dory's music is closely related to commercial models, her tunes tend to be diatonic, her rhythms square, both being subservient to words that are commentaries on the social scene as well as a consequence of autobiographical perplexities. Joni's songs reach back to grass roots and uncover aboriginal America. Dory's songs never do that. They cleverly, sometimes disturbingly, uncover her own origins, but artistically they live in, even if they do not accept, our commercialized society. Though in this sense Dory remains an entertainer, as she was in her childhood, rather than an artist, this indicates — since her numbers are intellectually enlivening and emotionally touching — how hazily defined the barriers between art and entertainment must nowadays be.

Chapter Ten

SOCIETY'S CHILD IN SMALL TOWN AND CITY

'Tea and sympathy'

Janis Ian

'Love out in the streets'

Carly Simon

Nostalgia ain't wot it used to be.

Wayside graffito

Carole King made her reputation in 1971–2, contemporary with Joni Mitchell and Dory Previn. Her verse and music don't open vistas, like Joni's nor, like Dory's, do they stimulate with an intelligence and wit at once stinging and pathetic. They have however their distinctive integrity: a quiet capacity and need for love is balanced with an insecurity that comes from not knowing where she belongs and to whom love should be directed. It is interesting that whereas Joni Mitchell's early songs evoke the small-town society she came from and the Californian world in which she spent her adolescence, and whereas Dory Previn's songs are, despite countryish elements, all urban, centred on Los Angeles, Carole King's songs are relatively placeless. She might be in big city, small town, or even village. Her melodic idiom is usually

modal and rural in origin; the beat, however, is often nervously
jazzy, and the harmony, despite a partiality for folky fourths, may
attain a bluesy ripeness.

'Tapestry', the title song of her most famous disc, encompasses
the rural bases of her art. The lovely poem is a permutation of the
old legend of the Frog Prince. The tune is as simple as a real folk
song, undulating by gentle steps, and if the modulations to keys a
second apart seem to compromise simplicity, they will be found
sophisticated only by ears trained on conventional academic harmony. Less mythic and closer to Carole's basic manner is 'So far·
away', a song about 'moving along the highway', admitting that
'nobody stays in one place any more'. The meandering modal line,
sometimes garlanded with pentatonic doodles on flute, expresses a
lost state with a tender melancholy that is – unlike that of Joni
Mitchell's highway songs – half pleasurable.

But the next song, 'It's too late', is tougher in facing up to a love
that has failed. Though

> We really did try to make it,
> it's too late now,
> something has died
> and I just can't fake it,

the beat, beneath the arching tune, is unbroken, while Curtis
Amy's soprano saxophone bleats in jazzy awareness of what life is
really like. A more generalized version of this theme recurs in
'Beautiful', an appeal that we should go on living exultantly,
despite the tears and madness rife in the world and in ourselves.
Rhythm has greater energy, and the tune spreads from speech-
inflected repeated notes into swinging lyricism. The modulation
that makes the passers-by pass, the sudden lift that makes us 'get up
in the morning', relate verbal sense to musical impulse as
unerringly as do Mitchell and Previn; and although Carole's vocal
production is less varied in range than Joni's and less expressive than
Dory's, it is apposite to her experience. Mostly in middle range,
undemonstrative, it is at once tender and tough – as an American
girl of the seventies, whatever her environment, had need to be.

Carole King's later work, of which the 1974 disc *Carole King
Music* may be taken as representative, doesn't extend her range of
experience, though the familiar themes sometimes attain greater
energy. 'Brother, brother' is remarkable for the charge it generates
from rudimentary material. The beat is breathless; the harmony

mostly plain tonic, dominant and subdominant; the tune, thrusting up slowly against the frantic beat, intensifies its pentatonicism with bluely flattened thirds. 'Some kind of wonderful' also restricts its harmony to the hymnbook's, and has a pentatonic tune that plunges to a low G. The song does what it promises, for the music sings the love that 'words cannot express'.

'Carry your load' brings in a more stomping beat and a melody jazzily syncopated, as she nervously asks her man to meet her 'on the highway'. The descending pentatonic phrase with which the number opens is answered by a phrase rising from fifth to tonic by way of a sharp seventh. This is the more enlivening because plagal-tending subdominants have been prevalent in the harmony; it promotes a mediant modulation. 'Music', with a particularly charming lyric, is about music's therapeutic powers:

Ah it's not always easy,
but the music keeps playing
and won't let the cold get me down.

Nor does it: for although the stepwise-moving tune is in country waltz rhythm and has a sonority like a merry-go-round, there's a Latin-American undertow that suggests that the brightness isn't merely childish; Curtis Amy's saxophone obbligati temper innocence with (s)experience. 'Growing away from me' makes (painful) experience manifest in blue notes in a line once more basically pentatonic. Anguish becomes overt in the middle eight in the upper mediant, when she admits that she would let the man go, if she could. The final number, 'Back to California', is regressive in being a stomping song in railroad beat, on tonic and dominant pedals that shift to subdominant for the middle eight. The pentatonic tune is peppered with blue notes; an instrumental interlude is basic barrelhouse piano and blue guitar. Even this gentle, love-lorn White American recognizes that her music cannot fully encompass the American experience without assimilating a tinge of Blackness.

Perhaps this is why she, like Joni Mitchell, has proved an impressive survivor. Her 1984 disc, *Speeding Time*, presents songs about the courage needed to survive, all in country–rock idiom, without much direct influence of jazz or blues. Without Joni's poetic mystery or Dory's mordant wit, the verses have the virtue of their honesty, and the music's lack of ostentation matches the words. Thus 'Computer eyes' defines musically the distinction the poem makes between a human being and a machine, demonstrating, in the lovely vocalized extension to the concluding phrase, that 'you're gonna have to learn to cry'. 'Crying in the rain' is explicitly about *going on*, in a fairly fast, even jaunty rhythm, whatever heartache another quasi-human being may inflict on one. 'Sacred heart of stone' has the same theme; the chugging beat is unremitting, though the rhythm is more nervy. The title song, 'Spending time', finds the enemy not in any recalcitrant lover but in time itself, which dispels illusion. Through and against time one must find 'the strength within and hang on – hold on – you gotta try to keep your love alive in this speeding time'. And the music does so, just.

The songs on the B-side offer tentative hope of renewal, for 'Standin' on the borderline' cannot be perpetuated: 'You either make your move or you turn away.' Again rhythm chunters while the tune unfolds, ready to cross the borderline but not quite making it. 'So ready for love' does make it, at least in the spacious tune, playing strong regular accents ('*I can see* by the way you *look at me*') against flickering roulades on key worlds like 'love'. It is not clear whether the man will respond to encouragement. Even if he doesn't the song – the longest and best in the cycle – amounts to a modest affirmation: which is not confirmed by the other numbers. 'Dancing', another appeal for honesty, is quite forceful; 'Alabaster lady' is a complementary admonition to the woman that she should 'keep on growing'. Both verbally and musically the piece has a hint of the pretentiousness typical of Joni Mitchell's middle years. None the less Carole King, in surviving, *has* grown, and pretentiousness may have been, as with Joni, necessary to growth.

Another artist to gravitate from small town to big city, although more traumatically than Carole King, was Janis Ian, a waif-like creature who came of a family that lived, during the space of fifteen years, in thirteen different places in New Jersey and New York. Like Dory Previn, she was something of a child prodigy: very clever, though at school 'music was the only thing that kept me going without freaking out. School was always absurd.' She was rescued from it by what she called 'the fame thing', for an album of songs, all with words and music by Janis, was issued in her sixteenth year. At school 'Most of the teachers were frustrated musicians; they didn't like it' – especially since the album's[1] commercial success was due mainly to its inclusion of a hit single,

1 *Society's Child.*

'Society's child', which earned notoriety through being about a love affair between a White girl and a Black boy – still a dicey theme in 1966. The lad, whose 'face is clean and shining black as night', is called 'boy' by the girl's mother, who thinks he's 'not of our kind'. The girl has to give him up because she is Society's child, conditioned by the world she came from. But notoriety wasn't the only reason for Janis's teenage triumph: the album as a whole shows precocious talent both verbal and musical, and an authenticity at once childlike and bleak.

This is evident in the first song she composed, 'Hair of spun gold'. The poetic imagery is worthy of real folk verse, and the modal line and virginal vocal production suggest unaccompanied monody. Yet the burden of the song concerns not life in small town or time-effacing village, but growing up too fast in a city. The girl, noticed by boys at the age of 10, at 13 has a leather-jacketed steady to replace her teddy bear, and at 15 is married and with child. By the time she has reached the age of 21, the wheel has turned. She looks at the child who has her own 'hair of spun gold' and promises that she will be given the chance to grow up slowly.

The effect of this song depends on the contrast between the prophetically autobiographical tale it tells and the manner of presentation. Normally, Janis's manner toughens to match the world she lives in. 'The tangles of my mind' is halfway between the legendary vein of ancient folksong and the dusty realities of the present; 'Pro girl', a toughly tender song about a very young prostitute, completes the hard image. 'Go away little girl' is an anti-mother song mimicking the mother's solicitude for her daughter, but concluding that the offspring has been moulded in the mother's image. 'Janey's blues' also scores off parental hypocrisy, almost as trenchantly as does Dory Previn. 'New Christ cardiac hero' tells of the downfall of a gospel–pop hero whose crown of thorns turns to ivory horns. Dismissively, Janis remarks that

We have no need of a God.
Each of us is his own.

Throughout these morally severe songs Janis's voice preserves a pristine purity in melodic line, though her rhythm grows wirier. A child's rural song acquires the harsher reality of the blues, and this is more pointed because her voice, speaking as well as singing, is of exceptional beauty. She does not offer a 'performance', neither as an artist, like Joni Mitchell, nor as an entertainer, like Dory Previn.

She simply offers what she is, in the loveliness of her voice; though that is inevitably modified by the society she finds herself in. Her instrumental backing, in contrast to her vocal simplicity, is elaborate; on this first album the scoring includes flute and harpsichord, as well as the obligatory guitars, piano and organ.

Songs as honest as Janis's first album, created by a 15-year-old, must have strained her emotional resources; she was neurotically disturbed both by the act of making the songs and by 'the fame thing' that was their outcome. Having met a boy on a peace march in 1967, she married him and retired to Philadelphia. Marriage didn't cure her depression, which 'was a sickness'. She came through it, and by 1970 was creating new songs, which are blander than those on the first album – sad, but without the nervous edge. The songs on *Present Company* are mostly in country idiom, closer to the spontaneity of folk style than are Joni Mitchell's ballads.

In the brief 'On the train' Janis falls asleep, lulled by the railway car's hypnotic motion; disarmed, she reveals her vulnerability. Sometimes she can, however, discover inner strengths – as when, in 'Hello Jerry', her little girl voice, speaking–singing over arpeggios on acoustic guitar, swells into a love song of affirmation in a crazy world. Gradually her voice grows in range, garnering blue inflexions as harmony shifts and tonality undulates to reflect the words 'can you reach me?' Such a metamorphosis of country style resembles the later Dolly Parton – who is also recalled in 'Alabama', which begins in Southern country style with a swaying tune in a slow 6/8. The middle section turns into country rag, with a sonority emulating plantation banjo. But the nostalgia is not as simple as it seems, for the return of the 6/8 tune brings odd tonal waverings and electrophonic distortion; the baby voice falters, and the song ends with a very blue flat seventh.

In 1975 Janis produced a disc called *Between the Lines*, which marks a development in that folk innocence and blue experience are mated. Her voice is lower and huskier, though still with bloom. Without forcing her range, she floats the line over an electric bass with enough tension to qualify as mild rock. Piano (played by herself) and guitar combine with electric bass, often cushioned by strings. Though the sound is mellow, honesty is not compromised. 'At seventeen' is a particularly affecting song about adolescence, presumably her own. It proffers condolence to those who, like herself, missed out on true love because of their 'ravaged faces and lack of social graces'; the lilting 12/8 metre, the calmly drooping tune and the triadic harmony invoke schoolday illusions and disillusions with a clarity that disarms. Another, more patently 'lost' number, 'The come-on', is not so much a revocation of childhood as an appeal from a girl who thinks there must be something 'terribly wrong' with her because men who will bed her won't wed her, or even care for and comfort her. Characteristically she blames herself rather than the men. Over an arpeggiated accompaniment the melody soothes the wounded words.

The simple verities of Janis Ian's verses, the symmetry of her tunes, the concordance of her harmonies, not to mention the halo of strings that may surround her piano, now relate her to fairly polite society, waif though she be. In these circumstances her finest songs prove to be those most tinged with the urban modes of jazz, such as 'Bright lights and promises'. Notated in a modal C minor and very blue in mood, this relates her personal distress to a wider theme, for the number is about the music industry. Janis says she is paid to produce 'bright lights and promises, a pocketful of dreams'. If she gave her employers what they asked for, she'd be untrue to herself; once having realized this, she cannot fulfil her commitment to them. The manager relies on the singer as source of income but the singer is dependent on the manager to produce the goods. They despise one another, but the manager holds the reins since he may censor, or fail to produce, the singer's songs.

Janis's verses ring changes on this theme. Though she is now 'gold lamé and diamonds', she still 'leaves and enters by the service door'. Making a familiar pun on the word 'light', she understates her need for help:

Have you got a light?
That's all it pays to keep in sight.

She has lost her own bright light of truth but will lose her livelihood if she cannot feed the dream machine. Ambiguity extends to the music, which mixes old-time country phrases with small-town blues and the Muzak of 'bar-rails and cocktails'. The tune, in slow boogie rhythm, begins lyrically, savouring the dreams and bright lights, but grows blues-infected the more aspiringly it soars. When the song seems about to fade in a memory of 'old-time melody' on parlour piano, it's yanked back to blue intensity, the last stanza being sung, in dialogue with wailing clarinet, in a timbre reminiscent of a Black blues singer. The tonality is twice hitched up, as anger and desperation get the better of self-commiseration.

In the 1979 album *Night Rains* Janis's expertly 'produced' compromise between country music and gentle rock suggests that she may be succumbing to the 'promises and pocketful of dreams' she deplored in her song about the pop-music industry. With familiarity, however, we recognize that the streamlined technique is part of the songs' expressive intention, since the point is the contrast between the 'guileless truth' of Janis's voice and the sophistication of her art and craft. A retrospect of childhood like 'Jenny', in which Chick Corea doodles in luxuriant romanticism on a second piano, or a ballad like 'Photographs of long ago', with an accompaniment adding harp to parlour piano, convince because old-fashioned clichés are accepted for what they are. This is why nostalgia can be metamorphosed into aspiration. 'Day by day' begins by depicting broken love in fragmented rhythms, but gathers itself together to sail into a fine bluesy tune, with a Black edge on Janis's voice, balancing the soaring soprano saxophone. Best of all is 'Fly too high', in which Janis's voice preserves its dewiness while dancing in Motown rhythms, with Steve Madaio's trumpet chortling aloft; the sonority recalls Weather Report or the later Miles Davis's fusion of jazz with rock. Presumably she is singing about herself who, like the girl in the song, did fly too high and run too fast. Viewing her teenage self retrospectively, she rides blithely over adolescent despair.

On her 1981 disc, *Restless Eyes* there is a new equation between Janis's folk-like immediacy and her technical competence. The verses are economically skilful in their internal rhymes and assonances; musically each number is artfully constructed, with well-moulded melodies, strong basses, and harmonic gradations that match the verbal patterns. Yet her folk-like command of verbal inflexion has never been more consummate, nor has her voice been more radiant. Some songs are slight, all know their limits; all entertain, some grow in the rehearing. 'Under the covers' is about Spanish or 'gypsy' boys whose capacity to hurt counteracts their capacity to afford sexual pleasure. Janis uses her two voices for verse and chorus: she's a little girl when hurt, an abrasive-voiced woman when 'under the covers'. Her grown-up voice matches the Latin-American flavour of the music; yet that too is vulnerable, and when Janis floats the word 'maybe' in the phrase 'maybe I'll let you be mine', we realize that she's singing not merely of her own hurt, but of that inherent in youth itself.

'Restless eyes' deals with a more complex situation: two young people each of whom knows he or she has married the wrong person, yet is committed to some kind of status quo. Again there's a divison between the verse, concerned with things as they are, and the refrain, concerned with the reality behind the façade. Yet there is no simple contrast. The song is enveloped in arpeggiated guitar, which blurs distinctions, wafting us between the two levels of experience. Janis's nuances on phrases like 'warm winds' and 'cold summer nights' themselves become music.

The longest song, with the punning title of 'Passion play', also deals in the ambiguities of passion. The poem is rich in internal rhymes and assonances:

Suddenly rootless
fashionably useless
magically fruitless and tame
like some Sunday scholar
who lives off the squalor
of yesterday's knowledge and fame.

The music not only creates a touching melodic–harmonic climax in the refrain, but effects a climax on the climax when, last time round, the 'passion play' phrase soars resonantly into the air. But perhaps the finest song is the most intimate, 'Down and away', in which the arabesques occasioned by Janis's response to particular words themselves create the form – as is appropriate, since the poem is about drifting. Yet nowhere is Janis's art more manifest than in these surrenders to a life of 'sensations rather than thoughts': consider how she sings the word 'time' in the second stanza, the 'flew away' and 'threw away' in the refrain, and the sundry references to 'drifting'

Whereas Janis Ian, born in 1950, began very young and grew up slowly, Carly Simon, born in 1946, was a slow starter who grew rapidly once she had found herself. Her tardy start may have been due to a privileged background very different from Janis Ian's. Her family belonged to the distinguished publishing firm of Simon and Schuster, so Carly has a 'cultured' background, and was musically nurtured on Beethoven and Chopin (her father played the piano), as well as on Gershwin and Broadway shows (to which her mother was addicted). At high school and college Carly sang folk music in Joan Baez style, but made no conspicuous impact. Friendship with men in or around pop and rock music introduced her to a musical world more congenial to her. Acquiring a recording contract from Elektra, she soon established herself as a singer specializing in her own songs, some of them no less artistically 'realized' than the later work of Janis Ian.

Carly Simon writes of the big city where she was born and lives, and of personal, usually sexual, experience, but she sees her own experience as typical of her tribe, supporting her voice with elaborate but lucid instrumentals, and with vocal backing in which she herself participates, along with notables such as Carole King, Rita Coolidge and James Taylor. Her songs are not only personal in theme, but have a distinctive idiom – evident in the first two numbers of her 1975 album, *Playing Possum*. 'After the storm' opposes a state of amorous turmoil to warmth and safety when the storm has abated. The music mirrors this ambivalence, the moderate beat being supportive, while the modal melody wanders irregularly, yet builds into a whole that paradoxically makes affirmation out of uncertainty. Carly's singing complements this; her middle-registered voice sounds like a sublimation of her speech, while her ornamentation imparts a jazzy flavour through blue arabesques supporting, rather than confusing, the melodic line. Compared with Janis Ian or Joni Mitchell, she does not employ much variety of colour, though such transitions as she does make are the more telling for their discretion: consider what the darkening of tone for 'your body seems so warm' does to the cool refrain phrase, 'after the storm'. Similarly, in the arrangement, as usual by Carly herself, the suavity of the strings balances the precision of the rock instruments and the jazzy reality of Trevor Lawrence's saxophone. Again as usual, Carly herself plays piano, presiding over the ensemble like a continuo player in a baroque orchestra.

The companion song, 'Love out in the street', presents the same theme negatively, for she and her man 'wash their dirty laundry in the alleyway'. Both beat and Carly's voice are harder, though the melody that unpredicably evolves is distinctive. 'Look me in the eyes' and 'Slave' form a comparable positive–negative pair of songs. The former, evoking a sun-baked Californian beach, is a love song in which Carly effects mini-miracles with her arabesques on phrases like 'no fancy dancing' and 'palm trees against the sky', the jazz flavour in her voice imparting a delicate eroticism. She is far more erotic than most pop singers because her sexuality, embracing both positive and negative impulses, is particularized. 'Slave' has a refrain in which she confesses, strident-voiced, that she is 'hungry, longing, burning' for her man; yet at the same time this is a feminist song in so far as she cries that she wants to be 'strong and free and brave', not just 'another woman raised to be a slave'.

The 'protest' elements in Carly's songs steer her towards a more rock-biased style. This is evident even in 'Are you ticklish', a very personal, indeed private, poem set to a country waltz that, through Carly's jazz inflexions, becomes an appeal for true love beneath the ticklishness. The words are half comic but the tune, reinforced by clarinet and trombone, grows gradually more shapely and emotive. 'Playing possum', on the other hand, is sociological commentary that turns into an enlivening rock song, charting progress from the 'hippest newstand' of Cambridge, to tilling the land in the country, to converse with a holy man in India, only to end up in a bookstore, with a wife and 'patches on your elbow'. As the trenchant words put it,

The wells they do run dry
and the speeches turn to words
and the woods are full of tigers
and freedom's for the birds.

By the time of the brilliant 1979 album *Spy* both the rock affiliation and the militant feminism of Carly Simon's songs have become overt. 'Vengeance' describes a confrontation between Carly and a traffic cop. She says she's put her foot on the accelerator as protest against his male predatoriness, and the ferocity of the music allows no room for a joke. The beat is remorseless, Carly's voice darker and rougher than anywhere on the previous discs, while Don Grolnick takes over on electric piano from the relatively gentle Carly. Jazz trumpet, clarinet and saxophone give immediacy to the hubbub which, compared with Carly's typical music, isn't subtle and isn't meant to be.

The title song, 'Spy', is more characteristic in that it is about a love relationship, as contrasted with a conflict between a private woman and a public man. But it is in part an anti-man song since Carly, though 'intrigued' by her lover, is spying on him, seeing through his prevarications. Here she uses her natural voice, with a jazzy edge. Beat is fast, electric guitars jittery, while Hubert Laws's flute flickers and flutters through the ensemble. Though this is a personal, jazz-orientated song about a wobbly personal relationship, it has a communal dimension because Carly is inviting other women to relish her spying activity. Even the lyrical, folky and balladic numbers are coloured, if not by feminist militancy, at least by a critical attitude to the male. 'We're so close' proves that its title is ironic, for Carly hardly ever sees her lover who, enjoying the jet life in some distant place, communicates only by long-distance phone, if at all. He says they're so close they don't need words, indeed don't need love, at all. Carly's melody is of the meandering type she specializes in, with odd modal shifts that reflect the failure of communication. Yet the truth of her love is still evident in the jazz intensity of her line, potently answered by an alto saxophone solo from David Sanborn.

The most remarkable song on this remarkable disc is 'Memorial day', which approaches grandeur in presenting similar themes of male betrayal objectively, in story form. The 'I' of the story appears to have run off with a man who is upbraided by his previous wife or mistress. The triangle meet in a Wild West valley ('the Indians knew it was a devil's sanctuary') and the woman rails at the Carly-figure, who 'watches safe and clean from the frosted windows' of her limousine. The tale ends with violence in 'the cruel and lovely valley' – a violence more appropriate to 'some alley in a low-down part of town'. The theme is complex and so is the music, with one of Carly's wandering tunes, with modally shifting triads. The effect – of Carly's voice and of the instrumental solos – is stark. As in Dylan's Wild West songs there's an equilibrium between the personal and the mythic such as may offer scope for development in future years.

Chapter Eleven

INTO THE GLOBAL VILLAGE

They circle and reach,
fixed in the whirling feet
of fire dancers, gypsy women,
early in their twenties,
learning,
early with a smoulder of sun
in their eyes and the skin of their cheekbones.

The singers discussed in the previous chapter were small-town and city women of the United States, which though United, are of their nature polyglot and polyethnic. One would therefore expect to find, in addition to the White–Black interlacings referred to throughout this book, subtler interracial complexities. These are revealed by way of comparison of key discs of Phoebe Snow, Melissa Manchester, Laura Nyro and Tania Maria.   On her fine initial album of 1973, called simply *Phoebe Snow*, Phoebe Snow sings and plays acoustic guitar, accompanied by rock-style electric guitars, with intermittent obbligati from frontline horn players, and with vocal backing from the Persuasions. Compared with Carly Simon, she has more explicit jazz affiliations, launching the disc with a traditional Black barrelhouse piece, 'Let the good times roll', performed fast and furious, no holds barred. She also includes the 'San Francisco

blues' of Jesse Fuller, a primitive Californian bluesman. The verses
are about a lost lover; the tune is pentatonic; the acoustic guitar has
the plangency of the country blues, which the beat of the acoustic
bass swings into the city. Phoebe's quasi-Black vocal production
sears, yet is undermined by a comically bleating tremolo,
distancing the poignancy of her grief. The high vocalise at the end
has a similar effect. Male primitive blues singers often used falsetto
for therapeutic ends, releasing pain in farce. Phoebe's more artful,
even romantic, version of the device is no less telling. A young
White woman adapts the Black blues to her own ends.

How she does this in her own numbers is movingly revealed in
'Harpo's blues', the charming verses of which present her as a little
girl lost and as a Harpo Marx-like clown – a persona often assumed
by Dory Previn. She would like to be a swaying willow, a volatile
lover, a mountain to pass 'boldly through the clouds'; she does *not*
want to be a grown-up trying to 'bear my life in pain'. Yet that is
just what the music does. True, the tune she starts from is graceful,
lilting in the elegant boogie-rhythmed piano of Teddy Wilson,
resuscitated from a forgotten world, supported by Chuck
Delmonico's bouncing bass. None the less Phoebe's vocal line, at
first responding to Wilson's twinkling pianism, darkens in her
transition from 'I wish I was a soft refrain when the lights were out'
to 'I strut and fret my hour upon the stage', the syllables accented,
breaking the floating rhythm. By this time Phoebe has been joined
by Zoot Sim's tenor saxophone. His answers to her phrases, and her
response to his response, intensify until the reiterations of the 'bear
my life in pain' phrase make the words incarnate. Phoebe has grown
up whether she wanted to or not.

In 'It must be Sunday' she betrays no desire to evade her scared
state by a return to childhod. She is watching the world from inside
a telephone booth – a telling image since she is cut off, behind the
glass, from the 'real' world, yet is in touch with a mechanical device
for communication. It might be Sunday, ' 'cause everybody's telling
the truth', or

It might be Monday
'cause everybody's drinking vermouth.

An atmosphere of alcoholic hallucination is generated, though the
regular beat ballasts the wavering line. Again Zoot Sim's tenor
steers her through the labyrinth. When the words tell us that

He pressed his cheek
in rainwashed streets
and he went into his gin
reincarnation
and he came back as himself

Phoebe's melismata make it happen. Synthetically electric strings
form a suave halo.

Others numbers attain jazz intensity without benefit of Zoot
Sims. 'I don't want the night to end' is a threnody for Charlie
Parker, growing progressively screwier until

In the night blue music's
all I seem to see
the drunks out in the rain
down on one knee.

More characterful songs tinge urban jazz with a bucolic flavour – as
in 'No show tonight', a number about opting out from the public
relations of show business because of personal crisis. The hint of a
bumpkin in the brief open-eyed tune stands for truth in a world of
deception. Most successful in this vein is 'Poetry man', who is
presented, over an exotic Latin-American beat, as another clown
figure, a 'bashful boy, hiding something sweet'. The vocal melody
enchants, in the literal sense, while around it a tinkling harp weaves
a spell. Again, however, Zoot Sim's thrusting saxophone pushes the
song towards reality: even a magic Poetry Man must sometimes 'go
home' to the wife and kids. The same point is made in 'Take your
children home', also in Latin-American rhythm and with harp
obbligato, though here the comedy of the magician–entertainer is
more evident than the pathos. 'Either or both' starts as a comic
countryish song, but gets jazzily nervous as the words speak of
'clumsy hands' that 'drop things' when, in a world commensurate
with her dreams, they ought to be 'signin' autographs'. The most
interesting moment is the modulation that follows Phoebe's
admission that 'sometimes this life gets so empty That I become
afraid'.

Though Phoebe Snow's later discs don't develop much from the
premises she'd established, they preserve her distinctive quality,
while her 1978 *Against the Grain* significantly climaxes in two numbers that respectively recall Dory Previn and Joni Mitchell. 'The
married men' Phoebe borrows from Margaret Roche, emulating

Dory in ragging it in old-time minstrel-show style. Its diatonic tune and perky rhythm opt out from care and commitment, as the small-time whore or good-time girl has fun 'snappin' that crazy apple off the stem, and givin' it to the married men'. She snaps her fingers, too, at 'all that time in hell', which a Southern heritage promises her as penalty.

The final song, however, doesn't seek an escape through Previn-like satire but, Joni Mitchell-like, faces confessional truth. 'Keep a watch on the shoreline' even evokes the seascape that Joni Mitchell started from, and momentarily in singing of the boat 'lost and tossed on the ocean', Phoebe's voice startlingly resembles Joni's. None the less this is an essential Snow composition, in which self-indulgence in the words —

> Every day you seem indifferent to my touch
> you may wake up glad to see I'll never be a crutch,
> feeling undesired makes a person feel tired

— is counterbalanced by the radiant music. Each time the chorus recurs Phoebe sings it more firmly, her voice changing from treble wistfulness to blue intensity, the choric voices growing louder and stronger. Despair over the wretched male fuels the truth of her love; we almost believe her when, squatting on the beach, she says she'll stay there 'until you reach me and come home'. Her melisma on 'much' in the phrase 'I will never give you up 'cause I love you very much' is both desperate and ecstatic.

Into her New York ethos Phoebe Snow often admits the Latin-American flavour that by the seventies had become indigenous to the northern scene. This trend is more overt in the work of Melissa Manchester, whose 1973 disc, *Home to Myself*, sums up, as its title suggests, her contribution. Melissa writes her own material, either solo or in collaboration with Carole Bayer Sager, herself a not inconsiderable singing poet—composer.

How basic Melissa can be is evident in 'Be happy now', which opens like a Negro work song accompanied only by clapping and stamping, but then garners guitar and banjo, and eventually bassoons and string quartet. The quite complex arrangement (by Chris Dedrick) transforms primitive incantation into Modern Jazz and relates this number to the initial track, 'if it feels good, let it ride'. Musically this is the most exciting track on the disc, with nervous rhythms and shifting harmonies on electric keyboards, over which Melissa spins a wide-flung, sung—shouted line, tinged with brown and black. The drumming and conga playing hint at Latin America; Melissa's marvellous unaccompanied cadenza re-creates the Black field holler in her coffee-coloured city.

The longest number, 'Easy', is likewise poised between worlds. It is about the relationship between love and sex, and Melissa's vocal timbre wavers between pale tenderness and smokey eroticism. The 'love' is contained in the slowish, lyrical, countrified opening and its *da capo*, the 'sex' in an aggressive, fast-rock middle section, Melissa's vocal equipment being equal to both. 'Pick up the good stuff' is a modified reprise of 'If it feels good', adding yet another mode to Melissa's repertory, for its angular, jerky string writing could hardly have occurred before Bartók and Stravinsky. On top her voice sings or yells with a wiriness distinct from a Black shouter. A Latin-American element is again catalyst between White and Black, whether or no Melissa is of part-Mexican descent.

Where Phoebe Snow's and Melissa Manchester's songs borrow elements of Black and Latin-American musics, Laura Nyro, being herself ethnically ambiguous – born in New York's Bronx and capable of passing as White American, Red Indian or Spanish–Hebraic – is able to integrate the disparate racial sources of her music and timbres of her voice into a seamless unity. The archetypal Global Villager, she hymns the New York city flat, describing herself as writer, composer, voices, piano and witness to the confession. *Eli and the Thirteenth Confession* was the title of her first representative album, issued in 1967. She wrote all the words and music, both being sophisticated – verbally in the manner of the Beat poets, musically in a style in which the obvious folk–rock prototypes acquire the urban lustre of Gershwin and Bernstein, Ellington and Miles Davis.

Laura's voice is remarkable, with a three-octave range that divides, like Joni Mitchell's, into two main registers, one a child's, the other a woman's. But this is too modest an account of Laura's vocal equipment: in the top range she can sound either like a frail little girl or like a metallic Viennese choirboy; in the lower reaches she may be huskily Black or cavernously Red. Somewhere in the middle she sounds like the jazzy soul singer she essentially is, with a precise rhythmic sense complementing the speech accents of her atmospheric yet incisive verses. Her ethos is that of global New York in the era and aura of the drug scene – Laura had a traumatic experience with acid. Not surprisingly, her music has an edgy febrility. 'Eli's coming', from the *Thirteenth Confession* album, opens

with quasi-Hebraic incantation to herald Eli's advent (he is, perhaps, a very sexy, secular messiah) but turns into the hard, nervous
sould music in which American girls may encase themselves, with-
standing lure and threat.

This nervous and physical brittleness is balanced by very slow,
emotive numbers such as 'Lonely woman' and 'December's boudoir',
which opens with voice and saxophone meandering in desultory
dismay over almost immobile harmonies on piano and guitar. The
pulse of the city, which in the daylight moods of the fast songs
never lets up, is slowed down to a nocturnal ticking. Although the
manner recalls the urban blues, the vocal melismata suggest other
ethnic musics – Hebraic, Spanish, Puerto Rican, as well as Negro.
Only one song, 'Emmie', hints at the white world of country music
and this is far from straightforward since electrophonics impart to
rural manners a hallucinatory quality. Bucolic Emmie may be
dreamed of, but cannot fully live in the brash city.

In latter years Laura Nyro hardly fulfilled the promise of her
initial album, though in her ambiguity she remains interesting.
But the most distinctive and musically accomplished talent in this
New York ethnic scene is Tania Maria, a genuine racial Outsider
who demonstrates how one who doesn't belong to the inside
community may become part of and ultimately help to shape it.
Tania Maria Correa Reis was born in north Brazil, of mixed Spanish
and Indian ancestry. Musically precocious, she was encouraged by
her father, trained as a classical pianist, and profited from her
technical accomplishment when she moved, as keyboard player,
towards jazz; this evolution coincided with her adolescent enthusiasm for the pop musics of her own country. So the roots of her
South–North American equation were deeply planted. One of
Brazil's finest musicians, Egberto Gismonti, has said that Brazilian
pop musics were beginning to make a worldwide impact because,
'we have something important to tell other people, something
about life, about friendship and energy. It's not about a new world,
but maybe about an open door to a new world.' Tania Maria herself
made a similar point when she remarked, 'Normally when you're
Brazilian and you play music, people want it that you always seem
very happy and very high . . . My music is an invitation.'

In a sense Tania's musical beginnings were easy since she grew up
in a spontaneously music-making community. None the less her
start was difficult in the sense that, as she sang and played in small
bars around Rio de Janeiro, she realized that a talent such as hers

could not be content with Brazilian euphoria. In order to grow to maturity she had to synthesize the two Americas, profiting from the example of jazz musicians like Stan Getz.

Specifically, she was helped by two pianists, Johnny Alf and Luiz Eca, who were among the first to encourage cross-fertilization between Latin-American bossa nova, samba and salsa and North American jazz. It was with their aid that Tania went to Paris and found fame as a club singer, mostly because of her exceptional talents, but also because her jazzily sophisticated Brazilian exoticism awoke echoes in the hearts of world-weary Europeans, as had the soprano saxophone of Sidney Bechet fifty years earlier.

On her first disc, *Tania Maria Live* (1979) – taped with French drummer and bassist at a club in Copenhagen, not Paris – we're immediately aware that as pianist Tania Maria ranks, among singing poet–composers, with Blossom Dearie in electric elegance and with Nina Simone in passion, power and precision. Tania opens the album with an extensive, hectic piano solo she calls 'Mr and Mrs'. Like almost all her numbers, this is her own composition, though 'composition' probably means incentives to improvisation rather than a rigorously notated score. Fusing Latin-American bossa nova, samba and salsa with jazz of the bebop era she creates a music related to that of her friend, the Brazilian New Yorker pianist and composer, Chick Corea. That she has preserved closer links with her native country gives her music a fiercer zip, with Afro-Cuban overtones similar to those in the later work of McCoy Tyner, whom she also admires. When, in 'Catoamante', she sings while she plays her voice is slightly savage yet wryly humorous; her acrobatic agility recalls Dizzy Gillespie's trumpeted excursions into Latin America. But the longest piece on the disc, 'Pingas da vida', reveals a darker level of reality, opening with a stark unisonal chant accompanied by a hypnotically syncopated ostinato. The chant, recurring rondo-wise with growing inexorability, counteracts the displacements of the ostinato's metre.

'Seu dia vai chegar' is hardly less intense: its Latin metrical complexities are frantic, both from bubbling piano and scatting voice. 'O que e amar', on the other hand, is a slow ballad, exceptionally not by Tania but by her one-time mentor Johnny Alf. The ripely chromatic yet lucid textures of Tania's piano here suggest comparison with another of her heroes, New York's Bill Evans; sometimes her resonant sonorities recall Duke Ellington as pianist. Certainly her voice, like Ellington's music, is at once mellow and tough – an effect on which the inflexions of spoken Portuguese may have some bearing. Here the text conditions both the vocal quality and the voluptuous pianism. In the final number, 'Carona', Tania releases a bomb of energy from her keyboard, using her voice only to enhance excitement with yelled vocalise and a tipsily scatting coda. This samba, though euphoric, is also dangerous. In Tania's phrase it is high as well as happy – remote either from the mindless jollity of White (blue-grass) or Black (Motown) Euphoria, or from the hysteria that sometimes afflicts distraught Janis Joplin or angry Patti Smith.

On this initial disc Tania Maria sings exclusively in her own language. When, on her splendid 1983 disc *Come With Me*, she writes and sings in English as much as, or more than, in Portuguese, she more thrillingly exploits the extremes of Southern and Northern idiom. The first piece, 'Sangria', is unambiguously Latin American, a very fast salsa-mambo in which Tania's piano is reinforced by the ebullient drums, percussion and electric bass of Steve Thornton and Lincoln Goines. This Southern number is followed by a Northern standard, Gershwin's 'Embraceable you', the only track not of Tania's composition. Tania's voice sounds more White than in any track so far commented on, with a throwaway quality reminiscent of Chris Connor. There may also be an affinity with Nat King Cole, whom Tania admires above any jazz singer, and it could be the Caribbean-flavoured sprightliness of his 'light' Black voice that preserves a memory of Latin-American fervour beneath Eddie Duran's 'talking' guitar and Tania's slow-swinging Bill Evans-style piano.

Certainly in the two remaining tracks on side 1 Latin America effectively absorbs Gershwin's city sophistication. 'Lost in Amazonia' is mainly instrumental, though the funky beat and the piano's glittering passage work stimulate Tania to lunatic scatting. From a 'lost' state in age-old Amazonia she makes a music apposite to New York's Asphalt Jungle – after which, in 'Come with me' she can invite music to 'bring sunny days into my life'. At a more moderate tempo, with words by Regina Werneck, the song audibly effects what it promises.

From this point Tania proceeds, on side 2 of her disc, to reanimate the world she came from, creating what she calls a music of *festa*. For her *festa* is not just 'people getting together to celebrate something' but a general frame of mind, 'our opium against sadness, a stimulator of our joys'. One couldn't hope for a more physically and emotionally rewarding *festa* than 'Semantes, graines and seeds', the title of which promises new life in Portuguese, French and American English, languages that represent three chronological stages in her progress. The worldless piece reinvokes Tania's adolescence: the babel and babble of the Rio piano bars where she'd started, with the Muzak of Afro-French *meringues* and *baiaos* tinkling in the background. Thus music grows up while Tania's acoustic and electric pianos are garlanded with intricate percussion and her own whirling vocalise.

'Nega' is also environmental music: a languid samba that suggests how Latin-American *festa* usually carries, beneath its life assertion, an undercharge of ferocity and death. Tania's voice mingles Indo-Portuguese eroticism with White-American laconicism. 'Euzinha', sung in Portuguese, is *Festa* in retrospect, for it recounts anecedotes of Tania's childhood in her birthplace Maranhao, in the company of her family, especially her beloved aunt Euzinha. The hubbub of life is incarnate in rapid speech and rapider Latin-American piano and percussion. Speech grows into frenetic scatting and song, still interspersed with chatter, but the vocal acrobatics do not disturb the continuity of the complicated beat – the sound world in which, as in authentic primitive music, we momentarily live, move and have our being.

Yet after this number evoking her Brazilian past, Tania Maria rounds off the disc with 'It's all over now', a song dismissing the past in favour of an American-styled present. With poignant irony the number belongs to the 'nostalgic' rather than the 'hedonistic' type of pop standard, so that in these two complementary numbers Tania sings of the past in a quasi-hedonistic present and of the present with quasi-nostalgic regret. The paradox makes sense: when she wails 'It's hard for me to see our lives go separate ways' we realize that she is singing not so much of a failed love affair as of the distance between her present and her past life. This is why her American nostalgia is not after all retrospective, let alone regressive. The long piano postlude incorporates Latin-American virility into its originally limp lope. As usual this marvellous artist not only looks to a future; she makes it an audible reality, here and now.

That Tania Maria is orientated towards a future means that she tends to get better with each disc. The 1984 album, *Love Explosion*, lives up to its title, being a bomb that promotes love and life. 'Funky tamborim' starts at home, in the manner of the Brazilian street music known as *Choros*. The minimal words are a simple invitation to the Good Life of funky song and dance. Electric instruments emulate the sun-baked stridency of the *choros* band, while Justo Almario, Harry Kim and Art Velasco swing in bossa-nova rhythm on Latin-American–African jazz saxophone, flugel horn and trombone. Tania's voice has a folky abrasiveness, though the idiom is urban. So is that of 'It's all in my hands', with lyric by Regina Werneck half in English, half in Portuguese. This bluesy love song is in the languid yet paradoxically intense manner of Getz's Latin-American-tinged numbers; Tania's voice is mellow, her piano resonant with tenths. In 'You've got me feeling your love' Tania's 'American' voice is unabashedly erotic, while her piano swings in Latin-American boogie rhythm, activated by Steve Thornton's hard percussion; Justo Almario's alto saxophone screeches like some lurid-plumaged Brazilian bird. Brazil's fetid jungle, its Indian villages, its tarmacked motorways and its New York-style night clubs are simultaneously present in Tania's potent 'natural' voice, accompanied not only by her acoustic piano but also by her Fender and Minimoog synthesizer.

'Love explosion', the title song, extends this process into an environmental *festa* similar to those on the previous disc. Caribbean percussion is vivacious, harmony transparent; Tania's voice, at first naive, singing a childish rune, is electrophonically echoed by choric voices that become a jubilating crowd midstream in carnival. That the energy of Tania's music sparks off so lively a sense of *promise* cannot be separated from her polyethnic nature: Indian, Portuguese, Spanish, French, Mexican, Cuban, Caribbean and American are only the main cultures that cohabit her Global Village. Again, 'environmental' immediacy is married to technical sophistication, to the advantage of both.[1]

---

1   It is worth noting that the leading Brazilian 'art' composer, the inexhaustibly fecund Heitor Villa-Lobos (1887–1959), resembles Tania Maria in making no distinctions between the artistic conventions he was trained in at the Rio Conservatory and later in Paris, and the rural and urban pop musics he imbibed from childhood. Some of his multitudinous compositions are 'advanced' modern music; some are well-turned salon and parlour music; some are directly derived from the street music of the *choros*; some create, even as they 'transcribe', songs and dances of rural folk. As with Tania Maria, jungle, village and industrialized city coexist in his work, in a way to which there is no parallel in European musics.

Chapter Twelve

THE ROUGH AND THE TOUGH

And what you own, in this erotic furtherance,
is nothing to do with response or that
times do change . . . you could call
it coming down to the streets and the seedy
broken outskirts of the town.

J. H. Prynne

The 'Global Village' singing poet–composers considered in the last
chapter manifest various shifts from folk to rock, with jazz as
formative agent. Each is a skin tougher than the previous one, and
the trend towards toughness carries with it an encroaching militant
feminism. This attains a climax with Janis Joplin and Patti Smith.
Though neither is strictly speaking a singing poet–composer, each
is sufficiently re-creative to earn a place in these pages.

   With Janis Joplin an assumption of Blackness – of spirit if not of
flesh – could not be more open. A 'smashed woman' victimized by
drink and drugs, she identified her alienation with that of the Black
woman, becoming a White Negress whose music not only resembles
that of blues singers like Bessie Smith and gospel singers like
Mahalia Jackson, but can challenge her Black peers in passion and
power. Although she used traditional blues material and sang
numbers by other people, she did on occasion make her own songs,

and in everything she did revealed that for her creation and re-creation were indivisible.[1] Her performance of Big Mama Thornton's 'Ball and chain blues' is even more agonized in its split pitches, its extension of song into screech and howl, than the original, let alone Elvis Presley's emasculation of it.[2]

Janis sings her own 'Turtle blues' with the same terrifying intensity; this is a real twelve-bar blues in which the 'Blackness' of her vocal production is reinforced by twanging guitar and thumping barrelhouse piano. Here Janis is a White woman creating quasi-Black music in a Chicago ghetto. A comparable 'authenticity' animates her habitual fusions of Black jazz with electric rock. 'Move over' is pentatonically blue in line, with an unremitting powerhouse beat, as though that alone prevents collapse – she may be compared, as rock musician, with the no less distraught Jimi Hendrix. At the same time she is capable of a painfully pinched tenderness, as in her version of Gershwin's 'Summertime', in which her voice coos, croons, whimpers, whispers, levitates, through an austere two-voiced polyphony on guitar and bass; here the counterpoint, as much as the beat, forestalls disintegration. Sometimes she protects herself in defensive irony, as in her own 'O sweet Mary', which infiltrates a country waltz into a fierce rock number.

Janis Joplin was at her peak in her 1967–8 sessions with Big Brother and the Holding Company,[3] a small rock–blues band that ballasted her anguish with the metallic precision of their rhythm and sonority so that her music, however furious, still offered incentives to life and love. Though she is not the composer of the numbers she sings, in performance they could hardly be more her creation. 'Misery'n' is a slow, hard blues marvellously manifesting the traditional equation between speech and song. Beginning with strangulated grunts and groans, the line, driven yet supported by the beat, grows gradually more rhythmically continuous and melodically sustained, so that victory is not after all with 'misery'. Something similar happens in 'Catch me daddy' when, after a frenzied start, Janis launches into a sinuous solo backed only by Dave Getz's savagely *precise* drums. In 'Farewell song', her last appearance with Big Brother, she opens with speech and wails over a spiky beat but grows cumulatively towards song. A tranquil

1   *Janis Joplin's Greatest Hits* and *Pearl*.
2   Elvis Presley's treatment of another Big Mama Thornton song, 'Hound dog', is discussed on pp. 33–4.
3   *Cheap Thrills* and *Farewell Song*.

episode in the middle drops like balm on her and our tangled nerves; then the thrust of the boogie rhythm through the beat sustains her, as she admits that 'your're gonna have to pay your dues'. One later track, 'One night stand', made in 1970 with the Butterfield Blues Band, complements 'Farewell song'. A one-night stand is what her life had become; yet she manages to speak–sing this tune almost bouncily, with positive rather than desperate energy. Superb jazz horn playing matches her resilience.

Janis Joplin was described by people who knew her well as 'a sweet person', and there is intermittent evidence of sweetness in her music. The psychological reasons why she became, with Jimi Hendrix, an archetype of youthful rebellion will probably never be fully known. In any case she, like Jimi, was incapable of lasting attachments, even quarrelling with the band that had played so significant a part in her success; her death of drugs at the age of 27 was, like Jimi Hendrix's, a martyrdom. In her music anger becomes heroic. The evidence of her genius lies in the fact that today her performances sound no less alarming than they did when first created – much as Stravinsky's *Rite of Spring* is a bomb that still, after seventy years, cataclysmically explodes. There is no true successor to Janis Joplin as a White blues–rock shouter, though Tina Turner has something of her raucous ferocity, and gives a sartorial gloss to her Wild Woman of the Woods image by dressing in tatters. Bette Midler, who impersonated Janis Joplin in a film about her, is a show-business performer rather than an instinctive artist in a jazz–folk context. She creates none of her material, but dynamic in performance and sexually attractive in her ugliness, can make a considerable impact, given a number as potent as Mick Jagger's 'You can't always get what you want', or as gruffly affecting as Tom Waits's 'Shiver me timbers'.

Not even Louis Armstrong had a 'dirtier' voice than Janis Joplin and she too, though far more smashed than he, discovered in dirt a triumphant ebullience. She demonstrated, the hard way, what Dory Previn sang *about* in her number concerning the muddy iguanas. Patti Smith's evocation of the iguanas is more conscious, even contrived, than Joplin's, though her rebellion, epitomized in her slogan 'Vive l'anarchie', had similar roots. Whereas Janis's songs were painfully wrested from the heart of her experience, Patti Smith makes imaginative statements aimed at the evils of modern technocracy on behalf of oppressed rather than smashed women. In being the archetypal singer of Women's Liberation she relates social

and political themes to the general plight of Western civilization.
Born in New Jersey in 1946, she had a Christian background which
she rejected on the basis of the Tower of Babel. It seemed to her
inadmissible that a jealous Lord should deliberately confound our
languages, robbing us of

> the universal tongue because we sought to create beyond the
> landscape . . . the artist in me was already aroused . . . and
> satan . . . the first absolute artist . . . the first true
> nigger . . . he was the first to have a vision of existence
> beyond what was imposed on him. He fell to disgrace not for
> being evil but for exhibiting the anxious passionate
> recklessness of the artist.

In this spirit Patti Smith, like Janis Joplin, cast herself as a satanic
White Negress. Moving to New York in 1967, she lived in the
famous–notorious Chelsea Hotel where Dylan Thomas died and
where archetypal dropouts like Brendan Behan, Andy Warhol,
William Burroughs, Jimi Hendrix, Jim Morrison, Bob Dylan and
Janis Joplin herself intermittently lived and consorted.

Trained as a visual artist, Patti soon moved into literature,
creating surreal verse and prose influenced by her culture heroes,
including Verlaine, Baudelaire, Rimbaud, Bataille, Artaud and
Genet, as well as figures nearer home such as William Burroughs,
Allen Ginsberg and Bob Dylan – not to mention the cosmological
William Blake, who has been appropriated by so many subversives,
and usually misunderstood in the process. Patti Smith's writing
does 'pay honour to the runner who would still seek glory in the
heart of failure'; but when she adds that 'all honour goes to the
guardian of ritual as he caresses the land with the entrails of
language' one wonders whether pretentiousness may not discredit
her authenticity. Read as literature, Patti Smith's writings are not
impressive; the reiteration of four-letter words, the 'shocking'
sexual and narcotic anecdotage, grow tiresome, and any genuine
startlements the language might offer are vitiated by verbosity, by a
lack of rhythmic vitality, and by a total absence of humour such as
she shares with another, rather greater, Messianic artist who wrote
almost as many words as notes – Richard Wagner.

But Patti Smith cannot be adequately assessed on the printed
page; she is a mediawoman whose words need to be spoken aloud
and which become, in her public readings, a theatrical experience.
Speech becomes incantation, incantation becomes song. Her 1976

disc, *Radio Ethiopia*, made with the Patti Smith Group, a heavy-metal electric band of considerable impact, can hardly be shrugged aside. Patti writes all the words and seems to collaborate on the music with members of her group, Lenny Kaye, Ivan Kral and Richard Sohl. 'Pissing in the river' and 'Pumping (my heart)' are heavy-rock numbers with something in common with the 'hymnic' numbers of Bob Dylan, though their tunes are more fragmented and their oscillating triads looser. Their cataclysmic effect is due more to their shattering decibel level, in which the electric sonorities lacerate like tearing cloth.

That 'first absolute artist and first true nigger' takes over in 'Radio Ethiopia' and 'Abyssinian', in which Babel let loose inverts the process of biblical history! And it's significant that the singer in this electronic powerhouse of tribal music is a woman: her voice, unalleviated in its bleak, dark tone, sounds minatory and is meant to. The deafening noise makes the words inaudible, but this is irrelevant because the message is 'beyond' words and incarnate in the 'ritual'. This is more movingly if not more powerfully revealed in 'Ain't it strange', in which the percussive ostinati and the vocal moans, groans, wails and howls suggest both Black African and Red Amerindian tribal musics.

This collocation is still more marked on the 1978 disc, *Easter*, a gallimaufry of verse and prose that fuses Verlaine, Baudelaire and Rimbaud with Black African rituals and the peyote-cult ghost dances of the Amerindians. The starker textures and metrical patterns of Red Indian musics prompt from Patti a raw flatness in her vocal production. In retrospect it is noticeable that her voice, even in her most uproariously 'African' moments, is seldom 'blue' in inflexion. By using the mechanized electrophonics of her Asphalt Jungle to unify her White, Red and Black musical sources, Patti is able to 'reanimate the ancestors', as the authentic ghost dance is supposed to. The cycle can justifiably end with a hymnic number in which plain diatonic concords are haloed by Easter bells. The text explicitly relates Christ to Promethean smiths (including Patti herself!), to Little Richard, and to Rimbaud as martyr; her personal anarchy seeks a universalized matriarchy, transmitting the patriarchal power of the aboriginal inhabitants of the American continent to today's alienated and oppressed.

Patti Smith's return to 'primitive' musical roots is less persuasive than that of New Yorker Grace Jones, who reinstates 'darkest Africa' in industrial America. Black, austerely beautiful, six-foot tall, with geometrically cut hair and regal bearing, she looks like an African idol. For the 1982 album *Nightclubbing* she devises, if she does not compose, all the numbers in collaboration with her exceptionally able instrumentalists, especially Barry Reynolds and Wally Badarou, who play electric guitar and electric piano respectively. In this music the jungle remains a jungle even when concreted – as we may hear if we compare her 'Feel up' with 'Demolition man'. The former consists of a sexual rune yelled in Grace's imperiously penetrative timbre against feverish African percussion, tribal rather than township in style, with twittering African flutes simulated on a synthesizer. The noise might come from an African village, but for its mechanistic precision. 'Demolition man' inverts this, beginning with a thumping rock beat as savage as the fiercest tribal music but industrial in connotation, with the synthetic sonorities emulating road drills, tearing cloth and crashing masonry, while Grace ungracefully blares vocal riffs. This demolition *man* – not woman – is not merely a part of the industrial landscape, for he demolishes human hopes and fears as well as buildings.

More subtly, the fusion of African and Asphalt Jungle appears in 'Nightclubbing', in which the beat thuds in forbidding and foreboding slowness, while Grace chants of nightwalking the streets 'like ghosts'. Grace's growls and hoots are often startlingly subhuman; we recall that Henry Thoreau found 'the hooting of owls admirably suited to swamps and twilit woods which no day illustrates, suggesting a vast and undeveloped nature which men have not yet recognized'. Yet Grace's forest is here urban: the words refer to nuclear bombs and attendant horrors. So the number makes its effect through its sinister discretion, having no need of rhetoric. None of these numbers has harmonic or tonal development; melodically they are virtually restricted to rudimentary pentatonicism. The African forest's primitivism and New York's technology reveal an uncanny identity.

Most numbers on the disc have more in common both with American rock and with urban African township music. 'Walking in the rain' recounts in dark-hued speech rather than song how Grace, 'feeling like a woman, looking like a man', tramps through incessant rain on some endless journey to no end, yet does so without desperation, for the polymetrical Township style is light and airy. 'Pull up the bumper' and 'Use me' (which is about abuse as much as use) are harsher, their patent affinity with hard electric rock also betraying resemblance to the fuzzbuzz effects beloved of many African peoples. This is an instrumental complement to Grace's vocal production: industrial technology imitates the noises made by so-called savages, just as Grace Jones and her backing voices bark or grunt in grimly primitive communication, rather than jubilate in choric solidarity like Gospel-singing Afroamericans.

The rewards this music offers are conditional on its avoidance of fanaticism. Scary though it often is, it is blessed with a sense of humour and even, to pun on the singer's name, with grace in more than one sense. 'Art groupie' is at once acutely satirical and charming, for the thirtyish raggy beat and the impudent, cornily harmonized tune beguile, while the electric sonorities have the jocundity of African street musics. The cheeriness may be innocent as well as 'emergent', but it is not victimized by that aggressively male Demolition Man. 'I've seen that face before (Libertango)' is aptly described by its subtitle, being a fast Afro-Caribbean tango, which Grace sings and swings *almost* lyrically. Yet both tune and sonority, pervaded by Jack Emblow's accordion, recall the Brecht–Weill songs. Here too there may be a suggestion that demolition of the old world may be a necessary preliminary to construction of the new.

This is a most invigorating album, and the final track, 'I've done it again', may tell us why, since for the last and only time the song is a lyrical ballad, in tango rhythm, with harmony and modulations that imply some development, compared with the 'African' numbers that exist like real tribal music, in an eternal present. Momentarily, Grace's voice approaches tenderness, though the refrain phrase 'I've done it again' hardens the tone as she sings something approaching a tumbling strain. What she has done again is to fall in love. The harshness of the refrain may suggest that although love remains positive, it cannot be easy, in our frightening world.

Grace Jones's 1982 disc *Living My Life*, carries on from this point being no less positive if less startling, and less African, than *Nightclubbing*. All but one of the numbers are by Grace, sometimes solo, sometimes in collaboration with her lead guitarist Barry Reynolds. The first track reveals a West Indian rather than straight African lineage, for 'My Jamaican guy' is in West Indian patois and in reggae-style rhythms. The instrumental patterns and Grace's dark-hued phrases are meant to be hypnotic, for the song is about the 'laid-back' state as a virtue. The presentation in Jamaican dialect is, however, reductive, and irony, if not parody, is inherent in the contrast between the singer's austere vocal production and the agility of the percussion. Irony becomes explicit in 'Nipple to the bottle', an anti-man song which, with woman becoming predator, reverses the basic relationship between man and mammary security. Yet again aggression is purged in the bouncy beat and sharp textures.

The only number not by Grace Jones, 'Waltz of the stork', is perhaps the most imaginative in her performance. Extracted from a Broadway musical by the rebelliously talented Black composer Melvin van Peebles, it offers in its verses a particularized description of a New York morning, spoken by Grace over bright, urban-morning percussion patterns. Her voice, controlled in rhythm and colour, makes a perfectly timed transition into the sung refrain, the only moment of harmonic and tonal movement in any of the songs. The refrain's lyricism – 'just the Apple stretching and yawning, just morning New York putting its feet on the floor' – flowers out of the grubby ephemera of New York streets. Again, purgation is achieved.

The four songs on side 2 form a sequence moving incrementally in a positive direction. 'Everybody hold still' is a briskly reggae-styled song of indecision. Animated regularity makes for stasis; there is no melodic, let alone harmonic–tonal, movement, since each phrase gets stuck, rotating on itself. It may be a song of fear also, since only if 'everybody hold still' will 'nobody get hurt'. This bears on the next number, 'Cry now, laugh later', in which movement is allied to crime and violence, with the implication that only by holding on, still and firm, can one hope to come through laughing rather than crying. The band's electrified and electrifying sonorities rend with a ferocity almost too much for the bouncy beat. But in the next number, 'Inspiration', there is no doubt that the Caribbean lilt is working on behalf of good. Although Grace hasn't *found* inspiration, her search gathers power, both in her sustained if sepulchral voice and in the unbroken humming of electric organ. There may be a way through doubt: 'The thing I wrote off as false came true'. The sibilant whistling that wafts around the vocal line and over the hypnotic beat is disturbing, yet contains more promise than threat.

Promise becomes incarnate in the final song, 'Unlimited capacity for love', even though 'the end's not in sight' and the world is minatory, as in some sense it always was and will be. Cataloguing the evasions we try out, Grace convinces us that she herself will 'never cheat unlimited capacity for love'. The instrumental parts enhance their habitual nervous agility, telescoping several metrical patterns from moderate to very fast. Against this agitation, the electric organ is serenely sustained; and what had been, in 'Inspiration', a remote whistling dubious in emotional effect becomes, in the long instrumental before the final stanza, heart-easing pentatonic song. The peroration, still hard and chittering, is also life-affirming, though there is only the prospect of 'another unwinning war'. Few fade-outs are as imaginatively justified as this. That 'unlimited capacity' stretches into an untold, untellable future and we recognize in Grace Jones a rare black bird who abides as well as forebodes.

While 'darkest' Africa, aboriginal America and industrial technocracy were discovering a common denominator in the New World, the Old Country had herself acquired an indigenous Black population. It is gratifying that West-Indian Britain should already have produced, in Joan Armatrading, a singing poet–composer of major talent, who creates her own words and music and puts them across with presence. Though the lot of a West-Indian woman in the brash British city is still not easy, her Caribbean temperament is too buoyant to prompt the minatory qualities inherent in Grace Jones's Africanism. Armatrading's songs[4] promulgate affirmation, not protest. From the West-Indian island where she was born she brought a measure of the guilelessness inherent in reggae, as in African Township musics. Protest creeps in, if at all, by the verbal back door, without overt modification of the music's sunniness. From the current musical scene in global Britain, however, Joan picked up the exacerbations of city life as manifest in soul, rock and Black American jazz. Her affirmation becomes stronger because it has more to ride over.

The 1975 album *Back to the Night* points to this with its title. 'So good' and 'Let's go dancing' are basically simple love songs with childlike refrains and vivacious reggae rhythms. Yet 'Let's go dancing' asks questions of the lover, to which answers are ambiguous – indicated by the abrupt harmonic shifts, usually a tone or a third apart, at the ends of the stanzas. So we're not surprised when other numbers reconcile this guilelessness with the nervous virility of jazz and soul. Beginning as a piano-accompanied ballad, the title

---

4 *Joan Armatrading* and *Track Record*.

song 'Back to the night' evolves towards jazz *ecstasis*; 'Body to dust'
ends in melismatic abandon, like Nina Simone or Deniece Williams
in full pelt. Joan Armatrading's voice thus demonstrates how
'ripeness is all', and does so with significant force in songs about
various kinds of travelling. 'Get in touch with Jesus' and 'No love
for free' are in part rejections of Gospel music and message. Tone is
bold, rhythm sprightly, phrasing clipped. The total effect is merry
but jittery – as is still more the case with 'Travel so far' and
'Stepping out', reggae-style paeans to freedom that, under jazz
influence, become slightly manic, with plangently blue if anonymous saxophone obbligati. 'Dry land', unusual in being a slowish
ballad, also acquires blue intensity, especially on the phrase 'been a
long time at sea'.

Most of Joan Armatrading's later songs may be categorized as in
this sense 'Caribbean blues'. The title song from the 1976 album
Down to Zero opens with a rudimentary tumbling strain over
chattering guitar and zipping percussion. Vocal rhythm bounces;
tone is open – yet the line builds to jazz intensity through its triplet
cross-rhythms, which in turn promote jazzy saxophone obbligati.
Even 'Rosie', ostensibly a merry song about a girl successful with
the boys, has a nerviness that safeguards it from Motown vacuity.
Although in songs of the early eighties, such as 'I'm lucky' and 'Me
and myself', the refrains are sometimes babyish, as are those of
African Township musics, there is evidence in the sharp textures
and tingling rhythms that Joan Armatrading, having grown up in
the big British city, has had to put away childish things. Her 1983
numbers preserve jazz tension while gravitating towards heavy rock.
'Frustration' sounds quasi-African in its remorseless ostinati, and
the horns blaze in Township ebullience gone sour. Yet even
frustration proves life-enhancing – and not so far from the 'Heaven'
of another 1983 number, which, touching on a hymn-like
Township style, has a grand modal tune over sustained chords on
electric keyboards.

Joan Armatrading makes her songs out of the everyday reality of
her life in Britain, using common words in common contexts,
without much metaphor; complementarily, her voice is bold,
direct, middle-ranged. Contemporary with her is Marianne
Faithfull, a White British woman also centred on London, who
started in the sixties as an 'educated' modern folk singer in the genre
of Joan Baez, singing real English folk songs and modern imitations
of them with dewy tone and delicate inflexion. A little later she was

singing folk–rock numbers, including some by Mick Jagger, still in relatively gentle, even genteel, English style. But her liaison with Jagger introduced her to the hard-rock world, where her jetting life-style transformed her into an urban singer responsive to the stresses and distresses of her time. Though she did not usually make up her songs, she coverted rock and soul numbers into her own property – as in her 1979 album *Broken English*.

The punning title number is presented as heavy metal, quasi-African rock Englished into a female equivalent of the Rolling Stones themselves. Over a primitively unremitting beat, Marianne Faithfull broods in a dark voice like a less raucous Patti Smith or a less vibrant Grace Jones. Though her vocal quality is not intrinsically remarkable, she has travelled far from the piping treble of her early remakings of folk songs. In all the *Broken English* songs her manner is incantatory, especially venomous in 'Guilt' and in a version of John Lennon's 'Working class hero' even angrier than the original.

By her 1981 album, *Dangerous Acquaintances*, Marianne is working consistently with Barry Reynolds, Grace Jones's one-time associate. She has become a singing poet–composer, though we have no information as to how the collaboration between her and Reynolds functions. She now responds more positively to the heavy-rock backing; her music is less morose, though Marianne's voice is still restricted to a very narrow range – not much more than a fourth – and is not only bleating, but also quavery, in tone. The best songs compromise between urban rock and folk music incantation, fierce or melancholic. 'Eye communication' has a near-hysterical beat, though a dignified modal tune is born, in the chorus, of the verse's lugubrious one-tone lament. The tenor of all the songs is desperate or forlorn, and the final number, 'Truth bitter truth', is certainly bitter, though its truth is loaded. The refrain – 'Where did it go to, my youth, where did it slip away to?' – is genuinely discomforting.

The discomforture prepares us for Marianne Faithfull's 1983 album, her most distinctive achievement. Many women singers have been obsessed, we've noted, with a recall of childhood. Marianne calls this cycle *A Child's Adventure*, but the emphasis is on the adventure that obliterates childishness. Again, it's a collaboration with Barry Reynolds, sometimes with the assistance of Wally Bardarou. An atmosphere of menace is soon established. 'Ashes in my hand' lives up to its title, being a drab tango that tries to rescue happiness from 'extreme despair', but finds that 'happiness feels like pain'. 'Running for our lives', faster in tempo, more lilting in rhythm, remains creepy as well as scary, and is a song of frustration in that 'we never get very far'. 'The blue millionaire', at first spoken over a jittery beat, is changed in the refrain, the non-singing point being that tycoonery inhibits life. Even when she does sing, Marianne's voice is restricted to its narrow compass, her timbre quavering.

The most personal songs are again those that infuse a dehydrated rock idiom into a gloom-infested folk modality, notably 'Falling from grace', which has a tune, though it is little more than a scale *falling* under its own weight. 'Morning come', dreaming of release on 'a humming bird's wing, beyond the back of the wind', alone aspires to evocative metaphor and lyrical flight, accompanied by restless modulations instead of the habitual, habituating drone. On the whole, however, this is a glum album and the glumness is its authenticity. It is a complement by opposites to the songs of Joan Armatrading. Where Joan, despite the odds, finds affirmation in her adopted home, Marianne Faithfull, as white Negro, finds her native environment increasingly alienating.

Chapter Thirteen

MAGIC AND TECHNOLOGY

Every moribund or sterile society attempts to save itself by creating a redemption myth which is also a fertility myth . . . The society we live in today has also created its myth. The sterility of the bourgeois world will end in suicide or a new form of creative participation . . .

Modern man likes to pretend that his thinking is wide awake. But this wide-awake thinking has led us into the mazes of a nightmare in which the torture chambers are endlessly repeated in the mirrors of reason. When we emerge, perhaps we will realize that we have been dreaming with our eyes wide open, and that the dreams of reason are intolerable. And then, perhaps, we will begin to dream once more with our eyes closed.

Octavio Paz

Return to primitivism is not the only possible liberation from a mechanized world. Heavy rock was often associated with drugs: and therefore with release into dreams, nightmares, and phantasmagoric realms of experience that may be foreboding, but may also be benign. Women, especially English women, have enthusiastically explored such 'fairy realms', which, if usually 'forlorn', are occasionally incandescent. Modern electronic media readily lend themselves to such exploratory magic – as we may observe in the case of Kate Bush, an English girl with simple English names, who creates an exotic world by enhancing confessional intimacy with modern technology.

With her, boundaries between reality and televisual fantasy are hazy, in an elaborately produced act involving mime, dance and visuals along with her singing, piano playing and the contributions of a wide variety of acoustic and electrical instrumentalists. Kate writes her own words and music, and has a hand in the arrangements and production. What comes out is highly sophisticated, yet also naive, in that she abandons herself to her dreams and nightmares with childish relish. One suspects that her methods of creation would bear this out. She is a real mini-poet, in a more artful sense than Joan Armatrading or even Marianne Faithfull, whose basic words are adequate to basic experience. Kate Bush's words make a virtue of inconsequentiality, veering between magical mystery, black comedy and quirky fantasy. Similarly her music, despite the complexity of the arrangements, sounds as though it were initially improvised at the piano, the clauses meandering and harmonies fluctuating according to whim. This is not necessarily a weakness in 'subversive' pop art, and may be a strength.

The 1978 album, *Lionheart* is typical. At the centre stands a touching little ballad, 'Oh England my Lionheart', about the Old Country renewed after (presumably atomic) wars. Kate's piano is haloed by antique recorders and harpsichord; the folky tune and concordant harmonies could hardly be simpler, while Kate's voice is a high treble, so little-girlish as to suggest ironic overtones, which to this song are inappropriate. They fit, however, Kate's more characteristic numbers, such as 'Symphony in blue', which begins in gently loping tempo, equating her state of mind with the blue environment she's made for herself, but shifts to red and the passion that engenders. The final stanza turns into near-farce:

> The more I think about sex
> the better it gets.
> Here we have a purpose in life,
> good for the blood circulation.

This may be true enough but, with its pseudo-rhyme, sounds comic after the fancy poetry of the first verse and the confessional intimacy of the chorus. Here Kate's stratospheric soprano, between pipe and squeak, is quaint, unnerving and ludicrous by turns. Nothing could be further from Joan Armatrading's direct middle register or Marianne Faithfull's sultry surliness.

Similar in effect is a kid's song, 'In search of Peter Pan', which is about the *advantages* of not growing up. 'Wow', about a failed actor, hinges on reality and illusion, the voice being comically dismissive. Perhaps the best song, 'Don't put your foot on the heartbrake', is so because it acts out the pun in the title, presenting the young woman's desperation in terms of a runaway car. The physical image gives direction to the agitated beat, supporting a swinging tune. In the circumstances Kate's squawks seem justified, and the song gains cohesion without surrendering the freedom of its long-ranging paragraphs.

The songs on side 2 grow more fantastical at the expense of personal immediacy. 'In the warm room' is sensual–sexual fantasizing, in which the words are moulded by free association and internal assonances ('mellow wallows', 'soft as marshmallows'), while the maundering non-structure of the melodic periods and harmonies is as apposite to the theme as is Kate's fluttery voice. 'Coffee homeground' is Grand Guignol black comedy, with wittily disturbing words, an obliviously corny tune, and vocal production of artful syrupiness. This serves as prelude to 'Hammer horror', which is what its title indicates, and gives Kate ample opportunity for squeaks and squawks. The horrors aren't really horrific, any more than are the cinematic and televisual versions. Kate Bush's songs, for all their art and craft, are gamey compared with Joan Armatrading's, though this is not to deny their flair and originality.

Even so, Kate Bush's talent, like her voice, is frail, and by the time of her 1982 disc, *The Dreaming*, little verbal and musical substance survives outside the multimedia gimmickry. The first number 'Sat in your lap', seems to be about the distinction between knowledge and wisdom. It is very fast, frantic and squeaky, and leaves us unable to distinguish between the 'real' world and the flickering images and ephemeral sounds of the television screen. Significantly, one of the numbers concerns the prince of stage magicians, Houdini. Others – 'Night of the swallow', 'Pull out the pin', 'There goes a tenner' – tell tales such as one might pick up from a desultory watching of the box, between sleeping and waking. The verses have poetic moments, but are too elusive, as well as illusive, to count for much; the music is submerged in the electrophonics. The only number to escape this is the simplest, 'All for love', which has a tender tune, sung in Kate's least affected style.

Usually on this disc events succeed one another with telly's arbitrary irreality, in which the boundaries between fact ('the news') and fiction are undefined. The title song is the most revealing example of this confusion. It's about the 'dream time' of Australian aborigines – which for them is a reality beyond the world of appearances. But Kate Bush presents it as an infantile rune, in a swinging 6/8, sung in a 'comic' (for her, very low) register. The aborigines' dream time ironically comments on the dream time of our technology, but Kate's *parody* of the 'savages' leaves us stranded, the more so because, with her customary opulence, she calls on real aboriginal didgeridoo and bull-roarer along with electrophonics simulating tribal gatherings and the bayings and babblings of bush beasts and birds. 'What is Truth?' as Pilate asked, watching wars and rumours of war on the telly.

Magic and technology meet more purposefully in the work of Toyah Wilcox, especially her 1982 disc, *The Changeling*. All Toyah's numbers are credited to Wilcox/Bogen, and it is not clear who is responsible for what. None the less both her voice and her theatrical presence are potent enough to establish her rights over the songs in which the words, if magical, are intelligible, and the tunes have pith and point. *The Changeling* presents a girl – a 'street creature' – in a modern technocracy who, joining 'the Castaways', contacts magical Druids of Antiquity, establishing connections between 'Angel and me'. This changeling may 'Run wild, run free', making 'A life in the trees', chanting in a 'Dawn chorus' – all titles from the album, animated by electrophonics and by Toyah's electric charisma. The rebirth of animal instinct and the invoking of supernatural forces convince because they are verbally and musically cohesive, and so can attain a hymn-like apotheosis in the epilogic 'Brave new world'.

Overtones of irony are not, as in Kate Bush, fuddled: Toyah absorbs enough of Joan Armatrading's sturdy affirmation into her media magic to evade Kate's arch self-consciousness. Her vocal line, strong enough to survive the technology, is itself an assertion of human survival. Perhaps it is not fortuitous that physical 'presence' has become more important in Toyah's work than music *per se*; she seems to be becoming an actress on the legitimate stage as well in films, rather than a singer.

Another fascinating tie-up between magic and technology is offered by Judie Tzuke, who also calls for complicated electrophonics. All her numbers are attributed to her in collaboration with Mike Flaxman, her lead guitarist, synthesizer, electric pianist and backing vocalist, sometimes with another member of the band, Paul Muggleton. It is not clear whether they work together on words, music and production, or whether their roles are distinct. What is clear is that they produce between them a distinctive, convincing whole. The words, though not verbally rich like Kate Bush's, are well designed for music, and the music has recognizable character, whether in fiery rock vein, as in 'Sports car', or in a tender folky ballad such as 'For you',[1] which opens with an entrancing choric episode in multiple tracking. Later this merges into lyrical writing for strings which shows some compositional skill, as is also evident in the string coda to 'Stay with me till dawn'. Judie Tzuke's voice, whether in fast rock numbers or in folky ballads, is high and wispy, with minimal vibrato. Like Toyah, she does not aim at expressivity, but educes magic through the precision of her rhythm and the lacy filigree of her folk-like ornamentation.

On her 1984 disc, *Ritmo*, her co-ordination with her brilliant instrumentalists opens unexpected vistas. 'Jeannie no' is a telephone call from one woman to another, pleading that she won't hurt the caller's brother. Judie's exiguous voice, reiterating a drooping rather than tumbling strain over nervously syncopated percussion, gives the experience more than topical and local application, becoming a cry from the void, if not *de profundis*. Still more remarkable are two songs of menace: 'Nighthawks', a portrait of leather-jacketed motorcycle boys in moonlight, and 'Walk don't walk', which tells a tale of incipient violence through pentatonic plainchant, like a Black Mass. Both numbers are mysterious; their menace is not so much destructive as a recognition of the dangerous unknown that surrounds us, not merely because of leather-garbed lads. The tensility of Judie's voice, contrasted with the choric sonority, contributes to this effect.

Comparable with Judie Tzuke is Annie Lennox, the name of whose group, the Eurythmics, telescopes rhythm, euphony and Europe, though Europe is seen and heard in a global context. All words and music are created by Annie Lennox and David Stewart. She is an academically trained musician who, inspired by Joni Mitchell, rebelled against the concert world, discovering that her talents ran to words, mime and dance as well as music; he started

1 *The Best of Judie Tzuke.*

out a professional rock guitarist. Between them they have created music ritual of remarkable originality, creating not so much songs as 'sound pictures'. The ingredients that make these sound pictures have affinities with folk cultures all over the world. Many of their songs are charms or spells; all create 'moments of sensation' in which an audience may participate.

This is why the words are usually simple and reiterative. But their simplicity is artfully artless and mysterious, and mystery, as with Joni Mitchell, promotes music. The Eurythmics' premisses are defined in their first exploratory album, which appeared in 1981 under the telling title of *The Garden*. 'English summer' evokes an Edenic childhood by way of the tingling of percussion and the glinting of synthesizers, through which Annie Lennox chants the words with the gravity of a child's rune. Cries of real birds and game-playing children are interlaced into the music. 'Belinda' is specifically a spell. Over a beat continuously thumping like a tribal drum, Annie summons rain to heal Belinda's fear, until the chant fades with double-tracked voice twining in parallel thirds, that age-old aural image of security. The loveliness of Annie's voice, used spontaneously in middle register without recourse to vocal gymnastics, makes the eternal rain a benediction against the thud of time. Magic and human feeling coalesce, as she sounds at once like a female shaman and a tenderly responsive young woman.

Sometimes there's a hint of threat as well as mystery: 'Sing-sing', chanted in French, merges into animal cries both comic and fear-ful; the final number confronts negative emotions of hate and revenge. Even so the music remains melodicaly, rhythmically and harmonically guileless, until it is gradually corrupted by giggling voices. Threat here is somewhat obvious; the disc as a whole might be called simplistic as well as simple.

Yet this rudimentariness was a process of discovery, necessary to the extraordinary advance effected in the two 1983 discs. The album called *Sweet Dreams are Made of This* asserts authority in the sheer quality of its sound. Annie's voice is projected with bell-like clarity; the electrophonic sonorities resonate cleanly; the rhythmic patterns are as exhilarating as they are precise. 'Modern' instability is healed rather than exacerbated by modern technology – as may be heard in 'Love is a stranger' and 'Sweet dreams are made of this', fairly fast songs with repetitive melodies over an ostinato bass and metrical figurations that themselves have melodic identity. Because the texture is so clear, everything being audible and worth listening

to, repetition does not degenerate into tedium. Polyethnic affiliations are overt – in particular, Polynesian rhythmic animation and
Balinese-like tinklings on synthesizers encourage us to 'hold your
head up – keep your head up – MOVIN' ON'. In 'Wrap it up' the
quasi-oriental pentatonics are jazzed up with bluesiness, as is
appropriate to the sexier theme. Again it's the lucidity of the sound
that refreshes. This applies hardly less to songs, such as 'The walk',
that deal with neurosis. Sustained chords on electric keyboards
make a magic background to Annie Lennox's pentatonic intimacies.
The upthrusting ostinato preserves melodic appeal. The number
turns on a dichotomy between 'the real thing' – introduced by the
refrain's change of tonal gear and Annie's harsher vocal colour – and
its illusory substitutes.

Personal experience usually acquires a mythological dimension.
'This is the house' sees and hears a particular human situation –

This is the family having a party
There's a crack in the ceiling

– in the context of 'the dust and rust of time'. Similarly 'This city
never sleeps' overlays the rumble of underground trains with the
beating of the girl's heart. The anonymous city breathes like a beast;
yet within its 'otherness' the ostinato patterns speak with melodic
and rhythmic identity, while above floats Annie's ethereal
pentatonic tune. Most magical of all is 'Jennifer', a ballad of a
drowned Ophelia with green eyes and orange hair. Again the
melody is as simple as a child's rune. Intoned in Annie's most dulcet
tones over a dully thumping, time-measuring drum, it is engulfed
in scintillating electrophonic sonorities. The aquatic waverings
suggest the waters of the unconscious, evoking the world of the
primeval fairy tale, as against the house of 'This is the house', which
is just around the corner, or the city that 'never sleeps' and is
London, the metropolis we're subject to. Levels of experience
merge, and that these levels include the 'matristic' and 'patristic'
impulses we've seen to underlie pop music in our time may be
suggested by the fact that 'Jennifer' is really a man – a boyfriend of
Annie's adolescence who tragically died. She herself deliberately
counteracts the natural 'femininity' of her voice and appearance by
cultivating an androgynous image, not necessarily through a desire
to project sexual ambivalence, but because she believes that her
intrinsic nature will be more fully appreciated without the
distraction of overt female sexuality.

The other 1983 album, *Touch*, explores similar themes with no less economy, perhaps embracing more menace yet attaining a more positive fulfilment. 'Paint a rumour' has an explicitly minatory subject, unfolding in crisp metrical patterns suggestive of Polynesia, Bali and even Japan as well as Africa, while synthesizers wail in arabesques that recall Moorish–Spanish flamenco. Jazz horns and Annie's soaring double-tracked vocalise enhance the air-borne effect – which ends by obliterating hostility through the elegance of the melodic and harmonic textures. So 'rumour' amounts to living dangerously in a dangerous world, finding deep satisfaction in so doing. Interestingly, the technique here is not far removed from that of the happiest number on the disc, 'Right by your side', a love song glittering in sonority, bounding in Latin-American–Caribbean rhythm, without a care in the world. Living so ebulliently in the present must always – we may recall Tania Maria – contain *potential* for danger. This becomes patent in 'Here comes the rain again', nervously energetic in rhythm, clean in sonority, radiant in vocal production. The song may qualify as a rain spell, balancing hope and hazard. 'No fear, no hate, no pain, no broken hearts' is another charm in which Annie's hypnotic repetition of the words exploits the therapeutic effect of the 'perfect Diapason' of the octave. There is a whiff of panic in the affirmation, just as, complementarily, 'Regrets' and 'Aqua' discover tranquillity within fear. Annie's statement that she regards the Eurythmics as European rather than British is supported by the French and Mediterranean flavour of this folk–rock ballad, both in the tune and in the accordion-tinged sonority. As we've noted, however, 'European' is too geographically limited a descriptive of the Eurythmics' Global Village.

It is slightly surprising, but also reassuring, that this lucid, relatively elegant yet never evasive music should have achieved spectacular commercial success. The phenomenon is paralleled by the woman singer who attained 'fabulous' celebrity on the evidence of her first disc. She is Sade Adu, who bridges gulfs between ethnic worlds in being of half-British, half-Nigerian descent. Sade writes her own words, which, concerned with sexual love and still more its frustrations, are fairly minimal but beautifully conducive to music. This too she is mainly responsible for, though apparently with a little help from her friends – whose instrumentals are often extended and always precisely projected. The on the whole affirmative tranquillity of the numbers on her record-breaking record, *Diamond Life*, springs largely from this diamond-like clarity of articulation. The metrical patterns of the percussion scintilate and the electrophonic sonorities unfold in sustained euphony, with an effect usually 'laid back' and leisurely, even when the rhythms are complex.

Sade Adu's naturally lovely voice floats or rides serenely through the textures, usually in middle range, though with occasional resort to a bell-like upper register, and more frequent intrusions of always controlled jazz 'dirt'. Stuart Mathewman's saxophone – especially in 'Sally' – complements Sade's voice both in sustained line and in jazzy intensity. Together they sound committed, yet at the same time cool, and this is a good way to live in the dangerous present. The polyethnic qualities of the music – British, American, West Indian, East Indian, African by turns and concurrently – condition the calm it induces. Responding to Sade's mellifluous vocal line and the easily loping rhythm of 'Why can't we live together?' we recognize that the question applies in a wider context than a specific man–woman relationship: riot is not the only possible reaction to ethnic differentiation.

Despite the charismatic appeal of Sade's *Diamond Life* it would be misleading to assume that its therapeutic 'cool' is necessarily the central strand in female pop songs of the mid-eighties. If less seductive and perhaps musically less rewarding, Alison Moyet might claim this centrality, producing all her own material in collaboration with Steve Jolley. More verbally articulate than Sade, she sometimes embraces social criticism ('Money mile' is scarily effective), while her love and anti-love songs have pith and sinew whether negatively, as in the fine man-debunking number, 'All cried out', or more positively, as in 'Honey for the bees' and 'Love resurrection'. The tunes are sturdily contoured, often modal; the ostinati figurations for the prevailingly electrophonic instruments are less lucent than those of Sade and – especially in the honey-bees number – have affinities with the process music of Steve Reich, or at least Philip Glass. Given the quality of the music, however, it's a strength that it *goes on* (all the numbers fade out rather than end); and although Moyet's voice hasn't the beauty of Sade's, she has a tough neutrality which, without calling for instant capitulation, ensures that her songs survive.

Less magical than Sade, she is more intelligent than the ebullient Cyndi Lauper, another supremely successful singer of the mid-eighties. All three of these talented women have been momently eclipsed by their contemporary Madonna, who has become the image of a generation without possessing either a distinctive voice or conspicuous musical ability. Ma-donna is 'my woman', if not lady, and at the same time an Eternal Beloved, as was the medieval prototype. Her ethnically grotesque, gypsyish attire identifies her with here and now, while her perpetual pout evades overt acceptance. This kind of 'neutrality' is easier to take than Moyet's and even Sade's, but while what Madonna offers can't be expected to last long, there is no denying the force of her impact on her own generation and on the pre-teenagers who will be the next.

Although a cool neutrality may be the distinctive pose of the mid-eighties, darker, more violent moods and modes are far from obsolete. Throughout the seventies heavy rock remained active in the songs of Chrissie Hynde and the Pretenders; Chrissie's 'direct' voice – a White complement to Joan Armatrading's – generated in the best of her songs,[2] such as 'Private life' and 'Back on the chain gang', passion and compassion enough to weather the destructiveness.

A little later a still more radical return to the jungle was advocated by Siouxsie and the Banshees,[3] whose aboriginal ferocity extended beyond their name. In 1984 the Cocteau Twins went a stage further, for their electrophonics create a dense *forest* of sound – an aural womb-tomb – which exists, non-harmonically and monorhythmically, not so much in aboriginal America or darkest Africa as in some space-age limbo. Through this sub- or super-human sound world Elizabeth Cocteau's weird voice moans and mumbles three- or four-note incantations, so electrically processed that mere human feeling evaporates. In comparison with the Cocteau Twins' *Garlands* (1984),[4] Annie Lennox's *Touch* and Sade's *Diamond Life* seem havens of normality. None the less, one cannot assume that because the Eurythmics and Sade are comparatively quiet they are not disquieting. Easy Listening is hardly likely to be, at this precarious point in the human saga, either honest or convincing. It is not fortuitous that the two female singing poet–composers who may be most crucially representative of the present moment, Rickie Lee Jones and Laurie Anderson, are Americans who have global affinities with Britain's Sade and Annie Lennox. Each, though fairly quiet, is deeply disturbing.

2 *Chrissie Hynde and the Pretenders.*
3 *Siouxsie and the Banshees: a Kiss in the Dreamhouse.*
4 Cocteau Twins, *Garlands.*

Chapter Fourteen

DEADEND KID AND ANDROGYNE

Circling the Sun, at a respectful distance,
Earth remains warmed, not roasted; but the Moon
Circling the Earth, at a disdainful distance,
Will drive men lunatic (should they defy her)
With seeds of wintry love, not sown for spite.

Mankind, so far, continues undecided
On the Sun's gender — grammars disagree —
As on the Moon's. Should Moon be god, or goddess:
Drawing the tide, shepherding flocks of stars
That never show themselves by broad daylight?

Robert Graves: 'Problems of Gender'

Rickie Lee Jones, one of the youngest singers considered in this book, may also be the one who, next to Joni Mitchell, most surely betrays a whiff of genius as poet, composer and 'performance artist'. Brought up in Phoenix and Olympia, Washington, she had a hazardous childhood; ran away often, usually to California, and at the age of 19 found herself working as a waitress in Los Angeles. Her days in 'the jazz side of life' were wild; out of her adventures and misadventures she made her songs, as close to the nitty-gritty of life-as-it-is as a girl could get. 'The stuff of my songs is real raw,' she said. 'I tell people it's fiction, but a lot of it is just fiction I happened to live.'

It is not clear how or when she acquired any musical education. What comes out sounds intuitively artless yet entails technical sophistication. For her first (1979) album, entitled simply *Rickie Lee Jones*, she calls on quite complex resources – keyboards acoustic and electrophonic, jazz horns, symphonic strings – and she seems to have had a substantial share in the arrangements as well as being totally responsible for the composition. Despite the sophistication, the sound is tough and sleazy, with no hint of Hollywood plush, not even satirically exploited, as by Dory Previn. This applies too to her verses, which are aphoristic and often, to people not reared on city scrap heaps, elusive. The voice, half speaking, half chanting or singing, matches; yet what emerges from seediness is poetry – the emptiness of 'all the underwriters on the boulevard', the lonesomeness of the girl who is 'in the wrong end of the eight ball black'. Even the witty songs, which may make us chuckle out loud, are sad if resilient.

The album opens with 'Chuck E.'s in love', which had been a hit single and deserved to be, for its spry boogie rhythm, its sharp textues and its lilting refrain charm while being grittily honest. Rickie's breathless enunciation, at once babyish and anguished, veers between talk, incantation and song; it is as though we're present in drugstore or poolroom, overhearing snatches of conversation trinkling through the jukebox Muzak. Yet it's a personal, even intimate song too. She's doing the rounds of her night-time haunts, searching for her boyfriend Chuck E. Only at the little wail on the words 'no more' in the middle section do we realize that the bitterness of the vocal line springs from the pangs of jealousy. Rickie is not going to be put down by any man, even one who has 'a cool and inspired sorta jazz when he walk'. Her jauntiness, if a bit desperate, is unafraid; so she prances through the present moments, but warily. The second song opposes to the first number's street scene recollections of childhood 'On Saturday afternoons in 1963'. Not being concerned with 'the jazz side of life', this substitutes for jukebox jazz the American small-town ballad, hymnically diatonic rather than modal. Starting from parlour piano, the instrumental texture sounds, as it garners horns and strings, slightly like Copland in his regionally American vein, and recalls him more specifically in telescoping tonic and dominant triads. The song concerns not so much the betrayal of innocence as its desuetude through the rub of time. Can you save from childhood 'your own special friend . . . when every day now secrets end?' The refrain 'Years go by' recurs three times, each more wearily than the last, turning a song of adolescence into a lament of premature maturity. The falling pentatonic phrase loses its innocence with the harmonic shift that reflects the 'foolish grin'; yet at the same time preserves it, since the voice remains pristine through the sighs that respond to the thud of the years.

The next five songs are back in the dusty present. 'Night train' is about an unmarried mother trying to escape the clutches of a welfare worker who wants to take her baby from her. A slow thumping bass enacts the girl's desperate 'walkin' with my baby in my arms', while the vocal line, more moaned than spoken, begins as a primitive tumbling strain. The rhythm stabilizes as she asserts her determination that 'they won't getcha cuz I'm right here witcha'; as the train approaches, promising a Blue Horizon, the vocal line swells more lyrically. When she has boarded the train the song becomes an uneasy lullaby, over a beat more connected, though still hard.

'Young Blood' is less involved in nocturnal frenzies; indeed Rickie is outside the action, keeping 'a third eye watchin' you. You never know when you're makin' a memory.' From such memories her songs are created – and couldn't be, were she not simultaneously involved and detached. This number evokes the night city in harsh texture and nervous, perhaps Puerto Rican, rhythm, mostly of 3 + 3 + 2 quavers a bar. Young Blood is 'hidin' there somewhere', looking for 'somethin' to do'. Although he may not be a type you or I would relish bumping into and although the rhythm is as menacing as the city itself, Young Blood is not necessarily sinister. Rickie at least can say that

> You feel real pretty
> when he's holdin' you tight.
> City will make you mean
> but that's the makeup on your face.
> Love will wash you clean
> in the night's disgrace.

So this song too hovers ambivalently between innocence and experience, even incorporating, within the city night, an enchanting interlude and postlude for folky jazz fiddle.

The same theme is latent in 'Easy money', though at its face value this seems to be about graft and prostitution.

> There was a joe
> leanin' on the back door
> a coupla jills
> with their eyes on a coupla bills
> their eyes was statin'
> they was waitin'
> to get their hands on
> some Easy Money.

The verses recount a squalid little tale about 'two dames who was losin' the same game'. The music, however, counteracts the words, the comic internal rhymes of which lilt into a tune in boogie rhythm over a stalking bass, with distantly nocturnal horns. The easy-money refrain sounds the more beguiling because it is cooingly sung whereas the narrative – about a predatory male who treats his women as toys – is *spoken*, with varied inflexion. The tale's climax in a 'turrible turrible fight' between the girls is outrageously comic yet frightening, for it accepts the bleak facts of human nature along with the calamitous consequences of no or minimal nurture. The tinkling glockenspiel that flits in and out of the song and takes over in the postlude dismisses graft with a shrug. The dismissal is inherent in the music. No moral point is scored.

'The last chance Texaco' starts out, in a slow, swinging 6/8, as though it's about a nocturnal car ride in which we're vaguely threatened by lights in the night, shortage of gas, dead battery or malfunctioning engine. The pulse gathers energy; oscillating triads are expectant; a chromatic shift to the harmony demonstrates how 'the cable won't reach'. In the middle, however, it turns out that the car is an urban metaphor for a woman:

> A blockbusted blonde
> who broke down and died
> and threw all the rods he gave her.

Although the figuration doesn't change, its effect does, exploding – on the words

> She just gets scared and she stalls
> She just needs a man, that's all

– in electrically charged vibrancy. The final stanzas establish Rickie Lee as a fine jazz singer: consider her wildly burgeoning arabesques on 'she can't idle this long, her Last Chance', and her near-bark on the words 'turn her over and go'. Here she presents woman as tragic victim, in an idiom recalling the blues at its most potent. Though Rickie may be a slight little waif compared with gargantuan Bessie Smith, Empress of the Blues, her cry in this phrase has heroic blue roots.

This tragic dimension, this impassioned, mechanistic-sexual cry on behalf of battered humanity, is the more telling because it follows the sly comedy of 'Easy money' and precedes the fast boogie of 'Danny's All-Star joint', where 'they got a jukebox that goes doyt-doyt' and where 'the vice is nice'. Rickie herself appears again, offering dollars to the dim dive's barman, Cecil – unlike the other kids in the place who, 'a quarter past left alive', are always begging dimes *from* Cecil for phone calls or coffee. Like the first number, the song creates an environment in which we live while the song lasts. The jukebox noise is cunningly emulated; through it flicker fragments of the kids' conversation and of Rickie's *doubles entendres* with Cecil. Though this may be a 'savage' life-style, it lacks the social purpose of real savages. The kids are idling around, waiting for easy money, a dime for the phone, a purloined Hershey bar – for the satisfaction of 'wishes', which have replaced dreams.

'Weasel and the white boys cool' creates the same milieu. The 'weasel in a poor boy's wool' works downtown at Nyro's Nook, auralized in chippy jukebox jazz and opposed, in the refrain, to the world of Mom, Dad and childhood pals, whose music, though sometimes metrical irregular, is homophonically triadic like march and hymn. Like 'Young Blood' (another weasel), this song is ambivalent. Rickie takes no side between Mom and Dad, the boy who

dances in the welfare lines
actin' like some jerk-off fool

and the easy weasel who prefers to lie out 'eatin' peaches on the beaches' with his girl or girls.

The remaining three songs don't, however, equivocate, but are strangely moving in their desolation. 'Coolsville', balancing the nostalgic 'on Saturday afternoons', seems to reject schooldays. Back with 'Bragger and Junior Lee', Rickie sings of 'the Real Right Thing back in Town', as contrasted with childhood fantasy. The song is infinitely sad, irremediably real, and poetically mysterious: consider the drum roll and vocal wail on the word 'Coolsville', and the painful steadying of the slow pulse on 'the real thing come, and the real thing go'. In the final statement of 'the way back to Coolsville' Rickie opposes a White baby treble to gruffly Black enunciation, exaggerating both to the point of parody. She piteously laughs at herself as a little White girl marooned in the big city, yet guys the tough Black mama image with which she tries to confront the harsh world. In undermining both White childhood illusion and Black grown-up disillusion she leaves us not with equivocation, but with paradoxical truth. Valediction to Eden and half-ironic acceptance of the grimey present offer a frail hope. Paradoxically and parodistically she *goes on*, in and from the deadest end.

This is also the burden of 'Company', the album's climax and the only number that Rickie *sings* from start to finish. Taking up the distinction between dreams and wishes that was the theme of 'Danny's All-Star joint', Rickie opts for dreams, auralizing her yearning in a lovely bluesy tune, very slow, but with more jazzy harmonic movement than she usually allows herself. The phrases soar upwards, with equal stresses on the syllables of 'lookin' for company'. This hints at the pain behind the hoping – which none the less becomes incarnate in Rickie's disembodied tone colour as her floating lyricism reaches 'across the galaxy'. Ecstasy survives even when, in the middle, the line grows agitated as she recognizes that, for all her love and longing, she has lost her man. There's a touch of bravado in her singing of the words

We'll *never* be the same,
and I know I'll never have this chance again,
no, no, not like *you*

until the dream of love recurs, not less heart-easing, yet stronger in its lyricism. So the song reveals how dreams may be more real than the reality most of the numbers tersely evoke.

The point is reaffirmed by the little coda to the cycle: a song of lonesomeness with a title, 'After hours (twelve bars past midnight)', which is a comically serious musical pun. But the jazzy flavour of the twelve-bar blues merges into the homespun ballad style of her songs about childhood, the tune being still simpler, the rhythm more halting, than those of 'On Saturday afternoons'. All the 'gang' – schoolmates and/or the kids she consorts with in drugstores and joints – have gone home. Standing on the corner, 'all alone', she whispers of how she and the streetlights will 'paint the town – *grey*'. The frail little tune floats up, then collapses, telling us how she and her generation are 'so many lamps who have lost our way'. Yet in singing 'Goodnight America, The world still loves a dreamer', Rickie assures us that lonesomeness need not be defeat. Though the love dreamed of in 'Company' may be fulfilled only in the song's soaring vocal line, that is enough to ensure survival.

In one crude sense Rickie's wishes, if not dreams, came true, as most people's don't: she must now have enough dimes for the phone and the Hershey bars. But although 'company' usually follows in the wake of dollars, there is no guarantee that love will. So Rickie, like the young people she sings of and to, still needs her dreams and fights for their truth. She had made her songs out of being a deadend kid; what would happen when, in material terms, she was one no longer? Clearly, she took the question seriously, for she didn't cash in on the success of her first album. It was two years before she produced her second disc, which is not less honest but bleaker than the first. Reality, she seems to be saying, has nothing to do with having or not having. Deadendishness is within the mind and heart.

On the new album, *Pirates*, the edge of nervous frenzy has grown sharper. None of these songs makes us laugh out loud, as 'Easy money' does, and the proportion of lyrical song to incanted speech is smaller. Though the title of 'We belong together' implies that it is a love song, it's a love born of desperation. The lover Johnny King is a juvenile gangster, for 'the only heroes we got left are written right down before us and the only angel who sees us now watches through the other's eyes'. Love cannot counter the alienation we're born to. So the lowdown argot in which the tales are hinted at is croaked or whimpered over sustained organ tones and a dragging beat. The spoken inflexions are so varied as to become themselves music, though only the refrain approaches song, as it asserts that 'It's better to face it, that we belong together.' Even so, the yelled assertion is ambiguous: it might mean that, despite appearances, she belongs to him and Love Will Find a Way, or it might mean that she belongs to him whatever she may pretend, and that's her plight. Most probably it means both simultaneously, and this is why the final refrain begins wistfully but ends vehemently.

Superficially, 'Livin' it up' sounds cheerier, opening with a lazy piano boogie that carries the lost lads Eddie and Louie and the (pointedly named) girl Zero through petty pick-ups and time- if not person-killing mini-violence. Against this the refrain —

> It's more trouble than it's worth,
> Oh Wild and the Only Ones

— appeals for a loving and caring that would fulfil timeless dreams rather than alleviate temporary trumpery wishes. Though hardly sung, it carries a high emotive charge — which is frustrated when the two anecdotical stanzas merge into a passage of rhythmic paralysis, simulating the 'magnets' that might bind the lost kids in togetherness. What in fact occurs, however, is a fast middle section dismissing dreams in self-intoxication: 'Oh yeah, we're living it up', mindlessly reiterated. So it is not clear whether the Wild and Only Ones are the truth of dream or a shibboleth — whether it is they who are 'more trouble than it's worth', rather than the round of adolescent escapades. The final narrative stanza returns, sad and lonesome, to a 'mean hotel'. Although the incantation to the Wild and Only Ones at last approaches song, it is not sustained. The music fades in pallid exhaustion as Rickie pleads

> Oh Wild and Only Ones,
> why don't you tell me where you are?

Since they don't answer, Rickie is left with 'Skeletons', a very slow number, the closest this disc comes to the childhood retrospections of the first album. Broken arpeggios on piano and sustained organ chords recall the parlour's cosiness and the chapel's solidarity as revoked in 'On Saturday afternoons in 1963'. But here the child is in a girl's womb, and although the slip of a phrase the song opens with, *sung* with vibratoless frailty, has the innocence of things waiting to be born, the words tell us that unless they move to 'the West side' the kid 'won't have half a chance'. In the second stanza the music remains wide-eyed as the words disclose a grim tale: the cops 'blew away' the baby's father in a robbery raid. The last stanza is deflationary. Children blindly goggle at Saturday cartoons on the telly, adolescent girls listen all day to records in solitary rooms, the boy the baby might grow into is up a tree, playing with a mechanical bird in the form of a model airplane, but catapulting real birds. 'Bird' was the nickname of his dead father; we're left with 'skeletons, skeletons', the ghost of a loss. This heart-rending little song is totally without evasion. We can understand why Rickie Lee needed time to face this sequel to her childhood memories.

She shakes herself back into the gritty city for 'Woody and Dutch on the slow train to Peking', which is not in China but off La Brea Avenoo. The placing of this basically funny number after the confessional ditty about the pregnant girl is no doubt deliberate. In the city, we overhear snippets of conversation, the clatter of subways and cars: that which is other than ourselves. That the words are impenetrable doesn't matter, since this is environmental music of the street corner, clipped in vocal line and in instrumental boogie rhythm, with clapping used percussively, in simulation of the slow train.

'Pirates', the title song and halfway house, is the most direct statement of the central theme: the gulf between deadend living and whatever might be revealed by a pirate lover on whose 'rainbow sleeves' Rickie might be carried 'far away'. But this rainbow has no affinity with Judy Garland's. The song's opening, if positive, is also fierce, embracing 'the jazz way of life on the edge of the corner' — which hardly sounds comfortable! Against this edginess the refrains are slow and lyrical, so that the valedictory 'So long, Lonely Avenue' becomes heartfelt longing. The number ends with a brief shot, prefaced by melismata in the vocal line, of the boy and girl, now perhaps man and woman, in their own identities, 'just like you, just like me'. This contrasts with the identityless street music of the previous number, though if the dream may be truth it seems unlikely to be realized. The last section, alternating cocky recapitulations of the number's opening with piano-accompanied childhood reminiscence, effects no fusion between them.

A consequence of this appears to be a retreat, in the next two numbers, into something like cynicism. 'A lucky guy' is the closest this album comes to the tough humour of 'Easy money'. Over an ostinato in displaced rhythm, the number chats rather than sings of a lover who is lucky because he takes things easy, as she can't. The music embraces both the man's ease and the woman's dis-ease, and appears to turn the tables when in the last stanza she pays him back in his own kind. Yet although this is comic, it is also lyrically broken. The song cannot sing, and we're left unsure whether the barbershop harmony at the end makes for solace or satire. Such wry acceptance is the most to be hoped for in Rickie's young–old world.

The penultimate song, 'Traces of western slopes', offers neither solace nor satire but nightmare instead of dreams. Rickie's voice, often virginal, is here cavernous as she tells us how the kids are

on the far side of the track,
lolitas playing poker and dominos
behind their daddy's shacks.

They'd like to escape to those western slopes (where that unborn baby might 'have a chance'?) but no liberating pirate arrives. The middle section tells us how she 'lied' to her 'angel' — perhaps the unhero who had 'watched' her and to whom she had yearned to belong. Lying relates nightmare, narcotically or alcoholically induced and electrophonically realized, to a personal failure of love, her own as well as the man's. The number dissipates in unanswered questions. Although the poem is haunting and Rickie's range of vocal timbre is astonishing, there is no *song*, let alone tune, and the electrophonic gibbers sound a little old-hat. This may be intentional, for the invoking of Edgar Allan Poe along with johnny johnson (the one with capitals, the other without) hints that a synthetic element may be endemic to the horror. This is the only Rickie Lee Jones number with a touch of the later Joni Mitchell's pretentiousness. The nightmare of lonesomeness, latent in the other songs, didn't need to be made patent.

At least the pretentiousness gives point to the little coda song 'The returns', which fulfils the same epilogic function as does 'After hours' on the first album. In that number Rickie was left 'all alone' in the night, after the gang had gone: solitary, but still forlornly *singing*. In 'The returns', admitting that 'after all there are such things as love and tenderness', she whispers rather than sings of turning 'memories into dreams again'. This is more than a desire to recover 'one of these days' the wholeness of childhood, for the stress is on a potential mating of destinies. Wanting a loved man, not merely a sexual consummation, she isolates the word 'close'. But what in 'Company' had been fulfilled in dreamful song if not in fact, is here dissipated. Against faint parlour piano, the little-girl voice falters, breathless; harmony is suspended beneath increasingly painful distonation of pitch. This negation complements the fact that the album has no comic–satiric number like 'Easy money' and no song with the incipiently tragic dimension of 'The last chance Texaco'. Rickie no longer asks what will happen to her dreams now that childhood is relinquished.

In a superficial sense one might detect a certain evasiveness in the short-play disc Rickie released after *Pirates* since it includes, apart from one number left over from that album, no song of her own.

She had made no attempt to capitalize on her first album; the relative failure, commercially speaking, of *Pirates* seems to have induced a temporary lack of self-confidence. Even so, her personal 'aura' is not weakened by her resort to other people's songs, for no artist, not even Janis Joplin, has effected more potent acts of re-creation than does Rickie Lee on *Girl at Her Volcano*.

The one original on the disc, 'Hey Bub', is a 1983 remake of a 1979 number intended for *Pirates*. It's a very slow, piteously broken, ballad hymn, comparable with the songs of childhood and of adolescent love on the first album. Both the frail vulnerability of the lyricism and the hesitancy of the piano playing resemble the childhood songs of her friend Randy Newman; only whereas Randy evokes childhood from the context of adulthood, Rickie is herself the child, and it is we rather than she who supply the nostalgia. Similar in vein is the lovely 'Rainbow sleeves', a number by Tom Waits who, as deadend kid and mini-bard of urban drugstore, bar, nightspot and caff, is Rickie Lee's male complement. Both Tom Waits and Rickie Lee Jones performing his song attain a piquant equation between the inflexions of urban speech and the lyricism latent within it. As this happens a tune as simple as a kid's ditty or a street rune garners the harmonic intensities of jazz. Significantly, this number has something like a climax in the 'middle eight'.

But 'Rainbow sleeves', a reissue of a single dating back to 1978, is no more representative of where Rickie stands now than is 'Hey bub', the leftover from *Pirates*. Among the new recordings only 'Under the boardwalk' seeks lyrical and rhythmic continuity, if hardly harmonic progression, and it does so because this Resnick–Young number is a Puerto Rican-style ghetto song which has an infantile insouciance supportable even in the sleaziest urban deprivation. More interesting, however, is what Rickie does with sophisticated standards.

Her version of Billy Strayhorn's 'Lush life' presents the haunting cocktail-lounge tune in a form piteously fragmented – not surprisingly, since lush life is what she, as deadend kid, is shut out from. The lush chords on the piano falter; the voice, with a Billie Holiday-like sensitivity of nuance, suddenly destructs its lyricism with a bleat or blare, even with a caw not far from a hoot. Something similar happens in her version of the Rodgers and Hart standard 'My funny valentine', though here the effect is less equivocal since the original number turns on ironic duplicity, half innocent, half knowing. Rickie's 'little-girl' voice here preserves its guilelessness, though she cannot aspire to continuous song. The breaks in the vocal line, the sudden sustained high note, the occasionally fluffed tone, recall the marvellous version of this tune by the young Miles Davis. Both Miles and Rickie here create a pathos too deep for words, if not for tears.

With her latest (1984) album, *Magazine*, Rickie Lee has returned to her own invention and to her own bleak world with a subtle, if slight, difference: whereas her first disc consisted of 'environmental' songs in which she was poised between the deadend gang life of joints and drugstores and the frail promise of her dreams, on *Magazine* she has more specific identity. A few years older, she makes attempts at personal relationships, without much hope that they can be other than aborted.

The first number, 'Gravity', presents her case as 'a young girl standing underneath the L train', having to 'wipe the hope' from her eyes as the force of 'gravity' punningly drags her down while surrealistically 'small things float up'. Intermittently babyish, her voice explodes in sudden exasperation through a limping pulse and a stark sonority. Though mysterious, like the first album's 'Coolsville', the effect is no longer nostalgic; indeed childhood dreams are wilfully dismissed. So are they in fast numbers like 'Jukebox fury' and 'It Must Be Love', for although they open with brief, incantatory phrases like a kids' street game, they become brittle in line, panicky in rhythm and clinky in sonority as particular passions about particular persons make for particularized pain: the baby rune, whispered or pouted to herself, erupts into petulance or frenzy. The coda to 'It Must Be Love' – in which the capitals precisely suggest the comic pathos of her enunciation – is desperate rather than affirmative: it *must* be love, only clearly it isn't.

The song that ends the A-side, 'Magazine', directly reinvokes 'Coolsville', forcing it to confront reality. Beginning cool enough, and very slow, it mounts to desperation as 'flagboys' warn her of impending danger – inherent in the mere possibility of 'their' or 'everything's coming'. The theme of the first album's climacteric 'Company' is desolately reversed.

Not surprisingly, the B-side begins at 'The real end': she transforms herself into a tough guy–girl delivering rather than receiving hurt, with clipped, snapped vocal inflexions over a jerky, lumpy beat with minimal harmony. Yet the ferocity of the coda suggests that toughness is an offshoot of despair. This is admitted in the lovely 'Deep space', in which she's metamorphosed from a Coolsville child into 'an Equestrienne of the Circus of the Falling Star'. The very slow non-pulse, the open fourths and fifths, the telescoped tonics and dominants envelop her voice which, projected into a circus performance, is not so much a child's as that of an adult capable of tenderness as well as fear. Though she asks 'What's the use of crying? It won't matter when we're old', cry she does, reinvoking 'dreams' that are 'like marbles in the pocket of a little boy' – something, elusive but not illusory, to hold on to. Tears sometimes dissolve the music in bitonal dislocation; this may be Rickie Lee's deepest, as it is her most hermetic, song, her frail voice being now 'like a beautiful girl', whose dreams reverberate in the secrecy of her synthesizer's echo chamber.

The 'interior' character of the song distinguishes it even from the childhood dreams of the first album; and no one listens to this still, small voice. The next number, 'Runaround', is about an easy weasel who treats her rough, emulating in its stuttering syncopations her atempts to 'shake the chain' that bind her in misplaced obsession. Through the stanzas, she shakes more fiercely, achieving continuous rock rhythm as she 'takes a deep breath and *breaks* the chain'. Though this hurrah is a mini-triumph, it's not clear what she's been freed *for*.

The final double number, 'Rorschachs', carries her into a different, less deadendish world but does so by momentarily *evading* pain. The wordless prelude, lilting in 6/8, in a sonority pervaded by mandolin and accordion, evokes a milieu remote from her customary downtown dives. Its ethnic flavours are ambiguous, suggesting a cosy Irish Catholic church, a Jewish mid-European café, a Puerto-Rican dance hall – to which she may belong by way of ancestral affiliations if not roots, yet which she distances herself from by *speaking* the words of the first song, significantly called 'The unsigned painting', with humorous tenderness, if not with overt irony. In the complementary song, 'The Weird Beast', Rickie gives a sinister – in the traditonally magical sense – twist to this ethnic variability, summoning not some easy weasel from her adolescence, but a gypsyish Weird Beast from 'the empty streets of Paris', or even a desperate 'Tartar', capable of un-Americanly 'Exiling the Tsar', and speaking the uncouth Russian tongue. The music hovers between dread and farce, prophesying untold terrors or delights. 'I have a Feeling a Weird Beast is going to come our Way' – the capitals again indicate precisely the funny–frightening effect of the by turns parlour-cosy, gypsy-melancholic, Russian-liturgical flavoured music. Though this may be a game, it would seem to be the beginning of the end of Rickie Lee's childhood and adolescence, carrying her out of her vividly delineated regional environment into the bewilderingly global village, with a hint, at the end, of the sci-fi limbos explored by Laurie Anderson.

We don't know where Rickie Lee will or can go from here. But it's certain that what's been most remarkable about her has been her refusal to cheat. Rather than that, she has remained and will remain silent. We may hazard that her songs will preserve their potency, though she will never make the biggest time.

Rickie Lee Jones's 'crisis' is a consequence of her integrity, whereby she precisely reflects the plight of 'our young', who, in A. R. Ammons's words

. . . don't believe in time as future and, so,
suffer every instant's death: they don't believe
in the thread, plot, the leading of one thing into

another, consequences, developed change: without retrospect
or prospect, they seek the quality of experience
a moment's dimension allows: thrill replaces

goal: threat lessens and fractures time, shortening
the distance to the abyss, immediate, a step away:
without calm, they can't see tomorrow unfolding.

Not surprisingly, the effect of such negation on music is to deny songfulness; and if – as I suggested in my book *Beethoven and the Voice of God*[1] – we may construe Beethoven's life's work as a search, from the heart of modern man's divisiveness, for the Hidden Song that is an aural image of the whole and holy, we may find the notion also relevant in the less sublime regions of pop music. We have noted that the songs of Joni Mitchell have veered 'positively' and 'negatively' to and from songfulness; we have seen that the younger Rickie Lee Jones has found song increasingly difficult to accommodate to her honesty. An ultimate extension of this occurs in the work of Laurie Anderson, who scarcely sings at all! A lowdown priestess of downtown New York – which used to be Greenwich Village but is now SoHo or the seedier warehouse areas between

1 Faber and Faber, 1984.

Houston Street and southern Manhattan – she offers 'performance art': an extreme version of the ritualistic element common to jazz and rock music. 'Performance', like ritual, exists in the moment, 'shortening the distance to the abyss'. It is as immediate as it is ephemeral.

Laurie Anderson came to New York in 1966, from a fairly affluent Chicago background, to study art and art history at Barnard College. Like many visual artists, she was fascinated by the music-theatre activities of John Cage and in her early twenties began to devise her own 'happenings'. She acquired some musical training, becoming a reasonably accomplished violinist. When, however, in her early thirties, she attained fame and notoriety in equal proportion it was as a multi-media woman whose written words deploy wit and pathos with telling economy; whose speaking and/or chanting voice is both ravishingly beautiful and starkly veracious; whose violin playing combines artfulness with folk-like immediacy; and whose technical command of electrophonics is not less imaginative than her use of cinematic visuals. All her creations may be described as one-person opera, making an aural universe from the computerized environment we are entering or being gobbled up by. Her first major project consists of a sequence of hour-long performances called *United States I–IV*, recorded live from a 1983 presentation. The series is now being extended into a series entitled *Natural History*, each number fitting into, and shedding oblique light on, a continuing chain of 'experiences'. Since the visual dimensions are no less important than the audible, Laurie Anderson's work cannot be adequately assessed on recorded evidence. None the less, the purely aural dimensions of these discs are impressive, owing their force to *precisely* distorted relationships between the science fictional limbos she invents and everyday situations in which we have all found ourselves.

In 'Dr Miller' there are no words but those two spoken, whether hopefully or minatorily, against a savage electrophonic jingle the more lacerating because we recognize, beneath the mechanistic hubbub, trite commercial clichés originally intended to comfort and assuage. 'Up in the mountains' inverts this, being a black comedy about an old-time Country Music Festival disrupted by marauding tigers, the only 'music' being electric tiger-noises and what might be human whimpers. 'For electric dogs' makes a collage of black electronic noises as backdrop to a still blacker anecdote, spoken not by Laurie but by the junkie novelist William Burroughs, in a voice as cavernous as his angular appearance. Occasionally the electronic instruments parody old-fashioned raggy pop music, as does Dory Previn, though Laurie's electrocuted retrospects are far more startlingly fragmented.

Musically, Laurie effects a more sustained 'performance' on the LP she calls *Big Science*, though again the disc inevitably misses out on the lighting effects, film clips and party props that are involved in the presentation. The title number introduces, with inane electrophonic glugs and burps, a science-fiction landscape in which the accoutrements of modern civilization – shopping mall, freeway, sports centre, drive-in cinema and bank – are maybe going to be built. But the cold windy set probably exists only in a movie. Since its morality is

> Every man for himself,
> All in favour say Aye,

it's hardly surprising that there is nothing to counter the 'cold dark and empy desolation' except a Disneyish Golden City, aurally evoked in a TV jingle interspersed with yells of Hallelujah and chortles of Yodellayheehoo! This empty-set landscape is a mini-hell we've all been in.

Still more scarily recognizable is the situation depicted in 'From the air' – which begins by emulating the captain's bland voice as he gives instruction and assurance to passengers on a plane about to make a forced landing. The verbal clichés and syrupy inflexions are horridly familiar – until electrophonics, jazz horns and drums gradually transform both voice and inane ostinato into an image of Doom: not merely a crashing plane, but a 'going down' into some horrendous Black Hole:

> Put your hands over your eyes.
> There is no pilot . . .
> This is the time.

Although such pieces are frightening, they are also funny – which matters because it means that Laurie Anderson's Performances behave like Art in that they help us to live in the world in which we surprisedly and perhaps surprisingly still find ourselves. This applies too to numbers concerned with personal rather than public relationships, or at least with the failures of communication consequent on mechanization. 'Sweaters' disposes of love abruptly, dismissing loved eyes and mouth as objects no more nor less significant than an unpleasantly coloured, discarded garment. Here Laurie uses no electrophonics, only her voice and violin, ballasted by acoustic bagpipes and rather frenzied drums. Even so, she employs these 'natural' resources to formidably negative effect, exploiting the propensity of both fiddles and bagpipes to distonation. Although such effects frequently occur in the wilder types of folk music, they seldom show such disregard for the lyrical potentiality of song. That Laurie here uses a wide vocal range, even hinting at a folk singer's childish treble, intensifies rather than alleviates the dismissive nature of the piece.

'Walking and falling', on the other hand, calls on electrophonics only as background to the spoken text. Oddly enough, this comes across as the most 'musical' number thus far, for Laurie's speaking voice is moving, even beautiful, in its variety of inflexion, subtlety of rhythm and precise timing, while the electronic gibbers exactly delineate the ambiguous psychological state the words describe. Since we have all to some degree been there, we may identify with Laurie – which may be why the cycle can move into a new dimension in the last piece on side 1. 'Born, never asked' is about 'a world I never made'. If there is a threat in the words Laurie speaks unaccompanied as prologue – we never know, but remain apprehensive about, 'what is behind that curtain' – the music eventually makes it possible for us to accept unironically the words 'You were born. And so you're free. So happy birthday.' If Laurie cannot sing a tune she can play one on her fiddle. Against slow hand-clapping and a coolly intricate ostinato on marimba, a rising scale, interspersed with pentatonic minor thirds, unfolds like a flower. Though it hardly achieves wholeness and holiness it does suggest that something, even from this limbo, is waiting to be born. The melody couldn't be simpler; its timbre is that of a genuine folk fiddler, the expressive distonation being slightly orientalized. It is not fortuitous that we should be reminded of the violin music of John Cage.

But the long number that opens side 2, 'O superman', returns to the creepy science fiction that may be fact before we've realized what's hapening to us. Electrophonics spookily present a Mechanized Mom who substitutes the Norm for love and justice; the attempt of acoustic flute and saxophone to create corny-cosy music such as was once associated with hearth and home proves impotent. The other numbers deal with non-communication, introducing vestiges of lyricism and of dance only in order to guy them. In 'Let x equal x' jolly holiday postcards exchanged between partners and amigos end up gaspingly in a burning building, from which 'I gotta go'. 'It tango', a dialogue between a mutually uncomprehending man and woman in which dual-voiced Laurie plays both roles, gives a bafflingly irresolute slant to tangoid jazz. Jollity stutters.

On the evidence of these discs, taken as aural experience, Laurie Anderson must seem, in comparison with Rickie Lee Jones, limited by her negativism. Rickie may not sing much or often, but when she does it's with an effect proportionate to its rarity. The element of theatre in her songs is always rich in musical potential, whereas Laurie Anderson's theatre is dependent on her brilliantly exploited electric gadgetry. This, however, is to discount the extraordinary beauty of her voice, which makes music even though she doesn't sing. The loveliness of her voice, like her wide-eyed wit, nurtures a childlike integrity in a wicked world. A young woman exploits minimal survivals of jazz and rock, and of rural as well as urban folk musics, to create in a context of film and electrophonics a dream or nightmare vision of the plight to which such technology has submitted us. Yet since even the nightmare is beautiful or funny or both, it is incipiently purgatorial – as her 1983 disc *Mister Heartbreak* (which overlaps with the USA cycle) demonstrates.

Here Laurie plays synclavier as main instrument, doubling on violin and on various acoustic and electric percussion instruments, with electric guitars and more percussion played by others. Like Annie Lennox and the Eurythmics she makes 'soundscapes' rather than songs; she too assumes an androgynous image and dissolves occidental menace in a timeless mythological world affiliated both to non-Western cultures and to sci-fi Outer Space. The first track, 'Sharkey's day', presents a 'day in the life' of an average American who, since his name is Sharkey and his nickname Mr Heartbreak, is presumably the archetypal predatory male – though in the final number, 'Sharkey's night', he turns out to be Laurie's one-time associate, William Burroughs, who can hardly be mistaken, as he speaks the words in his sepulchral voice from 'deep in the heart of darkest America', for the Man in the Street! If 'patristic' darkest America is confused with 'matristic' darkest Africa, there may be a suggestion of sexual abivalence too: the night's 'female' moon has ousted the day's 'male' sun, perhaps only just in time, before the cataclysm.

Such at least is the theme of this first number, in which our unheroic city dweller is awakened at dawn by electronic twitterings of birds and beasts to a routine of telephones and office desks he's 'never at'. The public-address system cannot locate him because for him the real world has merged into a video dreamland where 'little girls sing oooeee'. The piece is about the semiological confusion the media induce. Sharkey watches bugs crawling up his legs; he says he'd 'rather see them on TV: *tones it down*'. Seeing the world as a movie, teetering between reality and illusion, he is bereft of communication, left with his daydreams of the ululating little girls. The people in the movie, he says, knowing they have to find one another, ride off in *opposite* directions! Sharkey ends up 'on top of Old Smokey, all covered with snow', waiting for the holocaust. 'That's where I wanna   that's where I gonna   go'. Laurie's spoken words drop with bell-like resonance into the shimmering electrophonic sonorities and quasi-oriental percussion. The 'soundscape' ends in infinite stillness, the word 'go' reverberating through the mindless chitterings of birds and beasts. Yet the effect is purgatorial rather than doom-laden.

The relation here between the 'self alone' and nature electrophonically fulfils precedents suggested as early as the thirties and forties not only by Cage, but even more directly by Harry Partch. The aboriginal Californian experimentalist created ritual music-theatre for invented acoustic rather than electric instruments, though their Polynesian, Asian, Japanese, African and Amerindian sonorities strikingly anticipate the electric Global Village. Partch too used his new resources in protest against 'a world I never made', and in 'American musicals' like *US Highball* (1943) – based on hobo life of which he had first-hand experience – or *The Bewitched* (1956), adapts monophonic justly intoned chant, dance, mime, slapstick and juggling on the analogy of Japanese kabuki theatre to the demands of social–religious satyr, the punning spelling being his.

There are close parallels between Laurie Anderson's invented world and that of *The Bewitched*, in which the protagonists are clown hobos whose truth is to be true to the moment: 'Perception is a sand flea. Another moment must find its own flea'. The affinity is especially clear in the Laurie Anderson number that opens side 2, 'Ko ko ku' – which evokes a rootlessly Partched desert that sounds anti-occidental not only in being oriental but also in relating its super-nature to sci-fi. Laurie's 'lost' words are spoken and chanted within pentatonic incantation sung by Japanese Atsuko Yuomo and American Phoebe Snow. The dead rise again – 'strange animals out of the Ice Age'. Weird creatures from Outer Space with 'plates for hands and telescopes for eyes' approach our 'haunted planet spinning round'. If we shut our eyes tight, perhaps they'll 'just go away' — as they do if we're brave enough to turn off the telly. Then we can go on pretending that we are 'very pretty, very nice', and here Laurie's voice is so cool and the electric sonorities so entrancing that fear is purged. What happens in the more or less everyday world of Sharkey's day is extended to the weird worlds spawned by computer science. Although in our televisual teleological confusion we're not sure which is which, recurrently if impermanently fear is metamorphosed into love.

In two numbers the process works the other way round. 'Gravity's angel' is dedicated to V. S. Pynchon, author of the Laurie Anderson-like novel *V* and of *Gravity's Rainbow*, the immediate trigger to the number. At first Laurie pipes, very high, a two- or three-note rune about a wideboy lover whom 'everybody loves', who can 'charm the birds out of the sky'. Laurie, as a woman, has one thing over this cockily self-confident male: she is better at loving. The rune stops when an angel appears, to cut the lover down to size: 'The higher you fly, the faster you fall.' In speech, no longer in incantation, let alone song, the man is now presented as 'an also ran in the human race'. His funeral is described in deadpan black farce. Everyone is hanging around 'waiting for the ham and cheese sandwiches' rather than in valedictory tribute to a defunct hero. In the last section the ghost of 'your other lover' stalks in, 'made of thin air' yet 'full of desire'. Presumably he is the love that might have been, given a man instead of a puppet. 'There but for the grace of the angels go I', and we are left in fear rather than love, the 'empty room' being magically evoked in the sudden cut-off. Sharkey, in 'Sharkeys day', cannot distinguish between reality and illusion and so shunts between love and fear. Here fear is positive in that it frees us from self-deception.

'Langue d'amour' takes us back to the Garden of Eden where, as Henry James Senior remarked, Eve's courage released Adam from bondage. The soundscape, with bird-like quaverings and quiverings, electric conches and quasi-Balinese percussion, is Edenic yet also uneasy, and Laurie tells the tale in tones conveying both ease and distress. Man–Adam is safe but dull. Snake, walking on two legs, 'with his long tongue lightly licking about his lips', has 'a little fire inside his mouth'. Woman–Eve 'liked this very much'; gets bored with the man who is 'happy as a clam'; and loves Snake because he, being no clam, is unafraid to tell her of the world's perils – typhoons that level the landscape, sharks that walk out of the water 'right into your house with their big white teeth'.

When the language of love emerges it is in a 'confusion of tongues', a mingle of French and English neither spoken nor sung but hissed in serpentine sibilance. This reflects the Tower of Babel episode, a consequence of the Fall. There is a pun in the title itself, for the *langue* in 'Langue d'amour' means both tongue (and by inference the serpent) and language. Ambiguity of meaning involves emotional ambiguity for the point of the number – as of 'Gravity's rainbow' and 'Sharkey's day' – is that love and fear are complementary. In love and fear Laurie Anderson's 'sand fleas', like those of Partch and Pynchon, at once bite and delight. Being a performance artist Laurie Anderson exists in the moment rather than in the created artefact. While this is true to a degree of all pop art, the songs of a Bob Dylan, a Joni Mitchell, even a Rickie Lee Jones or a Tom Waits, do have, once created, an objective identity 'out there'. Laurie Anderson's sand fleas don't. Their agility and pertinacity matter the more because they are moments that are shaping our future, should we have any.

AFTERWORD: FOLK, JAZZ AND ROCK IN THE UNISEX GLOBAL VILLAGE

> Ah, why did God,
> Creator wise that peopled highest Heaven
> With spirits Masculine, create at last
> This *Novelty* on Earth, this fair Defect
> Of Nature?
>
> John Milton: *Paradise Lost*

> How can I live without thee, how forgoe
> Thy sweet Converse and Love so dearly join'd,
> To Live againe in these Wilde Woods forlorn?
> Should God create another *Eve*, and I
> Another Rib afford, yet loss of thee
> Would never from my heart; no, no, I feel
> The Link of Nature draw me: Flesh of Flesh,
> Bone of my Bone thou art, and from thy State
> Mine never shall be parted, bliss or woe.
>
> John Milton: *Paradise Lost*

The first part of this book examined the musical and cultural implosion among Black women singers in the New World. The frequent projection of the persona of the 'Black mama' reawakened long-dormant matristic impulses, both in the religious context of

Gospel singing and in the secular context of the blues. The impact of these Black musics was not confined to people of Afroamerican descent and had a decisive influence on the development of White musics, immediately in the United States and then gradually across the so-called civilized world.

During the thirties and forties Negroes, assimilated into the society that had enslaved them, increasingly performed as entertainers in White theatres and clubs. Still using techniques inherited from Africa and from Gospel and the blues, Blacks sang music, now mainly by White composers, which had originally been dedicated to escape, whether through hedonism or nostalgia. The leading singers were still Black women, who often projected a powerful sexuality. On the other hand, the most successful male singers of the dance-band era, designated 'crooners', adopted performance styles not conspicuous for aggressive masculinity.

The rock explosion of the fifties and sixties was in part an attempt by the young White male to exploit for his own ends the sexual energy he received in the performance of Black Gospel and blues. White rock and Black soul evolved alongside one another, then fused. The new age could grow only from a union of Black and White, and of the matristic and patristic principles.

Black women who sang for Whites, however, betrayed the ambivalent status of Eve in Eden's Garden. From one point of view woman is the serpent, to be degraded in being treated as a sexual object. From another point of view she is a maternal goddess to be worshipped in expiation of man's guilt; and in America White guilt had assumed forms both shameful and shaming.

When White women began to imitate Black women singing in club and cabaret, their status was less ambiguous. For the most part their singing expressed their frailty and their 'lost' state. None the less, their re-cognition of loss and of lost-ness was a step towards self-knowledge. White women, by assuming for themselves elements of the Black experience, became more aware of their social situation and of the need for liberation to counteract oppression and alienation. Complementarily, Black women, as they entered a White world, began to exploit their matristic power to pragmatic patristic ends.

By the seventies female and male soul singers have merged identities as performers, as we can hear in the voices of Odetta, Nina Simone and Aretha Franklin. A further stage in the inconsequentiality of sexual identity is represented by Black Grace

Jones, who, in embracing authentic African musics, develops an androgynous stage persona, as do White Annie Lennox and Laurie Anderson, entering the multi-ethnic Global Village.

This cross-fertilization is not restricted to the Afroamerican, White and coffee-coloured Latin-American blend we find in the songs of Tania Maria: consider too Nico, whose appearance and vocal qualities are German–Moorish–Spanish–American; Chaka Khan, whose singing approaches Indian *ecstasis* by way of the rocking Western body rather than through its denial; and Shusha, a Persian who sang indigenous music in a voice of velvety mellifluousness, later extending her range to embrace gentle folk–pop, her own included.

In this polyethnic context it is worth enquiring what the pseudo-science of cantometrics, as devised by Alan Lomax and his associates, has to tell us about the variety of vocal timbre displayed by women pop singers. According to Lomax's research there is a cultural correlation between singing styles and sexual permissiveness: tribes like the African pygmies who don't insist on masculine control of the female encourage relaxed vocalization from both men and women, whereas tribes like the Plains Indians, who demand total subservience from their women, communicate their raspy tension to their female property. (It is true that Plains Indians are an extreme case; other Amerindian tribes, such as the Pueblos, allow women their own music, low-profiled, syllabic, stepwise-moving, related to the feminine activities of bead and basket work.) Wherever masculinity dominates we encounter rasp, nasality and tightness. Plains Indian women are scarcely permitted to sing; if they did, we would expect to hear sounds comparable with what Lomax describes as 'the high wail of the muezzin, appealing for mercy from Allah . . . and the piercing silver tones of (Near-Eastern) café singers', giving vent to women's 'pain, fear and neurotic hysteria'.

We have noted that many of today's White women troubadours employ two or more voices, though one cannot simply categorize them as raspy-male and liquid-female. Joni Mitchell has a pale, little-girl pipe, a sensually 'dark' Negro woman's voice, and occasionally an Amerindian male rasp. Rickie Lee Jone's voice has the same triple identity, more tenuously nervous. Even Janis Ian, though devoid of masculine rasp, has a White and Black register. Janis Joplin is the Blackest of those White singers who being militantly feminist, almost metamorphose female eroticism into

256 AFTERWORD

male grating. Occasionally she calls on a very high, little-girl timbre, as in her famous version of 'Summertime', but her femaleness here, being inately conscious of victimization and rape, is not far from hysteria. Her female register becomes a screech, as it does with Patti Smith, another militant feminist who usually rasps, and on whose singing there may be some direct Red-Indian as well as African influence.

The genuine Red Indian, Buffy Ste Marie, is often raspy though low rather than high in pitch. When she employs a high, frail register it is to deal with the indignities her race, as well as women in general, may be submitted to. Siouxsie, a pretend Amerindian, is starker and raspier in tone, perhaps because she is putting on an act, playing the aboriginal American in protest against the world she came from. Laura Nyro, the most ethnically varied singer, plays little White girl, big Black woman, and mixed-race Jewish–Spanish gypsy as occasion offers. The genuinely Latin-American Tania Maria not surprisingly negotiates transitions between styles of vocal production more smoothly. Her rasp is that of the forest Indian *and* of the citified New Yorker. The vegetable and the concrete jungles merge – as they do in the singing of uncompromisingly Black Afroamericans like Grace Jones, not to mention the great Gospel, blues and cabaret singers from Mahalia Jackson and Bessie Smith to Aretha Franklin, Billie Holiday and Betty Carter. Basically, their vocal production is liquidly African; their rasp has been rubbed or scraped off the abrasive city, and becomes a further projection of their female sexuality, in a male world.

On the field of country music female sexuality makes less impact. Women like Hazel and Alice, in succession to traditional folk singers such as Aunt Molly Jackson, sometimes emulate men in their vocal timbre, though this is a consequence of their hard life-style, and not a calculated gesture. They don't want to be men, but have to rasp in order to survive. At the opposite pole are women working within the country music industry whose *raison d'être* is their femininity, whatever the odds. Tammy Wynette's voice is low, warm and yielding, as befits a doormat, but it is neither raspy nor liquid. Some interfusion of White with Black appears in the vocal production of Dolly Parton, who gives more edge to her femininity, for she grew up the hard way, however roseate her dreams. In general, women's variety of vocal production gives them an advantage over men. This is at once technical and experiential: the embryonic new–old world rests insecurely in women's larynxes and tremulous vocal chords, as we noted in commenting on the 'new-born' sonorities of speaking–singing Annie Lennox and Laurie Anderson.

With these performers the androgynous theme intermittently referred to comes into the open. The walking–talking snake in Laurie Anderson's parable of a new Garden of Eden speaks the *langue d'amour* that, in being international but ultimately unintelligible, reminds us of the legend of the Tower of Babel. That was a consequence of the Fall. It seems possible that at a level below consciousness pop musicians are attempting to heal breaches, both within the psyche and in the external world, between 'head' and 'heart', body and spirit, man and woman.

The Hebraic tradition that Eve was born of Adam's rib is a reversal of universal earlier myths whereby man was born of the Great Earth Goddess. One version of the Genesis story says that God created us in 'his' image, but that 'male and female created he *them*, and God said to them 'Be fruitful and multiply and fill the earth and subdue it'. In the Midrash, an ancient rabbinical commentary on the Bible, Adam himself is represented as hermaphrodite, split into two by God's axe – a myth duplicated in the account of human sexuality in Plato's *Symposium*. Gnostic permutations of Christianity presented Jesus the Fish as simultaneously male and female, and in Jungian terms spiritual perfection consists in integrating within ourselves both male and female sexuality. Some supreme artists – one thinks of Shakespeare and Mozart, possible Wagner – would seem, in their comprehensive and comprehending insight into both men and women, to bear this out. Either an All-mighty Father God or an All-embracing Mother Goddess is incomplete; God needs man as man needs God, and as man and woman need one another. No wonder Adam, in words ascribed to him by Milton, still feels

The Link of Nature draw me: Flesh of Flesh,
Bone of my Bone thou art, and from the State
Mine never shall be parted, *bliss or woe.*

No wonder Milton's Son of God, reborn in *Paradise Regained*, returns 'private', to his '*Mother's house*'.

Robert Graves, high priest of the White goddess, has summed up the psychological and indeed theological implication of this sexual ambivalence in his poem 'Problems of Gender', quoted as epigraph to my final chapter.[1] It would seem that the emergence of androgynous images in today's pop scene may be un- or semi-consciously fraught with precisely these 'curious problems of propriety' between sun and moon, male and female. And it works both ways: Grace Jones, Annie Lennox, Laurie Anderson acquire male characteristics; the phenomenally successful Michael Jackson aspires to near-soprano altitudes, not to mention the transvestite performances of Boy George.

Interpreted literally, androgyny would entail the extinction of the human race, for an androgyne is not, like a hermaphrodite, a bisexual creature biologically capable of reproducing itself but merely a being endowed with both male and female atributes, as to a degree we all are. No doubt the earth goddesses of the ancient matriachates would rightly find in our singing poet–composer androgynes only an inversion and perversion of themselves, since pop androgyny may mask an instinctive death-wish yearning for extinction by ways gentler than those advocated by heavily metalled Stranglers, Clashes, Sex Pistols and Boom Town Rats. Even so, pop androgyny has its more positive aspects, which the Eternal Mothers might recognize and revere: its men–women aspire to be more capable of loving and of being loved, in their masculinity and femininity alike. Today's unisex culture reminds us, in more than sexual terms, that Thoreau at Walden Pool, speaking of the renewal that 'unaccommodated man' (who may be a woman) may find in nature, said that *every child begins the world anew*. In the words of the Gnostic gospel according to St Thomas:

> Jesus saw the children who were being suckled. He said to his disciples: These children who are being suckled are like those who enter the Kingdom.
>
> They said to him: Shall we too, being children, enter the Kingdom? Jesus said to them: When you make the two one, and the inner as the outer and the outer as the inner and the above as the below, and when you make the male and the female into a single one, so that the male will not be male and the female not female, then shall you enter the Kingdom.

1 See p. 216.

DISCOGRAPHY

Recordings are assigned to the chapters in which they are first mentioned.

I BLACK WOMEN AS EARTH GODDESSES IN CHURCH, BAR, BROTHEL AND CLUB

1 Gospel Women, Eden and the Promised Land

Negro Worksongs and Calls, Library of Congress Recordings, AAFS L8
Brighten the Corner Where You Are, New World Records 224
Been in the Storm Too Long, Folkways 3842
Arizona Dranes 1926–28, Herwin 210
Sister Rosetta Tharpe, Mecca OSL 31
In the Upper Room with Mahalia Jackson, EMI 335X 1753
DUKE ELLINGTON, *Black, Brown and Beige*, Columbia JSC 8015
ARETHA FRANKLIN with the Reverend James Cleveland, *Amazing Grace*, Atlantic AD 2 906

2 The Rockbottom Reality of the Blues

Robert Johnson, 1936–37, Col. CL 1654
The Roots of the Blues, New World 252

Bertha Lee, Herwin 213
Memphis Minnie, Biograph BL 12035
JIMMY AND MA YANCEY, *Lowdown Dirty Blues*, New World 252
Ma Rainey, Milestone 47021
The Bessie Smith Story, CBS 62376–9
Ida Cox, Fountain FB 301–2
Ida Cox and her All Star Band, Queen 048
Great Blues Singers, Riverside RLP 12–121
Out Came the Blues, Ace of Hearts AH72
Victoria Spivey Reissues, Spivey Record Productions LP 2001
Louis and the Blues Singers, EMI PMC 7144
Sippie Wallace Sings the Blues, Storyville SLP 198
Classic Alberta Hunter, Stash ST 115
Helen Humes Comes Back, Black and Blue 33050
Big Mama Thornton, Vanguard VPC 40001
When Malindy Sings, New World 295
Dinah Washington, I Grandi del Jazz 27

3 From Tent Show to Cabaret: The Word and the Horn

Shuffle Along, New World 260
Big Mamas, Rosetta Records BR 305–6
The Vintage Irving Berlin, New World 238
Jazzin' Babies' Blues 1921–27, Biograph BLP 12025–6
Ethel Waters 1938–39, Victor 741 067
The Billie Holiday Story, CBS 68228–9
Ella Fitzgerald Sings Rodgers and Hart, Verve 4002–2
Ella Fitzgerald Sings Irving Berlin, Verve 4030–31
Ella and Louis, Verve 6 4003 and 4006–2
Porgy and Bess, Verve 2632 052
SARAH VAUGHAN, *It's a Man's World*, Mercury 20109
Sarah Vaughan and Count Basie, Emus ES 12010
Sarah Vaughan and Clifford Brown, Mercury 20055
SARAH VAUGHAN, *After Hours*, MFP 1130
Carmen McCrae: I Hear Music, Affinity AFF 97
Carmen McCrae, I fabri del Jazz 31
NANCY WILSON and GEORGE SHEARING, *The Swingin''s Mutual*,
   Capitol T 1524
Pearl Bailey and Louis Bellson, Everest FS 284
Abbey Lincoln: That's Him, Riverside RLP 12 251
Abbey is Blue, Riverside RLP 1153

The Betty Carter Album, Bet-Car Productions MK 1002
Betty Carter, Bet-Car Productions MK 1001

4 Soul, Motown, and the Fusion of Sacred and Profane

Odetta at Carnegie Hall, Fontana TFL 6003
Odetta Sings Bob Dylan, RCA RD 7703
Golden Hours of Nina Simone, Golden Hour 535
NINA SIMONE, *My Baby Just Cares for Me*, Bethlehem CYX 201
Aretha's Greatest Hits, Atlantic 40 279
The Dionne Warwick Collection, Arista Dionne 1
The Loving Sisters, Peacock PLP 176
The Best of Gladys Knight and the Pips, Buddah BDLH 5013
GLADYS KNIGHT AND THE PIPS, *Taste of Bitter Love*, Pickwick SHM
   3132
An Evening with Diana Ross, EMI TMSP 6005
The Pointer Sisters, Blue Thumb ILPS 9243
THE POINTER SISTERS, *That's Aplenty*, BTS 6009
ESTHER PHILLIPS, *Performance*, KUDU 18
Esther Phillips, Mercury 9111 030
The Best of Roberta Flack, Atlantic K50840
ROBERTA FLACK, *Killing Me Softly*, Atlantic K50021
RANDY CRAWFORD, *Nightline*, Warner 92 3976 1
DONNA SUMMER, *Bad Girls*, Pye CALD 5007
DONNA SUMMER, *Four Seasons of Love*, Casablanca 912 803–7
DENIECE WILLIAMS, *Song Bird*, CBS 86046
ANGELA BOFILL, *Angel of the Night*, Arista 201 304

II WHITE WOMEN AS URBAN AND RURAL SURVIVORS IN THE
    INDUSTRIAL WILDERNESS

5 The Jazz Singer as Little Girl Lost

BARBARA DANE, *Folk Festival at Newport*, Fontana TFL 6004
Mildred Bailey, I Grandi del Jazz 93
ANITA O'DAY, *Once Upon a Summertime*, Glendale 6000
CHRIS CONNOR, *I Hear Music*, Affinity AFF 97
JULIE LONDON, *Julie*, Liberty LPP 3096
Blossom Dearie at Ronnie Scott's, Fontana STL 5352
Sweet Blossom Dearie, Fontana STL 5399

BLOSSOM DEARIE, *Winchester in Appleblossom Time*, Daffodil BMD 104
BLOSSOM DEARIE, *Needlepoint Magic*, Daffodil BMD 105
PEGGY LEE, *Black Coffee*, Jasmine 1026
Bing Crosby and Rosemary Clooney, RCA DPS 2066

6   The Folksong Revival and the Real Right Thing

British Traditional Ballads Sung by Jean Ritchie, Folkways 2301
JEAN RITCHIE, *None But One*, WEA SPK 602 5
Joan Baez in Concert, Fontana TFL 6033
JOAN BAEZ, *Joan*, Vanguard STFL 6082
JOAN BAEZ, *Gulf Winds*, A & M Records AMLH 64603
JUDY COLLINS, *A Maid of Constant Sorrow*, Elektra 209
Judy Collins' Fifth Album, Elektra 300
JUDY COLLINS, *Amazing Grace*, Elektra 42110
Hazel and Alice, Rounder 0027
Cajun Swamp Music Live, TOM 2 7002
Kate and Anna McGarrigle, Warner K56218
KATE AND ANNA McGARRIGLE, *Dancer with Bruised Knees*, Warner K56356
KATE AND ANNA McGARRIGLE, *Pronto Monto*, Warner K56561

7   Women and the Country Music Industry

The Carter Family, RCA DPM 2046 & Col HE 7280
Tammy Wynette, Embassy EMB 31023
Loretta Lynn's Greatest Hits, MCA1
Coalminer's Daughter MCA 10
The Dolly Parton Story, CBS 3582
DOLLY PARTON, *New Harvest: First Gathering*, RCA PLI 288
Lacy J. Dalton, Col 36322
LACY J. DALTON, *Takin' It Easy*, Col 37327
EMMYLOU HARRIS, *Elite Hotel*, Reprise K54060
EMMYLOU HARRIS, *Luxury Liner*, Warner K53664
Crystal Gayle, UAG 30169
CRYSTAL GAYLE and TOM WAITS, *One from the Heart*, CBS 70215
BONNIE RAITT, *Taking My Time*, Warner K56254
LINDA RONSTADT, *Simple Dreams*, Asylum K53065
LINDA RONSTADT, *Livin' in the U.S.A.*, Asylum K53085
SUZI QUATRO, *If You Knew Suzi*, EMI SRAK 532

III   NOT FROM NEW ADAM'S RIB: WOMEN AS SINGING
POET–COMPOSERS

8   White Seagull, Black Highwaywoman, Red Squaw: Joni
Mitchell

To a Seagull, Reprise 6293
Clouds, Reprise K44070
Ladies of the Canyon, Reprise K44085
Blue, Reprise K44128
For the Roses, Asylum K53007
Court and Spark, Asylum 7E 1001
The Hissing of Summer Lawns, Asylum 7E 1051
Hejira, Asylum K53053
Don Juan's Reckless Daughter, Asylum K63003
(with CHARLIE MINGUS), *Mingus*, Asylum K53091
Wild Things Run Fast, Geffen GHS 2019
Dog Eats Dog, Geffen 2EF 26455

9   The Midnight Baby and the Hollywooden Dream: Dory
Previn

Mythical Kings and Iguanas, UAG 29186
On My Way to Where, Mediartis 41–1
Mary C. Brown and the Hollywood Sign, UAG 29435
Reflections in a Mud Puddle, UAG 29346
Dory Previn, Warner BS 2811

10   Society's Child in Small Town and City

CAROLE KING, *Tapestry*, Epic 82308
Carole King Music, AMLH 67013
CAROLE KING, *Speeding Time*, Atlantic 78 0118 1
JANIS IAN, *Society's Child*, Verve 2482 572
JANIS IAN, *Present Company*, Capitol SM 683
JANIS IAN, *Between the Lines*, CBS 80635
JANIS IAN, *Night Rains*, CBS 83802
JANIS IAN, *Restless Eyes*, Col 7464 37360 1
CARLY SIMON, *Playing Possum*, Elektra 7E 1033
CARLY SIMON, *Spy*, Elektra K 52147

11   Into the Global Village

Phoebe Snow, Shelter SR 2109
PHOEBE SNOW, *Against the Grain*, CBS 82915
MELISSA MANCHESTER, *Home to Myself*, Bells 233
LAURA NYRO, *Eli and the Thirteenth Confession*, CBS 63346
Tania Maria Live, Accord ACV 130005
TANIA MARIA, *Come With Me*, Concord CJP 200
TANIA MARIA, *Love Explosion*, CJP 230

12   The Rough and the Tough

Janis Joplin's Greatest Hits, CBS 65470
JANIS JOPLIN, *Pearl*, CBS 64188
JANIS JOPLIN and THE HOLDING COMPANY, *Cheap Thrills*, CBS 63392
JANIS JOPLIN and THE HOLDING COMPANY, *Farewell Song*, CBS 37569
PATTI SMITH, *Radio Ethiopia*, Arty 1001
PATTI SMITH *Easter*, Spart 1043
GRACE JONES, *Nightclubbing*, ILPS 9624
GRACE JONES, *Living My Life*, ILPS 9722
Joan Armatrading, AM LH 65488
JOAN ARMATRADING, *Track Record*, AM JA 2001
JOAN ARMATRADING, *Back to the Night*, AM LH 68305
MARIANNE FAITHFULL, *Broken English*, Island M1
MARIANNE FAITHFULL, *Dangerous Acquaintances*, Island ILPS 9648
MARIANNE FAITHFULL, *A Child's Adventure*, ILPS 9734

13   Magic and Technology

KATE BUSH, *Lionheart*, EMA 787
KATE BUSH, *The Dreaming*, EMC 3419
TOYAH WILCOX, *The Changeling*, Safari Voor 9
The Best of Judi Tzuke, HISPD 23
JUDIE TZUKE, *Ritmo*, Crysalis CDL 1442
ANNIE LENNOX AND THE EURYTHMICS, *The Garden*, RCA PL 70006
ANNIE LENNOX AND THE EURYTHMICS, *Sweet Dreams are Made of This*, RCA PL 25447
ANNIE LENNOX AND THE EURYTHMICS, *Touch*, RCA PC 70109

SADE ADU, *Diamond Life*, Epic 26044
ALISON MOYET, *Alf*, CBS CB 281
Chrissie Hynde and the Pretenders, RAL 3
SIOUXSIE AND THE BANSHEES, *A Kiss in the Dreamhouse*, Polydor
5064 2383 648
THE COCTEAU TWINS, *Garlands*, CAD 211

14 Deadend Kid and Androgyne

Rickie Lee Jones, Warner K56628
RICKIE LEE JONES, *Pirates*, Warner K56816
RICKIE LEE JONES, *Girl at Her Volcano*, Warner 92 3805–1
RICKIE LEE JONES, *Magazine*, Warner 25117–1
Laurie Anderson and William Burroughs, GPS 020–021
LAURIE ANDERSON: *United States Live*, Warner 25912 1–5
LAURIE ANDERSON, *Big Science*, Warner K57002
LAURIE ANDERSON, *Mister Heartbreak*, WEA 925 077–1.
Laurie Anderson Live, Warner 1–25192 (5 discs)

GLOSSARY OF MUSICAL TERMS

a cappella   literally, in chapel. The term came to be applied to
   unaccompanied polyphonic or later homophonic vocal music as
   sung in church, in the sixteenth century and subsequently.
Aeolian mode   represented on the piano by the scalewise sequence
   of white notes beginning on A: so the mode has minor third, flat
   sixth, and flat seventh.
appoggiatura   a dissonant note added to a concord, on to which it
   resolves. While it's usually thought of in association with
   eighteenth century, classical Baroque music, it's a natural fact of
   the language of music, more or less synonymous with the sigh: a
   point of tension which is then relaxed. The dissonant tone which
   resolves on a consonance is found in all musics everywhere,
   dissonance and consonance being scientific terms referring to the
   relatively complex or simple vibration ratios existing beween
   tones.
   The best way to experience this is for two people to sing the
   same tone; one moves up a semitone while the other stays put;
   the upper voice then falls, or resolves, on to the original tone.
   The meaning of the terms tension and relaxation, in relation to
   aural experience, will be then be almost physically evident.
blue notes   the blues is the classic form of the American Negro's
   poetry and music. Originally blues were sung to guitar

accompaniment, the melodic and to some extent the rhythmic techniques being derived from African sources, while the harmonic and metrical structure came from the White hymn and march. White harmony and metre tend to rigidity, whereas Black melody and rhythm are malleable, unnotable in White Western terms. Blue notes (simultaneous soundings of major and minor third) occur when African and American techniques clash in what appropriately came to be called 'false relation'.

boogie   an instrumental form of the blues, usually for piano and fairly fast. The boogie is an obsessively driving figure in the bass, often repeated as a dotted rhythmed ostinato (umtee umtee).

concerto grosso and concertino   the concerto grosso was the main instrumental form of the High Baroque era, perhaps because it was an instrumental microcosm of the techniques of *opera seria*, the heroic theatrical medium that reflected the values of a hopefully heroic age. The concerto grosso was usually in four movements, slow quick, slow quick, the second and last often being fuged dances, the third an aria, often in sarabande rhythm. The pieces were scored for a concertino of soloists who represented both musically and socially an élite, with a concerto or tutti of the main string orchestra, which represented *hoi polloi*. This was often literally true in the sense that the concertino consisted of the composer–leader employed by the Great House and his professional associates, while the concerto embraced both professionals and amateurs, and members of the nobility alongside household flunkies and serving maids.

da capo   literally, from the head. Applied most frequently to the eighteenth-century *aria da capo*, a symmetrical melody, followed by a 'middle section' in a related key, followed by a strict repeat of the first section 'da capo', usually embellished with (improvised) ornamentation. Later the term was applied to the repetition of the first section of a classical minuet or scherzo, after the middle section or 'trio'.

diatonic scale   the 'modern' diatonic scale, emulated by the white notes on a piano starting from C, is really only one of the vocally derived modes. When European music became harmonic in concept, the Ionian mode, now the diatonic scale, ousted the other modes and, in variously 'tempered' forms, became the basis of all harmonic music. The scheme of classical tonality, based on the cycle of fifths, grew out of this, the basic props of classical and then of nineteenth-century tonality being tonic, dominant, subdominant and relative. The dominant is a fifth sharper, the subdominant a fifth lower, than the tonic. The relative minor is the key having the same degree of sharpness or flatness as its major complement.

dirt   a term used by jazz musicians to refer to 'impurities' in their vocal or instrumental production, by the criterion of Western bel canto. Most folk musics and many oriental musics use dirt in this sense, for expressive purposes. Sometimes to be out of tune is to be in it; rasping and grating noises may be as essential as the blandest euphony.

Dorian   on the piano, the scalewise sequence of white tones beginning on D, so the mode has flat third, sharp sixth, flat seventh.

enharmonic   musical puns may be created by the identity, in tempered music, between (say) C sharp and D flat; thus the third of a dominant seventh in D might change to the tonic of the remote key of D flat. Such effects aren't common, of course, in folk-orientated pop musics, but they occur quite frequently in sophisticated jazz.

equal temperament   one of the techniques whereby – as indicated above in reference to the diatonic scale – the vocal modes were modified to make them harmonically amenable. The purity of justly intoned intervals had to be sacrificed if harmony and modulation were to be developed. In an equal tempered scale each of the semitones is of the same size; no interval is absolutely true, but none is painfully untrue.

fioriture   decorative arabesques embroidered around a (usually vocal-styled) melody, especially in early nineteenth-century Italian opera, and in Chopin's pianistic extensions of it. Often used of decorative passage-work in general.

heterophony   the same melody sung and/or played by several voices, some of which embellish or elaborate the original tune, thereby creating fortuitous ('heterogeneous') dissonances.

homophony   a musical style in which several – commonly four – voices or parts move 'homogeneously' together, note for note, instead of in independent rhythms, as in polyphony (many voices). The Victorian hymn is our most familiar form of homophony.

Lydian   the mode represented by the white notes on the piano, starting on F. The mode is characterized by its disturbingly sharpened fourth. It is also unusual in being the only mode –

except the Ionian which became the modern diatonic scale – to have a sharp seventh.

major, minor   the two established scales of the eighteenth and nineteenth centuries, associated with harmonic tonality. Though the minor form contains survivals of pre-eighteenth-century vocal modality, both major and minor forms exploit sharp cadential sevenths and call for some system of tempering, the artificial doctoring of pure intervals, to facilitate harmonic development and modulation. See 'equal' temperament.

mediant   the third degree of the scale and the key associated with that tone. Mediant transitions have become prevalent again, along with the modal revival.

melisma (pl. melismata)   an ornamental passage, especially in oriental and medieval musics. Strictly speaking on a single syllable, though the term is loosely used for any decorative arabesque.

mixolydian   the mode represented by the sequence of white notes on the piano, starting from G. Thus the mode has sharp third and sharp sixth but flat seventh.

mordent   as an ornament in seventeenth or eighteenth-century music, a rapid twiddle from and back to a notated tone, up or down through a semitone or tone. Frequently employed in folk musics and jazz.

obbligato   stictly speaking, an instrumental melody added to a vocal melody in an eighteenth-century aria. The term has been adapted to the instrumental soloist who dialogues with a jazz singer.

organum   in medieval music a technique whereby a monophonic melody, often plainsong, is embellished with another part, usually moving in parallel fourths and fifths, enhancing the music's awesomeness.

ostinato   an 'obstinately' repeated linear figure or even rhythm, usually though not essentially in the bass. The term comes from art music, especially that of the seventeenth century, though ostinati are prevalent in all primitive musics, in jazz and in pop.

pentatonic   the various forms of five note modes (represented on the piano by the black notes). Of all scalic formations the pentatonic are those mostly dirctly derived from the acoustical facts of the harmonic series; this is why they form the basis of primitive musics everywhere, and of most art musics that are melodically conceived. The modes – the scales in common use before the establishment of the major–minor hegemony – were acoustically derived from the behaviour of the human voice, and so naturally predominate in all musics melodically conceived. Hence the intuitive return to them in young people's pop. So basic is the pentatonic scale to these intuitive formulations that even today little children, brought up on equal-tempered music, still improvise pentatonic tunes. Pop musicians, emulating them, are children reborn.

plagal cadence   the progression from subdominant triad to tonic (Amen).

portamento   in singing a scoop or rapid glissando between notes. In art song the portamento is a special (dangerous, often deprecated) effect; but it is very common and expressive in all folk music and in much oriental music, which habitually includes microtonal intervals. See 'dirt'.

process music   twentieth-century types of music originally developed by Steve Reich in an attempt to reinstate so-called primitive techniques in the modern world. Reich studied in Africa and his percussion-dominated music has little to do with expressivity and temporal progression such as characterizes most European music. He creates a sound-world within which we live, move and have our being, while it lasts. Its ritual, unlike that of African musics, is often associated with mechanistic techniques appropriate to our industrial society. With other composers, notably Philip Glass, there is a direct link between process or minimal music and 'tribal' pop. The barriers between the genres are broken down.

riff   a melodic-rhythmic figure in jazz, incrementally repeated; indeed a spontaneous, originally improvised, form of process music.

roulade   a decorative arabesque or twiddle, in any kind of music.

shape note (hymns)   a technique for notating music developed by early American hymnodists of the eighteenth and nineteenth centuries to facilitate sight-singing on principles analogous to tonic solfa.

suspension   a note or notes held over, suspended while other, usually lower, parts move, so that dissonance and tension are created in place of euphony. The suspended dissonance then resolves on to consonance, as with an appoggiatura.

tierce de Picardie   a major third substituted for the minor third in the final cadence of a (usually modal) composition. Especially common in the sixteenth century, when modern harmony was becoming established, but recurrent subsequently.

trio the 'middle section' of a classical scherzo or minuet, (misleadingly) so called because it was originally written in three parts.

tritone the interval of the augmented fourth or diminished fifth. In the Middle Ages it was known as the *diabolus in musica* because it devilishly destroyed tonal order, being difficult to sing as a melodic progression and harmonically inimical to the perfect fifth (or perfect fourth which is the fifth inverted). To medieval people the fifth, being scientifically the most 'perfect' interval after the octave which is hardly a harmony at all, was a synonym for God. Imperfect fifths or tritones have preserved their devilish associations through the centuries, down or up to Liszt's and Berlioz's Mephistos, Vaughan Williams's Satan (in *Job*) and Scriabin's Black Mass sonata. In some twentieth-century music they represent a rootless, neutral limbo rather than a destructive force (Holst's *Egdon Heath*, the last movement of Vaughan William's *Sixth Symphony*); while for Messiaen they become moments outside Time, since their harmonic rootlessness deprives them of a sense of progression. Whether 'good' or (more commonly) 'bad', however, tritones are always rather special, a disturbance. If they occur in folk musics it is usually as intensifications of perfect fifths and fourths.

tumbling strain a phrase invented by the ethnomusicologist Curt Sachs to describe a frequent procedure in primitive musics whereby a vocal phrase starts at a high, strained pitch and then tumbles wildly downwards with an effect of uncontrolled libido. Fourths are the most natural intervals to fall through, though some peoples, especially Amerindians, tumble through intervals as wide as tenths or even twelfths.

INDEX

Adu, Sade, 228
Alf, Johnny, 205
Allen, Ed, 28, 29
Ammons, A. R., 244
Amy, Curtis, 188, 189
Anderson, Laurie, 244–51, 255, 257, 258
Anderson, Maxwell, 62
Arlen, Harold, 61
Armatrading, Joan, 217–18, 220
Armstrong, Lil, 34
Armstrong, Louis, 22, 25–6, 31–3 passim, 44, 52
Austin, Laurie, 30

Bacharach, Burt, 75, 76
Baez, Joan, 111–13
Bailey, Benny, 59
Bailey, Buster, 22, 34, 97
Bailey, Mildred, 96–8
Bailey, Pearl, 58–60 passim
Bardarou, Wally, 219
Barrett, Dolores, 7–9 passim
Basie, Count, 30, 47, 48, 56, 58
Beane, Reginald, 44
Bechet, Sidney, 33, 205
Beiderbecke, Bix, 47
Bellson, Louis, 52, 59
Berigan, Bunny, 46, 47
Berlin, Irving, 29, 41, 51–2, 71
Birch, Willie, 82
Blake, Eubie, 33, 41
Bofill, Angela, 90–1
Boland, Fanny, 59

Boswell, Connie, 96
Boy George, 258
Brasher, Henry, 43
Braud, Wellman, 34
Brown, Clarence, 35
Brown, Clifford, 57
Brown, James, 68
Brown, Oscar, 61, 62, 110
Brown, Ray, 52
Bryant, Ray, 63
Bush, Kate, 222–4

Cage, John, 245
Callender, Red, 119
Carmichael, Hoagy, 44, 53, 59
Carr, Leroy, 21
Carter, Benny, 44, 58
Carter, Betty, 63–5, 256
Carter Family, 124
Chambers, Paul, 60, 61
Chandler, Raymond, 108
Charles, Ray, 68
Christian, Charlie, 30
Clarke, Kenny, 59
Clayton, Buck, 48
Cleveland, James, 14, 15
Cleveland, Sara, 108
Cobb, Arnett, 35
Cocteau Twins, 230
Coe, Tony, 59
Cole, Cozy, 46
Collins, Judy, 113–15
Collins, Lee, 32
Comfort, Joe, 58

Connor, Chris, 99–100
Cooper, Gwendolyn, 7
Cooper, James Fenimore, 107
Copeland, Martha, 42
Corea, Chuck, 194, 205
Cox, Ida, 30–1, 42
Crawford, Randy, 88
Culley, Wendell, 37

Dalton, Lacy J., 127–30
Dane, Barbara, 95–6
Darker Shade of Pale, A (Mellers), 3–4, 81, 108, 115, 124
Davies, Jesse Ed, 85
Dearie, Blossom, 101–4
Dedrick, Chris, 202
Delmonico, Chuck, 200
Dena, John, 98
Dickens, Hazel, 115–18
Dixon, Charlie, 23
Dolphy, Eric, 62
Dorham, Kenny, 60, 61
Dorsay, Georgia Tom, 22
Dorsey, Tommy, 60
Dranes, Arizona, 8–10, 20
Duke, Vernon, 57
Dunbar, Lawrence, 62
Duran, Eddie, 206
Dylan, Bob, 3–4, 169

Eca, Luiz, 205
Eldridge, Roy, 47, 97
Ellington, Duke, 13, 33, 60
Ellington, Mercer, 58
Ellis, Herb, 52
Etting, Rose, 42–3
Eurythmics, 225–8

Faithfull, Marianne, 218–20
Farmer, Art, 59
Fawcett, Skip, 58
Fazola, Irving, 46
Feather, Leonard, 37
Fenton, Willie, 82
Fiedler, Leslie, A., 4

Fitzgerald, Ella, 51–5, 63, 65
Flack, Roberta, 87–8
Flaxman, Mike, 225
Fleming, Gordie, 120
Foster, Stephen, 40
Fox, Jimmy, 29
Franklin, Aretha, 14–15, 68, 73–6, 254, 256
Fuller, Jesse, 200

Gadd, Stephen, 120
Garner, Erroll, 100
Garcia, Russell, 54
Gates, David, 80
Gaye, Marvin, 15
Gayle, Crystal, 131
Gerrard, Alice, 116–18
Gershwin, George, 41, 54–5, 71
Getz, Stan, 205
Gillespie, Dizzy, 55
Gismonti, Egbert, 204
Goffin, Jerry, 80
Goines, Lincoln, 206
Goodman, Benny, 60, 97, 98
Gordon, Jamie, 82
Graves, Robert, 257–8
Green, Charlie, 22, 27
Greene, Freddie, 49, 98
Grolnick, Don, 197
Gumbs, Onanje Alan, 64
Gunning, Sarah Ogan, 108

Hall, Vera, 5, 17
Hampton, Lionel, 37, 63
Hancock, Herbie, 84, 85
Harris, Emmylou, 130–1
Hawkins, Coleman, 23, 62
Hawthorne, Nathaniel, 108
Haywood, Eddie, 34
Hazel and Alice, 115–18
Hemingway, Ernest, 108
Henderson, Fletcher, 23, 27, 43, 98
Henderson, Rosa, 42
Higginbottom, J. C., 30, 32
Hill, Chippie, 31

Hinde, Chrissie, 230
Hines, Earl, 56
Hodges, Johnny, 47
Holiday, Billie, 42, 44–50, 51, 53, 55, 256
Hooker, John Lee, 33
Hopkins, Lightning, 32
Hughes, Langston, 62
Hunter, Alexandra, 33–5

Ian, Janis, 87–8, 190–5, 255
Ingdahl, George, 98

Jackson, Aunt Molly, 108, 256
Jackson, Mahalia, 12–14, 256
Jackson, Michael, 258
Jackson, Paul, 85
James, Harry, 60
James, Henry, 108
Jefferson, Blind Lemon, 19
Johnson, Blind Willie, 17, 18
Johnson, J. J., 100
Johnson, James P., 27–8, 30
Johnson, Lonnie, 32
Johnson, Mary, 31
Johnson, Ossie, 58
Johnson, Robert, 18, 28
Johnson, Plas, 120
Jolley, Steve, 229
Jones, Bessie, 19
Jones, Grace, 213–17, 255, 256, 258
Jones, Jimmy, 57
Jones, Jo, 49, 98
Jones, Philly Joe, 61
Jones, Richard M., 9
Jones, Ricki Lee, 231–44, 255
Joplin, Janis, 36, 175, 209–11, 255

Katz, Dick, 58
Kelly, Wyton, 60, 61
Kern, Jerome, 41, 46
Kessel, Barney, 58
Khan, Chaka, 255
King, Carol, 187–90
King, Martin Luther, 12

Kirby, John, 46, 97
Knight, Gladys, 78, 82
Krupa, Gene, 98
Kyle, Billy, 97

Ladnier, Tommy, 30
Larkins, Ellis, 100
Lauper, Cyndi, 229
Lawrence, Trevor, 196
Laws, Hubert, 197
Lee, Bertha, 19
Lee, Peggy, 104–5
Legrand, Michel, 102
Lennon, John, 74
Lennox, Annie, 225–8, 255, 257, 258
Lewis, Meade Lux, 8
Lightsey, Kirk, 98
Lincoln, Abbey, 60–2
Lindsay, John, 32
Little, Booker, 62
Lomax, Alan, 9, 255
London, Julie, 100–1
Loving Sisters, 78–9
Lynn, Loretta, 115

McCartney, Paul, 74
McColl, Ewan, 114
McCrae, Carmen, 58–9
McFadden, Gladys, 78
McGarrigle, Kate and Anna, 118–22
MacShann, Jay, 35
Madaio, Steve, 194
Madonna, 229–30
Mallory, Eddie, 44
Manchester, Melissa, 199, 202–3
Manilow, Barry, 77
Mann, Herbie, 62, 100
Martin, Roberta, 7
Martin, Sara, 9, 31
Mathewman, Stuart, 129
Mauritz, B., 83
Mayfield, Curtis, 80
Melville, Herman, 108
Mills, Florence, 33
Milton, John, 257

Mingus, Charlie, 163
Minnesota Minnie, 20
Misso, Vido, 46
Mitchell, Joni, 137, 141–68, 185, 187, 255
Monk, Thelonious, 56
Montgomery, Little Brother, 32, 33
Moore, Phil, 60
Morton, Jelly Roll, 43, 97
Moyet, Alison, 229
Muggleton, Paul, 225
Munich Machine, 89

Nash, Johnny, 80
Nelson, Arnett, 32
Newman, Randy, 132
Nico, 255
Niles, John Jacob, 71
Nolt, Dorothy Law, 65
Norvo, Red, 97, 98
Nyro, Laura, 199, 203–4, 256

O'Bryant, Jimmy, 30
O'Day, Anita, 98–9, 102
Odetta, 68–71 passim, 254
Oliver, King, 31–3 passim
Oxford Greys, 97

Page, Hot Lips, 30
Page, Walter, 49, 98
Parker, Charlie, 55, 56, 201
Partch, Harry, 249
Parton, Dolly, 125–7, 256
Pastorius, Jaco, 163
Patton, Charlie, 19
Peterson, Oscar, 52
Phillips, Esther, 86
Pinckney, Mary, 6
Poe, Edgar Allan, 108
Pointer Sisters, 82–5
Poole, John, 98
Porgy and Bess (Gershwin), 41, 54–5
Porter, Cole, 58
Presley, Elvis, 36
Previn, Dory, 170, 171–86, 187

Procope, Russell, 97
Pynchon, V.S., 250

Quatro, Suzi, 137

Rainey, Ma, 8, 21–4 passim, 29, 42
Raitt, Bonnie, 85, 131–3
Randolph, Irving, 46
Redding, Otis, 68, 75
Reis, Tania Maria, 199, 204–8, 255
Reuss, Allen, 46
Reynolds, Barry, 219
Rich, Buddy, 52
Riddle, Almeda, 108
Riley, William, 21
Ritchie, Jean, 109–11
Rivers, Laura, 6
Roach, Max, 60–2 passim
Roberta Martin Singers, 7
Rodgers, R., 15, 63
Rogers, Ike, 31
Rollins, Sonny, 60, 61
Ronstadt, Linda, 133–7
Rushing, Jimmy, 35

Sade, 228
Sager, Carole Bayer, 202
St Clair, Cyrus, 29
Ste Marie, Buffy, 256
Salisbury, Tom, 83, 84
Sanborn, David, 198
Saunders, Gertrude, 41
Sauter, Eddie, 98
Scott, Tony, 58
Sharon, Ralph, 100
Shavers, Charlie, 34, 97
Shayne, J. H., 32
Shearing, George, 59
Shorter, Wayne, 161, 162, 166, 168
Shusha, 255
Sim, Zoot, 200
Simeon, Omer, 32
Simon, Carly, 195–8
Simon, Paul, 75
Simone, Nina, 68, 70–72, 254

Sissie, Noble, 41
Sister Rosetta, 10–13 *passim*
Siouxsie and the Banshees, 230, 256
Slim, Memphis, 32
Slim, Sunnyland, 20, 32
Smith, Bertha, 6, 7
Smith, Bessie, 8, 23–9, 42, 51, 256
Smith, Joe, 22, 26, 27, 43
Smith, Patti, 209, 211–13, 256
Smith, Warren, 120
Smith, Willie May, 7–8
Snow, Phoebe, 199–202, 249
Spann, Les, 61
Spann, Otis, 32
Spillane, Mickey, 108
Spivey, Victoria, 32–3
Stent, Theodore, 69
Stewart, Dave, 225
Strachey, Jack, 46
Summer, Donna, 88–9
Summers, Bill, 85
Supremes, The, 80
Swift, Kay, 63
Sykes, Roosevelt, 33

Tania Maria, 199, 204–8, 255
Tampa, Red, 22, 32
Tannenbaum, Chaim, 120, 121
Tapp, Joel, 119
Tate, Grady, 121
Tharp, Rosetta, 10–13 *passim*
Thomas, Hershal, 33
Thornton, Big Mama, 35–6
Thornton, Steve, 206
Tin Pan Alley, 67
Top, Brick, 33
Toussaint, Alex, 82
Tub Jug Washboard Band, 22
Tucker, Sophie, 96

Turner, Tina, 211
Turrentine, Stanley, 61, 62
Tyner, McCoy, 205
Tzuke, Judie, 224

Vaughan, Sarah, 55–8, 65
Villa-Lobos, H., 208n

Waits, Tom, 131
Warwick, Dionne, 76–7
Wallace, Sippie, 33
Waller, Fats, 33
Ward, Clara, 15
Washington, Dinah, 37
Waters, Ethel, 43–6 *passim*
Waters, Muddy, 32
Weatherly, Jim, 80
Webster, Ben, 46
Weill, Kurt, 61
Wells, Dickie, 47
Weston, Paul, 51
White, Ted, 75
Whitman, Walt, 108
Williams, Buster, 64
Williams, Clarence, 31, 32
Williams, Deniece, 89–90
Williams, Hank, 11, 13
Williams, Marion, 5, 9
Williams, Mary Lou, 97
Wilcox, Toyah, 224
Wine, Alice, 6
Winging, Kai, 100
Wilson, Nancy, 59
Wilson, Teddy, 46–8 *passim*, 97, 200
Wynette, Tammy, 124–5, 256

Yancey, Jimmy. 20–21
Yuomo, Atsuko, 249
Young, Lester, 48, 55